JIMMY
REID

JIMMY REID was born and bred in Govan, the proletarian and cultural heartland of Scotland. He was actually born in Whitefield Road, which some troublemakers insist is in Ibrox —Jimmy rejects this allegation. Ibrox, he indignantly claims, is part of Govan and not an entity in its own right.

As a young child, strange as it may now seem, he had blond curly hair and an angelic disposition; thus he was beloved by the local womenfolk. When he was about three or four his father cut off these locks, thereby incurring the wrath of the aforementioned womenfolk. When the hair grew back it was jet black, a phenomenon for which his dad was held responsible by the community at large. The resentment was such that the family had to move further into darkest Govan.

From then on, for young James it was all down hill. At fourteen he left school, got a job in a stockbroker's office and became the youngest transfer clerk in the history of the Glasgow Stock Exchange. He left at the age of fifteen and a half to become an apprentice engineer, explaining to his boss that with the advent of a majority Labour Government the days of the Stock Exchange were numbered, and he was therefore seeking longer-term job security in the shipbuilding industry. This was among the first of Jimmy's many mistakes in his journey through life—nearly half a century later the Stock Exchange is thriving and shipbuilding on the Clyde is knackered. Jimmy comforts himself with the thought that a man who hasn't made a mistake hasn't made anything.

In 1952 he led a UK-wide strike of apprentices. He served, if that is the right word, two years in the RAF as a conscript, later telling his three young daughters that he flew a Spitfire in the Battle of Britain and shot down a lot of German Fokkers. This was a bit of an exaggeration—he spent most of his time in an RAF band and was a somewhat slovenly soldier. His commanding officer was once heard to opine: "I don't think Reid was cut out for the military life." This is a view with which Jimmy heartily concurred.

When demobbed he returned to marine engineering, much to the disappointment of his employers. He led a trade-union-based campaign for higher old-age pensions. Fell in love with Joan, who in a moment of madness agreed to marry him. They moved to London, young romantic revolutionaries who would build a paradise on earth for everyone, with, of course, the help of a few pals. That sense of romance, in the personal and collective sense, has not really departed. It is still there, lurking beneath a thin veneer of cynicism.

Jimmy returned to the shipyards and got involved with a little stramash known as the Upper Clyde Shipbuilders Work-In. By that time he was a councillor in Clydebank, and is miffed that no-one even tried to corrupt him. He was elected Rector of Glasgow University. For more than twenty years he has been a journalist and broadcaster. He puts it this way: "All my life I've been telling people what I think, and for nothing. Now I'm being paid to do it. In the words of Mr Duke Ellington, 'I'm just a lucky so-and-so.'"

JIMMY REID

POWER
WITHOUT PRINCIPLES

NEW LABOUR'S SICKNESS
AND OTHER ESSAYS

First published 1999
by B&W Publishing Ltd., Edinburgh
ISBN 1 873631 89 8
Copyright © Jimmy Reid 1999

British Library Cataloguing in Publication Data:
A catalogue record for this book is available
from the British Library.

Thanks are due to The Herald,
*and to George McKechnie for his help
with selecting the articles*

Cover photograph: Jimmy Reid in Poland, 1992
Cover design: Winfortune & Associates

Printed by WSOY

CONTENTS

PREFACE

THERE have been two world wars this century. I missed both. Born fourteen years after the 1914-18 war and therefore too young for the 1939-45 war. My selfish gene or guardian angel, take your pick, must have known a thing or two. And yet, in a sense, I'm a warrior. A warrior who trades in words. For the last twenty-five years or so I've made my living from words; in books, press, radio and television. I try to be professional but don't think of myself as a professional, because I'm not. I've been in communications all my life. Argument, conversation, dialogue, discourse, debate, all made possible through the spoken and written word, are an integral part of my being. They are an integral part of all human beings, to greater or lesser extents.

I've been communicating with other human beings since nappy times and before. Communication is a two-way process. People talk back. When they don't it isn't dialogue but a monologue. I've been communicating all my life, for nothing, and happy to do so. Now people pay me for what I did for nothing and would have continued to do for nothing, if they hadn't started to pay me. Well, you don't look a gift horse in the mouth. In other words I consider myself dead jammy, hoachie, and any other word you can think of that means inordinately lucky. I make a living out of what I most want to do.

It is not that words are important in themselves, though some, in a particular context, have a resonance that can go beyond their literal meanings, and invest meaning with beauty. But words are basically utilities or tools. Together they become a conveyor belt for what we think and feel. They enable us to know what others think and feel. This communion enables us to pass on and accumulate knowledge and information. Without this humans are lost. Some of the lads I grew up with in the slums of Glasgow ended up in Barlinnie or Peterhead prisons because, among other factors, they were intelligent but owing to some cultural deprivation, which is not easy to pin down, couldn't articulate or express that inner intelligence. It smouldered within and became a rage that found negative and sometimes terrible expression. A few who had an opportunity to study while inside, who were encouraged to read, had access to art disciplines, intellectually flourished, and now live violence-free, law abiding, successful and creative lives. I know some of them, they've come back from the abyss through thoughts, words, and the acquired ability to express themselves with means other than fists or boots. They needed help not hectoring.

I'm getting fed up with religious fundamentalist evangalists, with their too respectable faces, too respectable to be true, and unyielding hatred for all who will not conform to their particular orthodoxy, whose fire and brimstone god is without love, except for them. They are grossly intolerant and full of hate. In the United States they have become big business and exercise a most destructive force on American politics. What we most need in today's world is the spiritually enriching power of human reason and discourse. That has been my faith since my earliest teens. The pace of technological change this century has shrunk the globe so that no country is an island. It has brought instability, insecurity and for many millions a shortened and pathetic life due to hunger and starvation.

Siren voices tell us that there is really nothing we can do. That these global forces and their global markets are omnipotent. Impossible to control. The new gods of the universe. To hell with that. These gods are simply a bunch of faceless men in control of transnational companies that want to rule the world without interference. We have had their kind before. Pirates. Despots. Dictators. They had to be fought because they made life a misery for the rest. The transnationals are more difficult to fight for they have no particular locus. No single centre, place or country. They transcend these things but can nonetheless be countered. They have to come down to earth somewhere for that is where they make their money. They have to ply their trade in places and countries. Playing off one against the other. Moving around the world like locusts on the prowl. Peoples and nations can and must curb their powers or be powerless and permanently at their mercy. Our democracy would then be hollow and effectively without meaning. Single nations feel helpless, though their helplessness is exaggerated. Nations have to resist in concert with other nations. The European Union could be the umbrella for such concerted action on behalf of all the peoples of Europe.

During the Thatcher years I had hoped that a Labour government would fight that good fight. It was not to be. New Labour instead has gone into the Councils of Europe and argued that the EU should deregulate its markets, as Thatcher did in the UK, to make them more pliable and amenable to the transnational companies. That would be to make Europe, as already is Britain, a place fit for the Rupert Murdochs to plunder.

This was a disappointment but not a surprise. New Labour, from the start, was not so much a disappointment as a disaster. It accepted the Thatcherite economic strategy which meant it couldn't possibly tackle the social degradations of the Thatcher years. In fact New Labour locked itself into an inexorable economic system that would intensify these degradations. New Labour is able to do things that no Tory government would have got away with. Attacks on student grants, handing over to the Bank of England the power to determine interest rates, the proposed privatisation of Air Traffic Control, are just a few examples.

These selected writings of mine, which hopefully you are about to read, precede and succeed the 1997 General Election. Long before the General Election I was sounding alarm bells. New Labour was in fact becoming Non Labour. It was becoming non-socialist, non-social democrat, non-Keynesian/anti-Keynesian, pro-laissez-faire capitalist. What the hell has 19th-century untrammelled free market capitalism got to do with modernity? New Labour is approaching the next century with the spin-doctored mantras of the last century. What was so devastating was how the Blairites could abandon every fundamental principle of Real Labour, and get away with it. How they could dismantle the democracy of Labour, and get away with it so easily.

The promise of power and jobs virtually silenced all potential critics within the Party, which seems to suggest the need for an addendum to Lord Acton's famous axiom to include that the prospect of power also tends to corrupt. The Scots rejected Thatcherism. They will also reject Blairism, Thatcherism with a New Name. Politics up here is in flux. New Labour in Scotland could collapse before the next General Election or at the very least be badly damaged. All these things I've touched on in these writings. Taken together they are a root-and-branch critique of New Labour or what many people refer to as Blairism. This wasn't in my mind to start with but when we brought the articles together, that is what we had. Inevitably there is some repetition because of the subject matter, but there is also diversity in that the problems facing humanity today are as sociological as techno-logical, as political as economic. Some of the questions raised by our predicament are philosophical, or at any rate can only be answered in philosophical terms. I think there is a growing mood which scorns the philistine values of the Reaganite and Thatcherite era, and all their simplistic dogma.

I have grounding but no great expertise in all these disciplines, but then who has? Yet everything in the world is interconnected. We have to be able to think in the knowledge of this inter-connectedness. We have to try and identify the most important connections, so that we might be able to do practical things that can improve matters. We have to have a multi-disciplined approach to life. We can't address, let alone resolve, ecological and environmental problems without taking into account their economic and political dimensions. Economists need sociology. Sociologists needs economics. Science needs the humanities. The humanities need science. We are social animals. We need one another. This is where I'm coming from and hopefully you too.

There are no matters so serious that they must absolutely exclude humour. Sure, we must try and change the world, make it better for ourselves, and those that come after. But there is no law that says we can't have a giggle along the way. I hope you enjoy my meanderings.

BACK TO REALITY AFTER BETTING ON A MIRACLE

15 APRIL 1992

SCOTLAND voted Labour and once more is governed by the Tories, who will only begin to listen if Scots learn to speak with a united voice. Why were so many people surprised and shocked at the outcome of the election?

The Tories had a massive majority of 102 seats. Yet people apparently thought that roughly the same electorate, voting under the same electoral system, in precisely the same constituencies, would wipe out that majority, in one go, by sweeping Labour into power, just like that, as the late Tommy Cooper might have put it.

To me that result would not have been a surprise but a bloody miracle, and life has taught me not to bet on miracles. To have expected a Labour victory last Thursday was the stuff cloud cuckoo lands are made of.

And yes, I do know that the election was held in the midst of a recession. I also know that popular mythology has it that the Tories are better managers of the economy. I also know that in the

1930s, in the biggest economic slump in the history of these islands, the Tories romped home in a General Election. There is absolutely no evidence, historically or otherwise, to suggest that recession is electorally favourable to Labour. In fact, the evidence points in the other direction.

I'm convinced that future students of political science will marvel at how a General Election in which the Tory majority was reduced from 102 to 21, and Labour won 42 more seats with a 4% increase in its overall vote, was interpreted by almost everyone as a crushing defeat for Labour.

Worse still, this misinterpretation of events has sparked off a panic in Labour's ranks which could cost them the next election. It was obvious on Friday that Neil Kinnock would resign as party leader. What has happened since has been an absolute disgrace.

The bad old days are back with a vengeance. Over the weekend, union bosses, with huge block votes in the college which elects the party leader, met Labour parliamentarians behind closed doors to stitch up a deal to instal John Smith quickly as leader. I wonder where they met? In Las Vegas?

What about the new model Labour Party? One man, one vote. Everything above board. Was it all a con, a public relations exercise for the duration of the election? How can Labour leaders talk about proportional representation when inside the party power-brokers are at work "fixing" the leadership before a single party committee or branch has had time to meet, let alone deliberate on the matter.

John Smith might well have all the qualities of leadership, but his accession by these methods will do him no good at all. Since the mid-Eighties, at his request, I've been sending Neil Kinnock, from time to time, my views and opinions about political developments, the economy, and so on. Others, no doubt, have been doing the same.

In the run-up to the General Election this task, of course, assumed greater importance. On February 4, I sent a fax to Neil warning: "Lest your calculations about what is needed to win in the UK as a whole includes an assumption that Labour's position in Scotland was somehow unassailable; it wasn't and isn't."

My concern was to curb dangerously unreliable expectations. I pointed out that in the 1987 election "the vagaries of the electoral system had exaggerated our (i.e., Labour in Scotland's) mass support, formidable though that is, as it had done for the Tories in England". In 1987, Labour, with 42% of the votes, had 50 of the 72 Scottish seats. But the same flawed electoral system which had disproportionately brought so many of them to Westminster had also cruelly rendered them legislatively powerless. The serried ranks of English Tories, sitting on the Government benches, ensured their parliamentary impotence.

There was another crucial factor operating which I explained as follows: "To this must be added the revulsion felt in Scotland to the perceived cruelties and crudities of the Thatcherite creed. This went beyond politics and was, in many respects, a cultural phenomenon. Without conceding an inch to the fanciful myths of Celtic romanticism, which, like intellectual cataracts, tend to obscure our vision, let me say that this revulsion has sprung from Scottish tradition and historically evolved values.

"In Scotland, individualism and collectivism were never seen as contradictory. This attitude nurtured a concept of democracy in which individual liberty and social responsibility were considered to be interlinked.

"To such a culture Thatcherism seemed barbaric. The Scots would have nothing to do with it. The Tories were routed at the polls, Labour with most of the seats had the main responsibility for marshalling Scotland's defences against the barbarians. Labour failed. That's the scenario." The constitutional issues were crystal clear and relatively uncomplicated. The United Kingdom, as its name suggests, is a unitary state embracing more than one nation. The stability of such a state requires that political differences run through the various nations. Where fundamental differences arise

3

between them, with conflicting views about values by which they want to live, and these persist over many years, then strains and tensions emerge.

In such circumstances the small nation feels disenfranchised, and it is. The small nation feels that values it despises can be imposed on it by the bigger nation. At best the relationship becomes demeaning. At worse, repressive.

We know, for it's been our lot since 1979. It's intolerable, morally unjustifiable, and essentially unsustainable when confronted, as it ultimately must be, by the united wrath of the Scottish people. This was the background to the election, in Scotland.

In the absence of tactical voting, made almost impossible by the hostility between the opposition parties during the campaign itself, all talk of wiping out the Tories this time was a load of nonsense.

In the circumstances the possibility of the Tories clawing back a few seats was always on the cards.

Yet essentially it's as before. The Tories were overwhelmingly rejected and yet will govern Scotland.

Labour cannot do as it did in the 1980s—fighting only in Parliament where it could not win and scorning the extra-parliamentary struggle where it could not lose.

As I put in my fax to Neil, and remember this was February 4: "The upshot is that Labour was seen as saying to the Scottish people there is nothing you can do except vote Labour at the next election. To which the people could say, 'but we voted Labour at the last election and got a Tory Government. The way things stand we could vote Labour at the next election and get a Tory Government'."

As we now know, they did vote Labour, and once again got a Tory Government.

Labour, and for that matter, the Liberal Democrats and the Nationalists, must wage an unrelenting parliamentary fight for the self-governing rights of the Scottish people.

At the same time they must bring the people into play in a mass movement, demanding our right to self-determination. A right denied us, as we have just seen, through the ballot box in a British General Election.

We have a moral and legal right to an official referendum. Trying to organise our own, I warn, is fraught with danger.

Let the parties rise above party, politicians above party politics. Let Scots unite across the divides, and governments, and even this lot, will surely pay heed.

LABOUR'S LEADERS GO TO GROUND

8 JULY 1992

IN ENGLAND, Labour is now unelectable, say many pundits. In Scotland, the Conservative Party is now unelectable.

If true, these twin developments raise profound constitutional questions about the government of Britain and the long-term rights of the Scot. Under the status quo it means that the people of England elect those who will govern Scotland and the Scots have no say in the matter.

If voting Labour in Scotland can have no influence in determining the government of Scotland, then why vote Labour? In such circumstances it's a wasted vote, or a senseless protest.

In General Elections, as we all know, people want to make their votes count. Wasted and protest votes are out. If the present constitutional set-up is allowed to prevail much longer then Labour could be finished as a serious electoral force in Scottish political life.

As a matter of principle, or even of self-preservation, I expected Labour to emerge from the last election with guns blazing. Once

6

again the Tories had been routed, overwhelmingly rejected in Scotland, with no moral mandate to govern.

What an opportunity for dynamic leadership, but our Labour leaders were nowhere to be seen. They had gone to ground in some bunker where they no doubt brooded about what might have been if only more English had voted Labour or even Lib-Dem.

Three months since the General Election and still no coherent lead. Then Norman Hogg, Labour MP for Cumbernauld and Kilsyth, ex-Labour Whip, gave us his considered opinion. He no doubt laboured mightily but still brought forth a mouse. He confided to the *Sunday Times*: "We have to recognise that public opinion is turning away from the Scottish Question. It is even being abandoned by the broadcasting media."

What relevance, even if true, has the latter point? Is his political agenda set by Kirsty Wark? Has he no input? If so then resign, and let Kirsty take over.

His first point is by far the more important. How can the Scottish people, and I assume he does mean us, turn away from the Scottish Question? He might mean that the Scots are now resigned for evermore to being governed by values which we have rejected en masse. If he does, he is wrong.

The constitutional government of Scotland is not, never has been, and never will be, an abstract question. It can't go away because it impinges on our everyday life. It won't go away because politics is about the values by which we want to live.

In Scotland there is a widely based belief that the moral integrity of a nation can best be measured not by the wealth of the strong but by the well-being of the weak. Take that moral dimension away and societies will degenerate into a cesspit of greed, which is where we were heading during the Thatcher years.

A couple of weeks ago I read in an English newspaper an investigation into Basildon man and woman; Thatcher's children. Those interviewed unashamedly proclaimed their greed, wallowed in their selfishness, chanted their anthem, "look after number one", and generally lived down to their well-earned reputation.

Basildon mores, fuelled by the Thatcherite momentum of the Eighties, may persist through the nineties. The growing underclass of have-nots, peripheralised in their ghettos, will be driven further downwards. These injustices are now woven into the social fabric of life in Britain. In Scotland they are seen, rightly so, as injustices not of our making; injustices which cannot be disentangled from the constitution of the United Kingdom which has imposed on us an alien political culture. Mr Hogg tells us: "There is not going to be a multi-option referendum. It is a non-starter." "Why?" you may ask. Mr Hogg explains: "If ever, in 13 years of parliamentary politics, I have seen Scottish Ministers determined in their resolve, this has to be it." The resolve of these Scottish Conservative Ministers can have nothing to do with electoral strength. They received only 25% of the popular vote. Much less than Labour. Their triumphalism could, however, have something to do with the puerility of the Opposition.

He then adds: "Labour's policy for a Scottish Assembly will survive, but only in the wider context of constitutional reform throughout the United Kingdom." Ponder well those words. They equate the national government of a nation, Scotland, with local government reform in England.

If this is the level of intellectual understanding on the national question within the Scottish parliamentary Labour Party then no wonder we're in trouble.

The powers of local or regional government in England cannot possibly be comparable to the authority of a parliament serving the social, economic, political, and cultural needs and aspirations of the Scottish nation. To suggest otherwise means you perceive Scotland as a region of England like Lancashire or Bedfordshire.

Mr Hogg records that "a couple of weeks ago the Prime Minister wrote to me ruling out a royal commission or body of similar status, to look at Scotland's constitutional future". He writes as if that's that. Book closed.

What does Labour tell those who voted for it in Scotland? "Well, we promised to fight on your behalf but we're afraid that John Major has written to Norman Hogg saying we're not on. So, in a manner of speaking, the game's a bogey. See you at the next election."

It seems to me I've heard that song before. Such an approach is an abandonment of leadership. If it prevails, the Scottish people will abandon Labour and with justification. What I can't understand is how Westminster MPs, including Labour MPs, can support the right of self-determination for Croats and Bosnians but not for Scots; how some of them will support a referendum on Maastricht but not for Scots to determine how they would like to be governed. If sovereignty is the name of the game then what about our sovereignty?

THE LONG PEDIGREE OF THE SOCIAL CHAPTER

27 JULY 1993

IN LAST WEEK'S Parliamentary debate on the Maastricht Treaty spokesmen for the British Government sought to imply that the idea of the Social Chapter was an optional issue, mischievously smuggled into the proposals, at the last minute, by federalist fanatics.

This is nonsense. The provisions of the Social Chapter were considered fundamental to the concept of the single market right from the very start and were being openly discussed within the Community nearly 20 years ago.

I can prove it. In the late spring of 1975 I was a member of the Engineering Union's national committee which was meeting in Blackpool. It had a packed agenda, including the revision of rules, and was going on and on and on.

Now, I've nothing against Blackpool, in short doses, but this was a bit much. In the third week I wanted to form an escape committee but other delegates chickened out, reckoning it would have been easier scarpering from Colditz.

10

One night, lying on my bed, dreaming of baked beans that didn't congeal, and other such luxuries, I got a call from the hotel reception. Two gentlemen wanted to see me. They were from the Commission of the European Economic Community in Brussels.

This was mystifying. What did they want with me? I was an anti-marketeer. They courteously explained. The Commission was setting up a study group charged with producing proposals on what was termed the "new characteristics of socio-economic development" and they wanted me to be a member of the group.

I remember thinking at the time that these Euro-bureaucrats did indeed have a penchant for grandiose formulations. But as they explained what it was about I became fascinated by the wide-ranging remit.

In Britain, at the time, short-termism was rampant and here was the Common Market seeking to initiate a debate about long-term strategic objectives.

As someone campaigning for a No vote in the referendum on Britain's membership of the EEC, which was due to take place on June 5, 1975, a few weeks away, I couldn't get involved, and so therefore declined. They then asked if I would be prepared to serve on the committee if the British people voted Yes. I suggested that such an outcome would certainly change matters, requiring a re-think of a lot of things by anti-marketeers like myself. That is how it was left.

Well, you know what happened. The result was a massive Yes vote and there is no way, in my opinion, that a democrat can refuse to accept the people's will, as expressed in a referendum.

We were in the European Community, to stay. That was the reality. After a while, in terms of economic and trading relations, there would be nowhere else to go. The new task was therefore to make the Community work, on behalf of the people.

In a matter of days the same gentlemen were back and I accepted the invitation and became a member of this study group. We met regularly at the headquarters of the European Commission

11

in Brussels. Members included some of Europe's most outstanding academics, economists, industrialists, bankers and a number of trade unionists. Across the table from me sat a young professor from the Université Paris-Dauphine. His name was Jacques Delors.

Our report was published by the Commission on December 1977. It was entitled, 'A blueprint for Europe—a discussion document'. What I particularly liked about the whole approach was that it recognised the interconnectedness of things.

Life has convinced me that experts whose expertise is singular aren't really worth a damn. For example an economist who doesn't understand sociology and philosophy is going to be a bum economist. Narrow experts, no matter their discipline, invariably can't see the wood for the trees. Often their strategic judgments, therefore, are flawed. This report, which I have re-read again after about 14 years, is still stimulatingly wide-ranging but implicit within it are certain logical assumptions which I would summarise as follows.

The concept of a free trade area in Western Europe (Central and Eastern Europe were excluded by the divisions of the Cold War) had developed into a common market and would ultimately progress into a single market.

The single market would have certain imperative ingredients including the free and unfettered movement of goods and services, the free and unfettered movement of capital, the free and unfettered movement of labour, all within the European Community.

This, it was recognised, would require a framework of law or legislation to protect the owners of capital, the basic needs of employees, and the rights of consumers.

For example, consumers would have to be protected against those who might unload on an unsuspecting public dodgy goods which could endanger health and even lives, by exploiting differences in consumer protection laws among the various countries within the Community. Clearly European standards of hygiene and safety were required.

There was another factor. Europe has produced monsters such as Hitler but it also produced an enlightenment from which emerged the ethical values of liberal democracy.

This was only possible when people no longer had their noses to the ground scrabbling for subsistence and could therefore raise their heads in search of the heavens. In other words democracy has to have a material base and economics a social dimension.

Europe's social and political culture, at its best, requires that social justice must be part of the criteria of economic decision-making. So on page 17 of this report, published, I remind you, in 1977, there is a call for "the principle and determination of a minimum social income guaranteed to each European citizen and measured in real terms (essential goods and services)".

The Social Chapter of the Maastricht Agreement is the reiteration and the redefinition of this principle. In essence it was there from the very start, integral to the whole concept of the single market. It wasn't a contentious issue. Nor is it today except in Britain. There was not a dissenting voice on the committee which produced this report, including representatives of big business and right-wing Christian Democrat politicians.

It didn't occur to me that the British Conservative Party would in any way challenge this principle, but then that was in pre-Thatcherite days. Winston Churchill, Rab Butler, Iain Macleod, Harold Macmillan, Alec Douglas Home, Ted Heath, supported in principle the British Welfare State. The Social Chapter is in the same caring tradition. I genuinely believe that none of these men would have opposed it.

The scandal of past weeks was not the shenanigans of the Tory Euro-rebels but that Britain's Parliament alone in the Community has rejected the moral dimension of Maastricht.

I think we still underestimate the extent to which Thatcherism has insidiously penetrated and coarsened British public life.

Triumphalist hymns of praise for the strong, and sneers of derision for the weak, have taken their toll.

As a society we are less compassionate; more crude. Sleaze flows. The City awash with scandal. Parliament deceived. The people kept in the dark. We now accept as natural that the British Government's only ally in Europe, in its fight against the Social Chapter, is Le Pen's neo-fascist National Front.

Last week was a watershed. The acceptance of the Social Chapter would have signalled that we were coming out of the dark years, but it wasn't to be. Thatcher's children still call the shots at Westminster. The new enlightenment has yet to dawn.

WHAT DOTH IT
PROFIT A PARTY . . . ?

21 JANUARY 1995

TIME marches on and leaves behind those who cannot adapt to change. I therefore welcomed the proposal that there should be a review of Clause 4, the section of Labour's constitution that enshrines the socialist principles of the party.

Only two options seemed possible. That the clause would be retained, as it is, as aspirational principles, or, that it would be revised to make our socialist principles more relevant. It's now clear that from the start there was a third option. The socialist content of Clause 4 was to be lost in a mess of amorphous generalities, and Labour remade into a non-socialist party. Those who control the commanding heights of the economy no doubt rejoiced at the prospect. Since Labour upset the applecart earlier this century, they have lusted for the return of a two-party system in which the parties could safely alternate in government, without endangering the status quo.

Back we would go to the "let's pretend" politics of minuscule

15

differences, dressed up as fundamental disagreements, known scornfully as Tweedledum and Tweedledee.

At the party conference, talk was of an open, tolerant debate. Labour's leader set the agenda. He started to make one-sided public statements before the debate had even opened. Shadow Cabinet members were told to conform. Anyone who takes a contrary view, in the party at large, is an "infantile adolescent".

There's something familiar about this kind of language. Shades of Leninism, which also demanded obedience to the leader and treated dissent within the party as an "infantile disorder".

My fear is that Labour, founded to change the status quo, is to be reshaped into a party of the status quo.

But as the Good Book more or less says: "What doth it profit a party, if it gains the whole House of Commons, and suffers the loss of its own soul?"

The Labour Party isn't an employment agency for career politicians. Tony Blair says: "I care about the Labour Party winning the next election." So do I, but not as an end in itself.

A Labour Government worthy of the name would have to address, as a matter of principle, the colossal inequalities rampant in Britain today. Some years ago, I read in the *Financial Times* an article by Jan Pen, the highly respected Dutch economist. He had analysed the distribution of wealth in Britain and concluded that, contrary to widespread belief, the disparity between rich and poor had not diminished but had grown in the post-war years.

To illustrate this he projected a model of wealth distribution in this country in terms of a march, past a fixed point, lasting one hour. The size of each group would represent their ownership of wealth. For the first 48 minutes midgets trooped by with only a very gradual increase in stature. Then with eight minutes left there was a jump of 10 and 20 feet. In the last few minutes giants, bigger than high-rise blocks, suddenly appeared.

But they were relative midgets compared to the leviathans who trundled past in the last few seconds. Their heads had disappeared in the clouds, reaching up to outer-space. The real guv'nors had arrived.

Since then the very rich have got richer, the poor much poorer. To think you can tackle the problems of the poor, while leaving untouched this vast concentration of wealth in the hands of a tiny super-elite, is disingenuous.

There is another reason why we must tackle this obscenity. In economic terms how can such giants look the rest of us in the eye and make human contact?

From their loftiness, might we not appear as ant-like creatures who can be trodden on without remorse? Think of the heartless economic decisions of recent years, people thrown on the scrapheap, communities devastated. Were we just wee beasties, abstract indices, to the decision makers?

Wealth is power. Super-wealth is super-power. Tony Blair had lunch with Rupert Murdoch. That's okay. Dialogue is a good thing. But Tony hasn't had lunch with me, my next-door neighbour, or anybody in our street.

Could it be that we aren't billionaires, don't own a big chunk of the media, and therefore don't merit a munch with Mr Blair? We do have votes.

Is Labour's leadership supping with the super-rich to plead that they and their newspapers be less vicious to the party, come the next election, than they were at the last? There would have to be a reason for them to do so, that has nothing to do with fair play. Is it an assurance that the super-rich have nothing to fear from a Labour Government? But a Labour Government which leaves unchanged the system that allows them to be super-rich, will not be able to do much, if anything, for the poor.

The irony is that I am a supporter of reform within the Labour Party and have campaigned for one person one vote since the Seventies. I've contempt for the arid sloganising of the hard left. I'm for the revision of Clause 4 so that it deals with economic democracy. If political decision-making has to be accountable to the people, as a matter of democratic principle, why not economic decision-making?

Experience shows that market mechanisms are a prerequisite of economic efficiency. Even Marx's Theory of Value presupposes a market. I don't believe in state control of industry. It's been tried and everywhere spawned bureaucratic and not democratic institutions. Nationalisation isn't socialism. Bismarck nationalised the postal services in Germany, and he was no socialist.

But I don't believe that the destiny of humankind can be left to the untrammelled play of market forces. Laissez-faire capitalism ruled the world from 1850 till 1950, and failed miserably. We've seen the past and it doesn't work.

During this period there were two horrendous world wars, numerous colonial wars, devastating slumps that produced a grotesque situation, hitherto unknown in human history, where millions starved in the midst of plenty.

Millions today still starve in a world of food mountains. Our technology has outstripped our sociology. Man, who should be the master of economics, is too often its slave. Modern economics lack a humane ethic. A social dimension. Socialist principle.

Without a socialist Clause 4, Labour is a party of expediency. Enmeshed in agendas not of its making. Led by events but never leading. Having accepted the status quo, it becomes part of the system, the same as the others. Why then vote Labour?

THE LOST VISION

13 MAY 1995

HUGH McILVANNEY, sports writer par excellence, told someone who was rubbishing wordsmiths that "words were handy if you had something to say". There was irony in Hugh's words, for his assertion was gross understatement. If you didn't have words you would have nothing to say anyway. A poet wrote of God: "He gave man words and words created thought." This link between words and thought is fundamental. One of my daughters made a little calligraphic poster for me. It sits on my desk and proclaims, "The very greatest is the alphabet for in it lies the deepest wisdom." Words and their juxtaposition can convey more than literal meanings. Your choice of words can reveal hidden or subconscious thoughts. We even have expressions for such a phenomenon. A Freudian slip, or in the vernacular, a dead giveaway.

Ponder these following words. "A monstrous religious icon, a graven image." "No longer do we have to worship false gods, utter prayers that have lost all meaning." They could be the words of an escapee from a nutcase religious sect in the American Midwest, or one of the Brontës on a bad day, but they were actually penned by Jack Straw, Shadow Home Secretary, writing about Clause 4 for the *Independent*.

There are dark thoughts in them there words. Strong feelings nudging on hatred, and for something written 77 years ago to convey concepts of common ownership and democratic control of wealth-producing resources. Hardly an issue for heavy-metal words which also jar with the cooing public reassurances given by Labour's leadership that the debate on Clause 4 was concerned with archaic language, the need for an update, a simple redefinition of principles in the language of the 1990s. Why, Brian Wilson could do it on the back of an envelope, travelling on a train, musing about Glasgow Celtic's history, no bother at all.

Then wham—doomsday talk, Labour in thrall to a monstrous religious icon, and as sure as words have meaning this meant it was a cult and not a political party. Monstrous religious icons have high priests who must be given short shrift. This might explain why there was hatred about. Arm-twisting and threats. It wasn't nice. Tony Blair's nice-guy smile is a put-on. He's ruthless.

Since he was elected leader a war of sorts has been waged to make Labour into a post social democrat party purged of all constitutional and linguistic vestiges of what had been party principles.

The differences between Blair and a Thatcherite Tory leader will then be minimal, guaranteeing rough times ahead, for, in some perverse way, maximum heat among human beings is often generated by minimal differences.

One group of Muslims fought another group of Muslims, with excessive ferocity, in the Iran-Iraq war. In times past Christians took turns at burning each other over marginally different interpretations of biblical texts, some are still at it in what was Yugoslavia and elsewhere. Trotskyists loathe Trotskyists with a passion that exceeds anything they feel for those who are supposed to be on the other side of the barricades, come the revolution. Stalin killed more Stalinists than Hitler. Thatcher hated Tory Wets but looked benignly on Denis Skinner. Ernest Bevin, told that Herbert Morrison, another right-winger, was his own worst enemy, growled "not while I'm alive".

As the parties huddle ever more closely in the same camping grounds this hatred for the nearly similar will become more emphatic. They can share everything but bonhomie. This lack of meaningful philosophical and ideological difference has spawned a political debate which dwells on effects but never the causes. Trivia prevails. This is also true of inner-party debate.

Despite what has been claimed, the debate on Clause 4 was bereft of intellectual depth. Reasoning became fraught. Jack Straw explained the process by which he came to hate Clause 4 and to love the free market. He was having lunch with the staff at the British Museum depot, prior to the 1992 General Election. The staff was, "mainly middle-class middle-aged women—classic swing voters. They talked politely, but they would not look me in the eye."

This comes as no surprise. People do tend not to look in the eye of those inclined to talk of monstrous religious icons and graven images, even employees of the British Museum, especially over lunch. But back to Jack's story: ". . . one woman said her husband was in private industry, building, and he'd been told there would be many bankruptcies if Labour won."

That was all she said, absolutely nothing more. But it was enough for Jack; his road to Damascus, blinding light and all, was at hand. With one quantum leap he jumped to the conclusion that Clause 4 was definitely a monstrous religious icon, graven image to boot, not forgetting the meaningless prayers bit.

With missionary zeal he declared war on the clause. "Many colleagues at Westminster gave me great encouragement, above all Neil Kinnock and Tony Blair. Neither could be too public about this because of their close association with John Smith, who would be less than keen on my ideas." So in the beginning it was rather hush-hush. A trifle conspiratorial. Where did Jack meet Neil and Tony, in the vaults? Alas, John Smith died. Tony Blair became party leader. The rest is history. But if that lady's husband hadn't been told that there would be many bankruptcies if Labour won, and she hadn't told Jack Straw over lunch in the British Museum depot, then Clause 4 would still be in Labour's constitution and the next Labour government would have nationalised everything, including the *Independent*. Phew. A close shave. Eh?

Note Straw's reasoning; it's absurd. His language is bizarre, a discussion within a secular political party couched in terms appropriate to holy war. But Straw is not just a political warrior, tilting at socialist windmills, he is a social scientist who now rejects the "false dichotomy between socialism and capitalism".

In essence he argues that after thousands of years of evolutionary development human society has reached its zenith and absolute pinnacle in modern capitalism. History stops here. In Voltaire's mocking words, "We are living in the best of all possible worlds."

Apologists for slavery and feudalism sang the same song. It's an old song, music to the ears of those at the top of the pile. The beneficiaries of a status quo fervently want the status quo to last forever. It's old hat.

New Labour is old hat. Among those who founded the Labour Party were Lib/Lab career politicians who despised socialism. Middle-class men with an eye to a career in politics who knew promotion was barred to them in the hierarchical Tory Party of those days. They were "agin" the political establishment because they couldn't be part of it.

They viewed the extension of the franchise to workers as votes which could take them to the heights of government. They found allies in some personally ambitious proletarians and trade union leaders who believed in the liberation of the working class, one by one, starting with themselves.

Ramsay MacDonald was of that ilk. Born out of wedlock to a poor Scottish serving girl, he betrayed Labour in the 1930s, and for a wee while was the darling of all the duchesses in London. A bastard in every sense.

Non-socialist Labour parliamentarians are extant unto this day. The Gang of Four were unable to uphold the socialist principles of Labour and left to form a new party. Blair and his gang, unable to uphold the same principles, worked from within to ditch these principles. History will judge David Owen to have been more honourable than Tony Blair. As a consequence Labour is now back to where it was before 1918, a party of the centre.

In a two-party system you can't have one party governing forever. The British establishment needs a party, to interchange with the Tories, that will not question its hegemony.

When Labour succeeded the Liberals as a party of government, members of the establishment must have been excreting bricks. Labour's constitutional commitment to fundamental social change, while mostly ignored by Labour governments, was a potential threat to the establishment.

Labour had to be made a party of the status quo and the then virtually non-existent differences between the parties could be dramatised to give the illusion of choice.

The needle between Major and Blair is real, not political but personal. It is a clash of contending career politicians, fighting for the same office and not to be confused with the clash of contending philosophies.

There are different social classes in our society, in every country in the world. To deny this is like denying the world is round. Yet we have a Labour leader who talks as if nobody out there was being paid wages or salaries for their labour. No-one out there paying wages or salaries to those who sell their labour. Nobody out there paying wages is tempted by the thought of paying less. No-one out there who is paid wages is tempted by the thought of being paid more.

There will always be a potential conflict of interest between payers and paid. Good industrial relations are best served by recognising this reality and devising procedures which seek to resolve the potential for conflict.

If this fails or isn't tried and conflict occurs Labour, founded to support those who are paid wages, declares itself neutral. There is no such ambiguity with the Tories. They have never supported workers in a dispute, yet by the law of averages, the workers were bound to have been right some time. The Tories take this attitude because they were founded to support the interests of those who pay wages, and they remain loyal to their roots.

If Tony Blair rarely mentions socialism, he never mentions capitalism, which is very strange. Capitalism dominates today's world. The free market is a fundamental part of the capitalist system. Capitalism is a precise and legitimate word. Its non-use is inexplicable unless there is a language difficulty. Think of capitalism and you might also think of capital and labour and trade unions, etc, etc.

New Labour has expunged from its vocabulary all words that remind people of Labour's history, its raison d'être. It has abandoned its distinctive philosophy. The cumulative effect of these factors has led to semantic chaos. How to say nothing and make it sound like something. Bright people end up speaking gobbledegook.

In the speeches of Labour's leader, the vast complex of social problems—crisis in the health service and our schools, alienation, the hopelessness and despair of millions in our inner cities and peripheral housing schemes, drugs, lawlessness, the contrast of wealth and poverty, urban squalor, the atmospheric pollution which sent people flocking to hospitals where they were put on ventilators when the sun shone in London—have nothing to do with the prevailing socio-economic system. It's all down to ministerial incompetence. There are no objective factors operating, only subjective deficiencies.

The Shadow Chancellor recently spoke of how he will deliver a dynamic market economy. Does he mean a constantly dynamic market economy not subject to recessions? The implication is that if New Labour had been in power during the past four years it would have steered Britain to dynamic growth despite the recession in the global market economy. That cannot be true.

The capitalist free market is subject to cyclical recessions which destroy or atrophy resources, while contradictions between production and consumption are resolved, often in the crudest of ways, by the destruction of jobs and communities. That's not an opinion but a fact. Governments and economists have sought to alleviate or modify this negative phase in the productive cycle of the global free market economy and have not yet succeeded. To judge by what it has to say on the matter the phenomenon of capitalist economic crises doesn't seem to exist for New Labour. But then neither does capitalism.

In all of this it's difficult to discern, in terms of actually managing the economy, what a Blair government would do that is significantly different from what the Tories are already doing. There is certainly no economic or philosophical critique on which a new strategy could be based.

Within two years New Labour in government will have alienated millions, destroyed hopes, and have split Labour as in the 1930s, only this time there will be no world war to lead Labour back from the wilderness.

Principles do matter. They are not high-falutin' abstractions. Philosophical ideas are important. Political parties and governments consumed by immediacy end up with no goals beyond winning, and clinging to, office. We need perspective.

Of course, in a democracy parties have to relate to the concerns of people, yet they can't simply mirror existing attitudes. That's a cop-out. Parties of principle seek to change as well as reflect the minds of the people. We hear nothing now of the battle of ideas because our politicians have no big ideas. You can't lead a crusade on ministerial incompetence. The function of political parties will now be to provide career opportunities for career politicians.

New Labour has silenced the distinctive voice of true Labour which could appeal to conscience and not just wallets. What do

25

you stand for? asks a voter. What do you want us to stand for? is Labour's reply. This perception of Labour is growing, breeding a deadly cynicism. Jokes are already current about Tory Blair. Those obsessed by the prospect of office can end up in government, hamstrung by the concessions they made to get there.

New Labour lives by the soundbite, the smile, the glad hand, photo opportunities, and the superficiality that accompanies the absence of principle. Yet we have in our grasp the productive and technological means of creating an abundance to meet the material needs of humankind. The elimination of poverty throughout the world is now feasible. Only outmoded sociology stands in the way.

Market mechanisms are necessary for economic efficiency. This is a lesson of history. The absence of market mechanisms wrought havoc with the Soviet economy. The alternative was a price-fixing committee and the command economy. But the acceptance of market mechanisms doesn't mean accepting untrammelled market forces. The market has no moral imperatives. It cannot say "poverty is not to be tolerated", but we can say it. Human beings must control economics, or economics will control us. The Labour movement, reflecting these values, put people centre-stage. All of this has been lost. Progress has always meant hard, down-to-earth work. But progress is fuelled by dreams.

My dad wept with joy when Labour won in 1945. He was dreaming of a new Jerusalem. John Smith would have understood, but not Blair and Mandelson. Their souls were never seared by the vision splendid.

A SAFE BET WITH
GOD IN THE SADDLE

13 JUNE 1995

HORSE racing is fascinating because you have to take account of so many factors. First of all the horse; its abilities, has it been overworked or underworked, has the handicapper got its measure or has it something in hand; the distance; the going; the contours of the course; the jockey—and if you get these things right, there are the imponderables.

On the day of the race the horse might be cheesed off for no apparent reason. A young stallion, despite the bromide, might still have his mind on other things. That's why they geld some. It apparently concentrates the mind.

I backed the winner of the Derby and was delighted, more for getting it right than for the winnings. There were doubts about whether many in the field could get the distance. Others were gallopers and lacked the class for the Derby. The hot favourite had shown he wasn't happy with less severe undulations than he had to confront at Epsom. This left Lammtarra who had only one outing to his credit, which he won, but such inexperience is no recommendation for the most difficult flat race in the world. On the other hand, no flaws had as yet been revealed, and he was superbly bred.

My theory, which might be scientifically flawed, is that the genetic pool of modern thoroughbred horses has been so refined that it is now a more reliable guide to potential than ever before. This reasoning pointed to Lammtarra.

According to Walter Swinburn, the winning jockey, this victory had nothing to do with breeding, training, the skills of handlers and his own jockeyship. God had willed that this horse should win and, of course, it duly obliged.

According to Walter, who must have a hotline to Heaven, God's reasoning was as follows: Alec Stewart, a Scot, who was an outstanding trainer and judge of horses, and Lammtarra's original trainer, had been shot dead last year. He was such a good guy that God decided to reward him by giving the race to Lammtarra.

Why do people fork out lots of cash for thoroughbreds and employ skilled and gifted trainers, with expensive facilities, experienced stable-hands, veterinary back-up and so on when all that's needed is a word in the ear of God? Cancel *Sporting Life*!

Light some candles and remember the wee ones are for greyhounds. Face Mecca in the morning and ask Him to mark your card. Go dutifully to the synagogue and implore that one a day would do nicely.

Now according to some, God is riding shotgun on football as well. After a Scottish Cup Final, which Celtic won, Tommy Burns, the manager, came to the press conference, entwined his hands, looked to the heavens, and said: "I want to thank God for our victory."

Did Airdrie know of God's involvement? Is this allowed under SFA rules? Alex McDonald could have said: "My boys knew they would be under the cosh when they heard that God in mufti was sitting on the Celtic benches at the right hand of Tommy Burns."

There is at least one snag in this. If Celtic had lost, would Tommy have blamed God? Would he have told the assembled scribblers: "God let us down. He never really got into the game. Maybe he needs a few days at Seamill."

Nobody minds a "Thank God" or a "By Jove"; it's when they get serious that it becomes worrying.

I remember Peter Aliss commentating on an Open golf championship. A young Spaniard was forlorn in the depths of a bunker. Peter described the difficulties of the shot and the mechanics of good bunker play. Just before he struck the ball, the Spaniard made the sign of the cross. Peter, in a hushed voice, opined: "He's appealing for help to an outside agency". The ball hit the lip of the bunker and dropped back to where it was before. Peter concluded: "See, you can't trust nobody nowadays."

If you seriously believe that in sport God is on your side then by definition he's against the other side, unless they have another God who is on their side, and sport becomes a Holy War or fatwa, and that sure as hell ain't good.

But the idea of God floating around with a mobile phone ready to act as a fixer in sport is highly insulting to Him who must have his hands full with ethnic cleansing in Bosnia, the starvation of millions of helpless souls in the Third World, the pollution of our atmosphere and its threat to life on this planet, not to speak of Aids. If He has time to intervene in horses and football then his priorities are all wrong.

There is an old saying: "God helps those who help themselves." Jack Nicklaus once said: "The more I practice the luckier I get". And that's about it. God or genetics give us potential talents and abilities. The rest is up to us. To suggest that someone or something else is responsible is a cop-out.

A PRICE TOO FAR
FOR LABOUR

27 JULY 1995

TALK about biting the hand that feeds you, fed you, nurtured you through good times and bad, and even gave you that most precious of gifts, life. Well, that is New Labour's attitude to trade unions. The Labour Party and the trade unions are indivisible. Without socialism, already abandoned, and the trade unions, about to be abandoned, Labour is just another party. Its unique historic role and relevance is being dumped, and without these Labour will wither and die, for who needs another Tory or Liberal party?

In the short term Labour's leadership wants to keep the unions at a distance (they are deemed electorally embarrassing), but still within the fold, for their money is currently needed to keep the party afloat and to fund the next General Election. In the longer term a Blair Government would legislate for the state funding of parties, and the unions will then be ditched.

Yet the trade unions were fundamental in founding Labour and played a key role in shaping its destiny as a reforming party of government based on socialist ideals. In their hour of greatest need, following the carnage of Thatcherism, they are treated like pariahs by a party it founded to represent the interests of organised labour. As an act of ingratitude this takes some beating, and it's short-sighted folly as well.

The trade unions can survive without the Labour Party. Can Labour survive without the trade unions? I think not, and for reasons which have little to do with money.

We can only marvel at the gross insensitivity of those who have taken a cleaver to the finely evolved structures of what was a pluralist political party uniquely designed for the task of changing Britain for the better through a democratic parliamentary process. This has been a century of social upheaval and turbulent technological change which wrought havoc in the economic and political landscape of our planet. Humankind in the past 100 years has acquired more information than in the previous 10,000 years. Our technology has outstripped our sociology. In the midst of potential abundance millions have starved to death. Many millions more have been socially alienated. It has been a century of colonialism, fascism, communism, political convulsions, two world wars, countless "lesser" wars and in Bosnia the beasts are once again on the march. In certain parts of the world capitalism brought a general level of material living standards never seen before. This happened in Britain which was very much involved in colonialism and two world wars. Yet through these years there was relative social stability. The recently much-maligned old Labour Party was a major factor in ensuring that the fight for change in this country was channelled through the ballot box and civil war as a means of social change was eschewed.

It was able to do this because of its nature, its character, which was determined by its founding fathers. The TUC, at its Congress in September 1899, passed a resolution to invite "all the co-operative, socialistic, trade union, and other working-class organisations to jointly co-operate on lines mutually agreed upon, in convening

31

a special congress of representatives from such of the above-named organisations as may be willing to take part to devise ways and means for securing the return of an increased number of Labour members in the next Parliament".

Congress referred this resolution for further elaboration and implementation to a special joint committee comprising four members of its Parliamentary Committee, Will Thorne and W C Steadman, supporters of a new party of Labour, and Sam Woods and Robert Bell, who were Liberals; the Independent Labour Party was represented by Keir Hardie and Ramsay MacDonald, the Social Democratic Federation by Harry Quelch and H R Taylor, and the Fabians by George Bernard Shaw and E R Pease. Their deliberations resulted in a conference at the Memorial Hall, Farringdon Street, London, on Tuesday, February 27, 1900 which effectively founded the Labour Party. Present were 129 delegates representing 65 trade unions and three socialist societies.

At this founding Congress it was agreed that an executive committee of seven trade union representatives, two each from the ILP and the SDF and one from the Fabians, should be elected not by Congress as a whole but by their organisations.

This established Labour as a federal party. The broad kirk. A federation of trade unions and socialist societies with their own identities and their own directly elected executive members. A coalition of social forces. The trade unions organised workers who were non-socialists as well as those who were. They tended to act as a restraint on the idealism of the socialist societies.

On the other hand the economism and narrow "practicalism" of some trade unions were subject to trenchant criticism by the socialist societies. The tensions thus generated from these two wings of the party were dynamic, and often resolved in a positive synthesis. The new party's structure ensured that it could not be an exclusively class party. The trade unions provided a working-class base. The socialist societies involved people of all classes attracted by the vision of socialism. Many were middle-class intellectuals whose contribution to the cause of Labour has been greatly under-valued. Labour could and did appeal to all that's good in the middle classes without pandering to their baser elements.

There were no individual members of the Labour Party until 1918 when the constitution was amended, but the federal principle was maintained. Individual members joined a constituency party, not the national party, and the constituency parties became part of the federation. They could send delegates to the annual conference and elect their own representatives to the executive.

National conference was the supreme policy-making body. The national executive was the custodian of conference decisions. The Labour Party was the most democratic party in Britain, arguably in the world, and rose swiftly to become a party of government. Its core electoral base is massive. The unprincipled wooing of those groups fundamentally alien to Labour's core values is undermining that base.

The decisions of national conference are now ignored. The NEC is a rubber stamp. The party machine is controlled by the leader's office. The trade unions are diminished except as providers of money. New members are being recruited through the national office. Dues are paid by banker's order. Participation by the membership, in and through various and varied affiliates, as part of the process of decision-making, is being rendered innocuous.

Changes were necessary. The democracy of the Labour Party was damaged by those trade unions whose internal democracy was flawed. The election or appointment of union leaders for life was outrageous. It should never have required legislation to guarantee the rights of workers to a ballot on whether they should go on strike. None of this, however, can obscure the fact that trade unionism by its nature is more democratic than any commercial or financial institution.

The monolithic block vote was an anachronism. Greater internal union democracy could have broken down the block vote so that it could more accurately reflect the views of the union membership.

But the bottom line was much more crude. The British economy was in crisis. Thatcher needed a scapegoat. The unions were cast in that role. Blamed for all our economic ills. This was preposterous but the scale and ferocity of the attack intimidated Labour's leadership. There was no robust and coherent defence of the unions, no critique that laid the blame where it belonged, at the door of the real masters of the economy. Labour's current leader is still recoiling from this onslaught. He considers the unions to be an electoral liability, and in this is behind the times. The pendulum has swung. In industrial disputes the public no longer automatically blame the workers or their unions.

Tony Blair projects an image of even-handedness. "I'll listen," he says, "to unions and the employers", which is jolly sporting when you consider the unions are part of the party he leads and pay affiliation fees, and employers on the whole tend to do the exact opposite. But in fact Blair talks tougher to the unions. Read what he said at the conference of the TGWU and then compare it with his honeyed words to Rupert Murdoch's top executives.

The Tories can be beaten at the General Election. The swing in British politics today is against the crudities and cruelties of Thatcherism. Labour can win people who previously voted Tory and now believe they were wrong to do so. But Blair seems to be making a bid for unreconstructed Tory votes which can only be successful if he persuades them that Labour is a party of newly constructed Tories.

Some party members tell me that it's all a Machiavellian ploy. Once elected he will start introducing more socialist policies. That I suggest is naive in the extreme. This guy is dead serious. He is dismantling the party that presided over the most far-reaching social changes in the history of our country without recourse to violence or social strife. We do not sufficiently appreciate the significance of this achievement.

Labour's federal structure diffused power through affiliates. This developed an internal democratic culture. No Labour Prime

Minister was ever as dictatorial as Thatcher. No Labour leader has ever been as dictatorial within the party as Mr Blair. He obviously admires Thatcher's imperiousness and has been practising it on trade unions before donning the toga of Number 10.

Labour can win without surrendering everything it believes in, but if the price of victory is that Labour become the heirs of Thatcher, then it's a price too far. Such a government would finish Labour.

THE SEEDS OF ALIENATION

5 AUGUST 1995

ADAM SMITH was posthumously appointed and annointed a Thatcherite by the Blessed Margaret. The lady boasts she is absolutely not for turning, which means she is not for turning even if going the wrong way. Hardly a rational approach to life.

For Lady Thatcher, mere opinions were too supine. Her mind is inhabited by beliefs and convictions. Those who lacked the strength of character or native wit to see the indisputable wisdom of her ways were wet or wimpish, or both. Some Tory parliamentarians, with lascivious memories of an overbearing nanny who ruled their early years with a rod of certitudes, fell at her feet. She, of course, walked over them, and they seemed to enjoy the experience.

Adam Smith—a Scot of independent mind—would not have lasted a week in her Cabinet. He was a scientist open to new information which might prove him wrong, for this was better than continuing to be wrong. He pursued truth that he knew couldn't be absolute, but would be constantly modified, and amplified, by expanding knowledge and new investigative skills.

In his introduction to *The Wealth of Nations,* he wrote: "Political economy considered as a branch of the science of a statesman or legislator, proposes two distinct objects: first, to provide a plentiful revenue or subsistence for the people, or, more properly, to enable them to provide such revenue or subsistence for themselves; and, secondly, to supply the state or commonwealth with a revenue sufficient for the public services."

His work was, therefore, dedicated to helping those in government fulfil their responsibilities, which he defined as providing the means by which people could earn a living, and also secure for the state the revenues by which the commonwealth could fund public services. Political economy was, for him, a branch of political science. He was a political economist who sought to understand the laws of economics so that others might use them politically for the betterment of humankind. He advocated laissez-faire capitalism against a backcloth of feudal restraints on trade. He lived at a time when manufacturing was conducted by a multitude of small-to-medium sized companies. Competition was real. The emergence of big companies, monopolies, multinational and transnational companies lay in the future. He was a philosopher, a sociologist, as well as a political economist.

Smith would have scorned those who argue that economics should be depoliticised, as if it were possible to abstract economics from the society of which it is part.

In times past, our universities abounded with professors of political economy. Not so long ago political economists from universities were consulted about economic matters by the media. Today the media consults experts who work for big stockbrokers and merchant banks, and they're introduced as economists, not political economists.

In fact, "political" mysteriously disappeared from political economy. No-one knows how or why, it just happened. But nothing just happens, not like that.

In the context of political economy, the word "political" derives from politics as meaning the complex or aggregate of relationships of people in society as a whole. If you divorce economics from these human and social relationships, then economics becomes unhuman. Karl Marx, like Adam Smith, was a political economist, and is as much to blame for the crimes of those who used his name as Smith was for the crude marketeers who purloined his, or the gentle Christ in whose name dastardly deeds are done.

Marx was wrong in many respects, but his analyses of the market economy are worthy of study. In his *Critique of Political Economy* he wrote: "Man is in the most literal sense of the word a *zoon politikon* [Greek for political or social animal], not only a social animal but an animal which can develop into an individual only in society . . ."

Marx rejected as absurd the idea of an isolated man outside of society possessing within himself the dynamic productive elements of society as a whole, and called this ". . . as great an absurdity as the idea of the development of language without individuals living together and talking to one another".

Smith would have agreed. All political economists agreed that economics must explain how men make their living, and deal with the production and distribution of the materials needed to live, including food, shelter, clothing etc. It was generally agreed that man couldn't live by bread alone, but that he also couldn't live without it. The satisfaction of material needs was viewed as a liberating force which would enable mankind to stand upright and look at the heavens—as is right. Liberal democratic values could not have come from societies in which men and women scrambled in the dirt for sustenance.

There was also wide agreement that from earliest times human beings had worked together in order to live, and that the process by which we produced goods to meet our needs was a social process. The social aspect of the productive process has grown and got more complex as time goes by. Today, the production of the most mundane objects involves the co-operation of many.

The tin-opener in your kitchen started with the mining of ore; the ore was then put on wagons or ships and transported to a mill to be refined into the material prescribed by those who designed your tin-opener; the raw material is transported to the factory where the tin-opener is made, packaged, and transported to a shop near you. You bought it and took it to your kitchen. But thousands were involved, directly and indirectly, in the process of producing and getting this tin-opener to you. And far from being costly, it costs much less than if produced by yourself, or any individual or any small group of individuals.

The social character of production, distribution, and exchange was, in a capitalist market economy, the property of private owners. Some argued that this contradiction should be resolved by taking into social ownership the social processes through which wealth is created, and gearing them to social need and not private greed. These people became known as Socialists.

The others didn't argue a direct negative. Most suggested that inevitably, as the productive processes got bigger and bigger, they would lead to larger companies which guaranteed access for the public in terms of share ownership. In other words, there would be open and wider social accountability in public companies, underpinned by a legal framework of company law, within which these companies would operate. It didn't really work that way. Access to the ownership of shares in public companies was determined by whether you had the money to purchase shares, and the poor, by definition, had no money.

Many within the middle classes became small share owners, but there is little evidence that their interest went beyond the rate of profit. Even where shareholders did take up wider issues, the financial institutions and the company apparatchiks generally saw them off. There was a recent example of this at the annual general meeting of British Gas, where small shareholders turned up to vote out company officials who had awarded themselves share options and vast salary increases while closing showrooms and sacking staff.

A majority voted to sack these officials. The financial institutions which own big chunks of the equity had the power to override these shareholders, and did so. It is worth noting that those who condemn the block votes of trade unions are somehow less horrified by the block votes of financial institutions in public limited companies.

In any case, political economists argued, government, in a democracy, would have to act on behalf of society as a whole, if the power of big companies was used against the public good. Efforts were made throughout the twentieth century to equip governments with the means by which they could regulate the market economy for the public good.

The devastating impact of periodic capitalist recessions and slumps made an overwhelming case for such regulation. These recessions were unique. There was no historical precedent. People had starved in the midst of droughts and natural disasters, but that millions should starve in the midst of plenty was a new phenomenon.

It made capitalism look absurd. The slump of the 1930s was, for many, the last straw. No-one could morally justify a socio-economic system that produced such ludicrous injustices. Political economists sought a solution. One man came close to providing this, John Maynard Keynes. He advocated political intervention to try to regulate the market economy, to smooth out its booms and slumps, and thereby avert widespread suffering. If the economy was slithering into recession or was in recession, he proposed public spending on public projects which would permanently enrich the capital infrastructure of the nation. At best, Keynesianism created jobs in the short term which could stimulate an upturn in the economy, or stop the onset of recession, or precipitate an earlier recovery from recession. At worst, it was an economic drip-feed which helped keep the patient alive.

The American New Deal was largely based on Keynesian precepts. Post-war Western Europe promised that never again would its citizens be confronted with the economic ravages of the inter-war years which destabilised society and became a major factor in the rise of Hitler, and the drift to world war.

A new political and economic consensus emerged, influenced by Keynesianism and Socialism. The main political parties in Western Europe accepted as a function of government the creation of jobs and full employment. They accepted minimum welfare provisions as the guaranteed right of every citizen—from the cradle to the grave—thus giving birth to the welfare state.

Enlightened Tories like Harold Macmillan and Rab Butler, sickened by what they saw in the 1930s, were willing partners in this new political consensus. The years from 1945 to 1975 were the best in the history of these isles, warts and all.

The physical marks and diseases of poverty, such as rickets and tuberculosis, disappeared. Our children walked tall. Working-class women, who in the past were old by 40, were now taking holidays abroad in their sixties and seventies, and cavorting about like young things. This was achieved through politics, meaning the complex relationships of people in society, and the insistence that these relationships should be part of the criteria guiding macro-economic decision-making. Then siren voices came from across the Atlantic. From Chicago a gang of economists—the monetarists—emerged who wanted to drive government and politics out of economics, who insisted the market should determine everything as it had in the 1930s.

Keith Joseph heard these voices and relayed them to his disciples, including a young woman from Grantham who became a zealot. The Blessed Margaret was up and running, and became the boss of Britain. Economics were disconnected from social values and social responsibility. Personal greed was not only made acceptable but sanctified as the catalyst of economic activity. It reminded me of that character in Joseph Heller's *Catch 22*, Major

Major's father, who tells his followers: "The Good Lord gave us two hands to grab everything we could for ourselves."

Economics which eschew the human dimension create a society in which, as Marx observed, the only nexus between man and man is callous cash payment. The individual becomes a unit of consumption, a unit of labour, a state statistic, and the seeds of alienation are sown. In pursuit of this credo, NHS patients have been redesignated "customers". The only thing missing is a cash register or credit card machine at the foot of the customer's bed, but it's coming.

Such an economic ethos treats everyone and everything as a commodity, with a price tag. No wonder there is sleaze in Parliament and elsewhere. No wonder there seem to be more crooks in the City than in Barlinnie. No wonder the commercial exploitation of sex is at an all-time high. If everything is a commodity, how could sex be an exception? Mrs Thatcher said: "There is no such thing as society." Which means that instead of human beings living together, independent and interdependent, one with another, we are simply a multiplicity of self-seeking individuals; or as succinctly described by some punters: "Bang the bell Jack, I'm on the bus".

The market and market mechanisms are essential for economic efficiency. The theories of value and exchange of Adam Smith and Karl Marx, which were remarkably similar, presupposed the existence of a market. But neither believed in the absolute dominance of market forces to the exclusion of everything else—and anyway both are dead, and since their deaths the world has changed enormously.

The absolute dominance of market forces has been tried and has grotesquely failed. It is economics without a soul and, therefore, amoral. It led to the most horrendous world wars in human history. We cannot take our youth into the new millennium lumbered by such outrageous and outmoded baggage.

We need political economists. We need politicians who assert that it's impossible in a civilised society to take economic decisions abstracted from their social consequences. We need such an option available to us, at the next election—but it looks as if we won't get it. The Tories are still ideologically imprisoned in Thatcherite market and monetarist dogma. Labour is adapting itself to Thatcherite dogma in the belief that it is a vote winner. If Labour wins it will hand to the Bank of England the right to determine interest rates, an important economic tool in the hands of government in pursuit of full employment and other socially desirable objectives.

Banks take decisions on an evaluation of market forces and economic indices—that is their job. Governments are there to serve the public interest. If political parties give up the powers and instruments by which, in government, they might serve the public interest, then they are powerless to do good for the people, which is what socialist politics is supposed to be about.

If we go back to the economics of the past, we will have the problems of the past, writ large. The past has value in memories that might guide us to better ways.

STATUES TO MAKE
THE HEART BLEED

28 SEPTEMBER 1995

IF CHRISTIAN statues can weep what's wrong with Hindu statues drinking? But why milk? Why not a good swally, like an 18-year-old malt. Religious statues seem twee in their manifestations. Milk has a gentle image. The milk of human kindness and all that, though this is cow's milk they're swallyin', and weeping signifies sorrow or sympathy. But there must be times when the Deity gets cheesed off with antics that deserve something more condemnatory than tears or milk. He could make a statue urinate as a sign of his contempt for the fleshpot materialism so rampant in today's world.

Maybe He has and it was hidden by respectable adherents because statues are not supposed to pee in public, and anyway a urinating statue has less box-office appeal than one that weeps. Such believers would turn God into a kind of candy-floss celestial impresario. A mixture of Mary Poppins and Sir Andrew Lloyd Webber.

Such a god would be a dead loss. I prefer the Christ who stormed the temple and couped over the tables of the money changers. He wasn't respectable, kept the company of publicans, befriended a lady of the night, and would have been more at home in the company of Rab Nesbitt than He would the average Kirk elder. He was also a subversive to boot. Why should God do tricks to sustain the faith of the faithful? What kind of faith needs buttressing by having Him act like a cosmic Paul Daniels? What evidence is there that He ever did? The case for divinely inspired healing places is not helped by the fact that there is no record of anyone going into these places with one leg and coming out with two.

In the New Testament we read of a man beseeching Christ: "Look upon my son . . . And, lo, a spirit taketh him, and he suddenly crieth out; and it teareth him that he foameth again . . . And Jesus said . . . bring thy son hither . . . And as he was a coming the Devil threw him down, and tare him. And Jesus rebuked the unclean spirit, and healed the child, and delivered him again to his father." This affliction the youngster suffered from we now know as epilepsy.

Contrast this with Hippocrates writing 400 years BC about the same illness: "Men regard its origins as divine from ignorance and wonder, since it is a peculiar condition and not readily understood. Surely then this disease has its physic and causes whence it originates, even as have other diseases, and it is curable by means comparable to their cure . . . Such things are divine or not—as you will, for the distinction matters not—nor is there need to make this distinction anywhere in nature, for have not all a physic which can be found by those who seek it steadfastly?"

There is no proof of the veracity of biblical miracles unless you believe in the absolute literal truth of all that is written in the good book, which means we would have to rewrite the physical history of the planet, for Earth would then be only a few thousand years old, and not the millions of geological science.

Mainstream Christianity believes in the allegorical and not the literal truth of the Bible. Jesus Christ did exist. He was just over 5ft, dark, and slightly stooped, yet we've got Him looking like a young Peter O'Toole with the disposition of a delegate to a Liberal Democrat conference.

Jesus was a member of a Jewish sect, the Essenes, who lived in highly organised groups and held all property in common. The message Christ preached in the Sermon on the Mount was Essenian. His belief that we were all children of the same heavenly Father was a revolutionary doctrine in the context of the Roman Empire, based on slavery. Jesus Christ must have been an outstanding preacher. His message comes powerfully down through the ages and is more relevant today than ever before. For Him it was how you treated others that mattered: "What you did unto the least . . . you did unto me."

Try judging our political masters by this standard. What have they done unto the poor, the mentally sick, the weak and defenceless except make them poorer, sicker, weaker and more defenceless?

I find it impossible to believe in a supreme being who made the world and invented phlegm. But I know why believers believe and sometimes wish I could too. If some believe their statues are getting tore into milk, then so be it. If I ha'e doots, then so be it, but we can agree that children everywhere should get the milk they need.

Believers and non-believers might not agree about Heaven, but we can agree not to make Earth a hell. No messiah will save the environment that our greed endangers. No saviour will save our economy and give it moral purpose. We have to do it for ourselves.

In the film *Viva Zapata!* Marlon Brando, playing the peasant leader who became President, is resigning because he fears that power is corrupting. His lieutenant tells him, "Our people need a strong leader," and Zapata replies, "Only a weak people need a strong leader; our people must learn to be strong." That is true of all peoples. And anyway, "strong leader" is a euphemism for actual or apprentice despots. From Herod to Maggie.

Every time I board an aircraft I wonder. Flying tenements. For humans who lived in past centuries such a phenomenon would be a miracle to surpass anything. Maybe God gave us the capacity to work these miracles, but we have to make them work for the good of everyone. Here the words of Christ come into play. "What you do unto the least of men you do unto me", and me, and you.

OH FOR A NEW JANE AUSTEN

5 OCTOBER 1995

I KNEW an old guy who told the truth about something and was jailed for sedition. He started reading the novels of Jane Austen found in the prison library and thought them sublime. Halfway through the last book they told him his time was up and he must leave the premises. He pleaded for another day inside, that he might finish it.

That's the magic of Jane, maiden aunt, daughter of a country clergyman. In her novels nothing much seems to happen. People die considerately, off-stage, lest they remind us of our own mortality. Her heroines seldom leave the drawing rooms or gardens of the landed gentry except for forays to Bath and London for the "Season".

She lived through the French Revolution and the wars of the Napoleonic Empire, yet not a word of these events appears in her writings. It seems like a formula for mind-boggling boredom, but it isn't.

Her books fizz with excitements, comic caricatures, and barely containable understated passions which stimulate the imagination in a way that a more sexually explicit writer cannot do. There are minor and major dramas, and a wicked sense of humour at work. She was one of the best novelist-satirists ever to breathe a genteel breath.

She never went beyond the confines of the social groupings to which she belonged. But it's wrong to interpret this as acceptance of a status quo whose banalities she obviously loathed. Her writings are an onslaught on the values and cruelties of her times, in which young ladies were bred for breeding and marriage, preferably with sires of great wealth. She was a feminist before the word was coined, but wouldn't have been seen dead in dungarees.

She wrote for the enjoyment of family and friends and had to be persuaded to have her writings published for wider circulation. The rest is history. Two hundred years on we are still mesmerised by her insights. The BBC's serialisation of *Pride and Prejudice* is outstanding and brings Jane to a new generation, hopefully sparking off renewed interest in her novels.

Viewers will already have noted that young Army officers in *Pride and Prejudice* are portrayed as brainless twits, and that's because they were brainless twits. These were times when the landed gentry bought commissions for the less intellectually endowed of their male progeny. The NCOs ran the Army while the officers rode with hounds and whored in brothels. The intellectual vacuity of most officers was still extant when I was doing my National Service in the RAF. During initial training we were given political lectures and at the opening session the officer said that in here, the lecture room, there was no rank, and we should frankly express our opinions, without fear or inhibition.

We took him at his word and it soon became clear that he hadn't a clue, nor did any of the other officers. They were simply reading a briefing, written by others, probably descendants of Attila the Hun. Another factor was operating. We were sick to the back teeth of being bawled at by skin-headed, bone-headed bampots called drill instructors who operated a system calculated to take away our dignity and make us more malleable to their every command. The lecture room was where we could hit back with impunity, and did.

Our squad became the talk of the NAAFI, and a funny thing happened: our drill instructors became rather proud of their rookies, who were dancing rings round the officers in debate and showed plenty of bottle in doing so.

To be honest, dancing rings round these officers was no great thing, for they were spectacularly dense. The intellectual failures of the British middle class were still being dumped in the armed forces. But things changed. You couldn't hand a hi-tech, multimillion pound military aircraft to unintelligent Hooray Henries. As the military became more hi-tech, officer recruitment and promotion had to be based on ability, and nothing else.

We now probably have the most intelligent officer cadre in the history of the British armed forces. Listen to them explain operational difficulties in Bosnia, and you know you're listening to intelligent men.

In July 1988 I received a letter.

"Dear Mr Reid, Along with many other Servicemen I very much enjoyed your recent television series, *Reid About the USSR*, and found it compelling viewing. As we move, hopefully, to a Europe with fewer tensions we are trying to follow and understand the seminal changes in the Soviet Union. Your insights and those of your colleagues help to put flesh on the dry bones of official assessments."

Then followed an invitation to a black-tie dinner in the Royal Artillery Mess, Woolwich, with about 40 flag, general, and air officers. Later, in the more informal atmosphere of the Music Room, I was to speak and answer questions.

The letter was from Lieutenant General Sir Anthony Walker KCB, Deputy Chief of Defence Staff. I accepted the invitation. The dinner was splendid in a room that only lacked Errol Flynn fencing on top of the table. But the questions and discussion were a real eye-opener. There were no blimps. Instead there was intelligence and a firm grasp of the complexities of a deadly critical situation in what was the USSR. The Soviet economy was doomed, it didn't work. A quick collapse would lead to anarchy which could destabilise the whole landmass. The pace of economic change had to be managed and moderated. The military top brass understood, our politicians didn't.

Britain today, as the Army of yore, is led by dunderheads. Politicians reply to debates with speeches written before the debate, and get away with it. Spin doctors make crass career politicians look like St Francis of Assisi. Oh for a new Jane Austen to mock their evil pomposities. In the meantime, enjoy the old Jane, courtesy of the Beeb.

"HERE'S FREEDOM TO THEM
THAT WAD WRITE"

19 OCTOBER 1995

KEVIN MAXWELL'S old man was indeed a bully, and anyone who knew him knows that to be true. A bully needs to surround himself with people who can be bullied. Those bullied by brutes in domestic circumstances or in schools have little choice and evoke our sympathy. Others allow themselves to be bullied for base reasons.

Bob Maxwell had the enormous unelected power that goes with the ownership and control of enormous wealth. He used his wealth to buy executives whom he bullied. They could have told him to get stuffed, but his money bought their compliance.

I was in the *Mirror* building in London one day and he phoned down and boomed: "Jimmy, I heard you were in the building, come up and see me for a minute." It was to be for more than a minute.

His waiting room was crowded with Mirror Group executives. He came to his office door, jacket off, broad galluses, the fashion accessory to come of the busy young executive, valiantly holding up his trousers. He ushered me into his office without a glance at those waiting. Cap'n Bob wanted to talk about everything under the sun. When I made moves to leave he would immediately branch into some other subject, suggesting more tea or coffee and sandwiches, a brandy perhaps. Eventually I had to go or miss my plane. He walked me to the door, bade me bon voyage, then closed it without even a peep outside. The same people were waiting. Some I knew. We swopped pleasantries. One let it drop that they had been waiting since 9 o'clock that morning. It was now after 4pm. I was shocked and angry.

Angry at Maxwell for treating people like this. Angry at those who let him treat them this way. I was just a Mirror Group columnist at the time but wouldn't wait hours for anyone, unless there was a bloody good reason, like a near fatal accident, and nor would any other punter. But these guys hadn't the bottle of the punter. Executive status and salaries, not to mention the executive toilet, meant more to them than humiliation.

In 1986 Kenny Gallagher, *Herald* scribe, jazz fan extraordinaire, Glesgafied Dundonian, and good friend, told me that Kelvin McKenzie, editor of the *Sun*, was very keen to have a word with me. I was intrigued. My political viewpoint and the editorial line of the *Sun* were diametric opposites. We met in a hotel restaurant near the Embankment. Kelvin wanted me to work for him as a columnist. Free to write what I wanted.

I explained the need for me to have discussions with others, particularly with some political friends. He understood. I discussed the proposition with Neil Kinnock, then leader of the Labour Party. Neil wanted me to accept for they desperately wanted a friendly voice within the tabloid he considered a priceless vote winner for the Tories. Later Glenys joined us for a meal in an Italian restaurant in Covent Garden. It was delightful. When relaxed, away from the public eye and able to be themselves, they are excellent company. It was a great pity that their natural likeability was overlaid with media hype and gloss by the spin doctors during General Elections.

But Neil had decided, I think in consultation with others, that it would be prudent to explain everything to Maxwell, who promptly exploded. The upshot was that I was to stay put, as they didn't want to antagonise the owner of the Mirror Group and the only tabloid newspapers that gave it support.

I wrote to Kelvin McKenzie and briefly explained the circumstances. He wrote back saying his offer still stood, etc. The outcome was that I ended up writing for the *Mirror* and the *Record* at a time when contracted to the production of television documentaries. It was a bit of a bind. Maxwell explained the position to me and asked if I wanted paid offshore. My "What!" spoke volumes and he quickly changed the subject. This it seemed, was standard practice for some, in this bastion of "socialism".

It was quietly resolved by myself that Labour's leader would eventually have what he thought best for the Labour movement, without bringing down the wrath of Maxwell on his head, and so it came to be. Neil's fear of antagonising Maxwell, whom he thought mad, was perfectly understandable, given the hostility to Labour of all other mass circulation papers. But the issue had to be faced sooner or later, and not just by Labour. Why should the likes of Maxwell or Murdoch have such political clout? They hadn't earned it by the display of social virtues. They weren't noted for their advocacy of a moral philosophy which might add to the sensibility of civic and public life.

They were wheelers and dealers, made money, and therefore had power. They bought newspapers and television outlets and thus political power. Party leaders court them as if they came to where they were by divine right, feudal kings in a free-market economy.

The Mirror Group de-recognised trade unions. Labour promises to legislate for trade-union rights for the workers at GCHQ, Cheltenham, but will not declare itself in support of trade-union rights at the *Mirror*, because it doesn't want to offend the new owners.

Murdoch is wooed by Blair and Major though he hasn't even got a vote in this country. Neither will take a stand against the extent of his cross-media ownership because they fear the hostility of his papers. The right to vote is a fundamental factor in the democratic equation. Access to information is equally important. An uninformed, misinformed electorate devalues the vote and makes nonsense of democracy. Vast concentrations of media ownership, unconstrained by public accountability, are a violation of the democratic ethos.

Every dictator starts by seizing control of the media. Why in a free society should a few people be allowed to buy it all up? Our democracy needs smaller groupings of independent newspapers which would be more likely to reflect the plural views of our society, and near monopoly control of commercial television should be taboo.

> Here's freedom to them that wad read,
> Here's freedom to them that wad write,
> There's nane ever fear'd that the truth should be heard,
> But they whom the truth would indite.

We Scots don't need spin doctors, we've got Rabbie and he spun the truth in beautiful language.

UNIONS MUST LOOK
FOR NEW ALLIES

16 NOVEMBER 1995

A SCOTTISH Labour MP protests at the de-commissioning of a nuclear submarine. This, he complained, would reduce Britain's nuclear arsenal. New Labour, it appears, is now a more vigorous advocate of nuclear weaponry than the Tories.

A Scottish Labour MP outlined New Labour's plan to force unemployed youngsters to go on "training" courses. Youngsters who have been on various gimmicks before and are still unemployed might well say, "Gies a job but stuff your gimmicks", and then have their already meagre benefits slashed by a New Labour government. If the Tories had any sense they would have included this in the Queen's Speech. It is, after all, their kind of thinking.

A North of England Labour MP says that if the Government introduces tax cuts in the forthcoming Budget Labour should support them. The health service is in crisis. If we have a cruel winter more pensioners will die of hypothermia. Serious problems endanger the fabric of our social life. And back at Westminster the Government squalidly pursues cuts in social provisions to fund tax cuts for the don't-give-a-damn greedy.

Will this MP's worthiness as a Labour candidate be challenged by the Labour leader, as was the worthiness of Liz Davies? The answer is no. One thing is certain. If there are tax cuts in the Budget, New Labour's attitude will be determined by tactical considerations, principles won't come into it.

Blair attacks Major for lurching to the right, which really is rich. He is the most right-wing Labour leader there has ever been, including Ramsay MacDonald. MacDonald joined the Tories. Tories now join New Labour.

Blair is a master of the ambiguous. Rory Bremner makes a telling point about his rhetoric. He perorates. New Labour. New Britain. New Labour Britain. New Start, New Labour. His speech is verbless. New Labour's action man is verbally actionless, except when ditching Labour principles.

In his conference speech he was absolutely specific about one thing, he did a deal with British Telecom to let this company, the third biggest in Britain, have access to cable. John Major, Tory Prime Minister, then lectures the leader of New Labour on the dangers of such an awesome concentration of power in the hands of a private capitalist monopoly.

Pause for a moment. Think of it. A Tory Prime Minister has to warn a Labour leader about the dangers of capitalist monopolies. The same Labour leader then accuses the same Tory Prime Minister of lurching to the right.

Mr Blair spoke this week to the national conference of the CBI, and there is nothing wrong with that. Business is a vital component of any society and the captains of industry are important, but so are others. Workers are important, without them there is no industry.

Blair's speech to the CBI was cooing, wooing, placatory, reassuring about taxes. He was speaking to companies which have bankrolled the Tory party for years. New Labour. New Britain. Nothing to worry about.

Compare this with his speech to the TUC. Bambi then becomes John Wayne. Straight talking. Shooting from the hip. A man's got to do . . . The unions pay millions into Labour's coffers. Then they are told in cooingless and wooingless words that they can expect no favours from his government. Fair enough; the unions should tell him, more graciously, that his government should not expect too many favours from them.

Long before Blair and New Labour I had come to the conclusion that trade unions should play a more independent political role because the interests of their members and their families were often fundamentally affected, one way or another, by the decisions of all governments.

In the 1970s trade union leaders did get too involved in quasi-governmental institutions. At the time I argued that if trade union leaders wanted to play a part in governing the country they should resign their union posts and stand for Parliament.

The danger of such involvement is not that unions dominate government, but that government dominates the unions. Free trade unions, like the judiciary, have to be independent of government, all governments, any government.

Unions might campaign for Labour in a General Election but if Labour is elected then a principled distance has to be maintained between the two. If not, one suborns the other, and I know who does the suborning.

Trade unions should be campaigning for their own specific political objectives, including union rights and a raft of social demands which would benefit their members. They should be raising these with all political parties, reaching out to new allies in the civic life of the nation. Not to do so is a dereliction of professional duty.

Many trade unionists are not Labour Party members, some are not even Labour voters. There is no reason why trade union politi-

cal demands should conform to Labour policies. There is no reason why they shouldn't go beyond Labour policies. In present
circumstances there is every reason why they must do so.

In the fullness of time, a New Labour government is likely to
introduce constitutional reforms that will lead to the state funding
of political parties. New Labour will then seek to sever its organic
links with the trade unions. Such links will be deemed incompatible with the electoral programmes of a party that now recognises
no special links with the working class or wage earners, which is
true.

I think New Labour will be the losers, not the unions, for unions
have an objective existence in society whatever the fortunes of
political parties. On the other hand the union link is Labour's roots
among wage earners, even among those wage earners who aren't
union members, and among the working class in general. It's a
matter of deep-rooted ideas, psychology, class, community, and a
sense of identity and belonging, that defines who, and what, we
are.

I have no time for the ultra left but the ultra right are worse, and
more cold-blooded. There is talk of an emerging consensus, within
the higher echelons of the British Establishment, that the economy
can no longer afford the welfare state, that a Tory government
would not be allowed by the people to dismantle the welfare state,
but a Blair government, driven by the internal logic of its own
right-wing rationale, could and would. A chilling thought.

THE TRIVIALITY THAT
STARTED AN AVALANCHE

7 DECEMBER 1995

WHAT have O J Simpson and New Labour got in common? No convictions. One of many jokes ridiculing New Labour's propensity for abandoning principles, at the drop of a hat. Mind you, conviction politics has connotations of fanaticism, a touch of the Margaret Thatchers. Conviction politicians, rattling out certitudes, rat tat tat, like a Gatling gun and stamping all over our sensibilities in their mental tackety jackboots, are not a pretty sight. Stick to principles, I implore, instead of convictions, and you won't go far wrong.

Without principles you are un-principled. You can live without principles, slugs and worms do it all the time, but it isn't a life for the Homo sapiens, whom God or nature decreed should walk upright. Principles can change, and if it's an honest change then you're none the worse for it; you might even be better. But to change or drop principles in the pursuit of power, corrupts. Let me give you two examples from the history of the British Labour movement.

In 1951 Nye Bevan resigned from the Labour Government because Hugh Gaitskell, then Chancellor of the Exchequer, was proposing to make patients pay for medical services that had previously been free. The proposed charges were minimal. One shilling (five pence in current coinage) per prescription. Today it's £5.25 per item.

Bevan believed these charges were an abandonment of a profoundly important principle. Fellow Labour MPs accused him of trawling up trivialities.

In his resignation speech to the House of Commons, Nye gave them a most appropriate history lesson. "I remember the triviality that started an avalanche in 1931. I remember it very well, and perhaps my honourable friends would not mind my recording it. There was a trade union group meeting upstairs. I was a member of it and went along—the first subject was an attack on seasonal workers. That was the first order. I opposed it bitterly, and when I came out of the room my good old friend George Lansbury attacked me for attacking the order. I said, 'George, you do not realise this is the beginning of the end. Once you start this there is no logical stopping point'." Nor was there.

In 1929 a Labour Government was elected. Ramsay MacDonald became Prime Minister. His Government, loyally toeing the Treasury line, was trying to resolve the economic difficulties of the global market economy by exacting more sacrifices from the poor. They started betraying one principle, and then another, till the cupboard was bare.

With no principles left, MacDonald and other members of his Cabinet were drawn inexorably into an alliance with the right wing of the Conservative Party. MacDonald and those Labour MPs around him joined a coalition government which made immediate and savage attacks on relief benefits for the unemployed and their families.

By the late Thirties, according to John Boyd Orr, more than one third of Scotland's population was suffering from malnutrition;

61

many starving to death. Rickets was rife. TB and other killer diseases stalked our land. It was the slaughter of the innocent. Scotland became a killing field for babes in arms, with the highest recorded infant mortality rate in Europe. Three of the slaughtered innocents were my sisters, a factor which shaped my entire outlook on life.

Twenty years later Bevan was again warning of the consequences of abandoning principle. Let Labour impose charges for the first time within the health service "and there will be no logical stopping point". Nor has there been. Henceforth there would be no moral argument about a free health service, that principle had been surrendered in Gaitskell's Budget. The debate in future could only be about the severity of charges. When proposed by a Tory government, Labour protests are drowned by Tory cries of "you started it. You first brought in charges." I heard it again this year in a televised parliamentary debate.

At some stage the NHS edifice will collapse. We will have a well-equipped and funded private health service for the rich, and a tenth-rate underfunded public health service for the poor.

Rich ladies will do charity work for the sick poor; pub raffles might purchase a second-hand dialysis machine; failing that Princess Diana will hold the hands of the poor till they die. That's how it's going. That's where it will end. Discard your principles and you become ideologically naked, forced to pinch the clothes of others and claim them as your own.

This week New Labour decided to abstain on a Government proposal within the Budget to cut one penny off income tax. It might appear to be a "triviality", as the health charges of 1951 were perceived by many on Labour's side. There was, however, a principle involved.

A penny off income tax will cost the Exchequer nearly £2000m—money that can't now be spent on badly damaged public services. By abstaining the parliamentary Labour Party was, in a very real sense, an accomplice to an unprincipled misuse of public funds. Even to vote for tax cuts would have been more dignified than cowardly abstention, simulated opposition, or the parliamentary equivalent of a fake orgasm.

I have never seen a British political party scatter its principles to the wind as New Labour has done in the past 18 months. There is no discernible difference with the Tories on economic, social, and foreign policies. New Labour is really New Tory.

There is no distinctive philosophical base to New Labour's thinking. It reacts to electoral phenomena and nothing else. A philosophical ambiguity as reflected in the leader's peculiar verb-less mode of speech. Tough on crime. Tough on the causes of crime. It's a soap powder sales pitch. New Labour. New soft soap. New Labour soft soap. Tough on dirt. Tough on the causes of dirt. Can even erase memories of when Labour had principles of its own.

THE PERNICIOUS EFFECT
OF WISHY-WASHY RACISM

23 DECEMBER 1995

THERE are more than two million Asians in Britain. Many have been born here. All are British citizens. More than 77% vote Labour. Seven British Asians stood for selection as Labour parliamentary candidates for the impending General Election. All were rejected.

The last to be rejected was Mohammed Sarwar in Govan who lost the nomination by one vote. Fifty-two votes of accredited party members were ruled ineligible. The majority had been cast for Mohammed Sarwar.

Maybe in each of these constituencies racism played no part. But one thing's for sure, if Mohammed Sarwar was called Maurice Smith there wouldn't be a fraction of the public and media interest we now see focused on the Govan Constituency Labour Party.

I remember once sitting in the control room of a television programme on the results, which were flowing in, of local government elections in Scotland. On the screen came up the news,

Bashir Maan wins in Glasgow. The director who was, as you would expect, directing the operation, cried out to his minions: "Scotland's first coon cooncillor." Everyone laughed. I didn't. The man wasn't kidding. He was a full-blooded racist.

Our main problem, however, isn't the full-blooded racist but the wishy washy one, who quite likes blacks as long as they know their place and they don't forget it as in the America of 50 years ago. Negroes voted Democrat. The Democrat bosses welcomed negro votes, but not negro candidates. Negroes determined to be candidates were considered uppity niggers. There are those today in Scotland who consider Mohammed Sarwar an "uppity Paki". To deny this, is dishonest.

In a very real sense it couldn't be otherwise. Until fairly recently, in the timescale of history, our country was the centre of the biggest empire the world has ever seen. Empire implies subject peoples. The Romans had no qualms about their empire and subject peoples. They simply saw them as the legitimate booty of conquest.

But after the Enlightenment, European nations had to disguise their empire-building, and dress it up as a humanitarian crusade. The savages had to be civilised. We could subdue them, no bother at all, our cannons against their spears. But as they were unfit to govern themselves (though they had been doing so for thousands of years), we would govern them instead, and the missionaries would come and try to show them our ways.

This whole approach was based on a hierarchical delineation of peoples, which defined their fitness or unfitness to govern, based on a concept of superior and inferior races. To the colonialist, unfitness to govern was in practice permanent. The inferiority of colonised people was genetic and not cultural. A view which differed in degree, but not in substance, from the Nazi concept of race.

Read the popular fiction of those Empire days, still very much in our public libraries. Agatha Christie wrote a book *Ten Little*

Niggers. Her non-white characters are, shall we say, invariably dubious. She was also a rabid anti-Semite. So was John Buchan, author of *The Thirty-Nine Steps*.

Some of Britain's most revered twentieth-century poets were anti-Semitic and racist. There are existing photographs, taken this century, of official British posters, in the coastal towns of China, which state: "Dogs and Chinese not allowed on these premises."

British writers and film-makers glorified villains like Cecil Rhodes, who went into the African hinterland with a gang of mercenaries, armed with the latest machine-guns and cannons, and slaughtered all who stood in their way. Rhodes gave vast tracts of land, and the people who lived on the land, to his henchmen. Mineral rights he kept mostly to himself.

Queen Victoria blessed his deeds. He became a national hero. Rhodes and his gang did to a big chunk of Africa what Al Capone and his mob did later to Chicago. They split it up among themselves. Each had his own territory. The bigger rackets, which transcended the individual territories, were bossed by Cecil, as with Al in the windy city.

But even Al baulked at calling Chicago, Caponeville. But Cecil's backers, back home in the mother country, for whom he was making an awful lot of bucks, had no such inhibitions. They called a vast area of Africa, Rhodesia, which for sheer chauvinist arrogance takes some beating. Clive more or less did the same kind of dirty deeds on the Indian subcontinent.

The question to be answered is simple and to the point. Can it be true that a people brainwashed for centuries by the implicit and explicit racism of Empire are now completely free of even the vestiges of racism, due to the principled leadership of successive governments that made all of us come to terms with the negative and shameful features of our past? The answer has to be, it isn't true. Just think again of the last night at the Proms and see that jingoism.

The British Empire pioneered the concept of the concentration camp in Southern Africa. The Nazis turned the concept into a grotesque obscenity. Britain, which played such a noble part in the defeat of German fascism, demanded, along with our allies, that the German nation and German people should acknowledge their guilt.

It would do us no harm and a helluva lot of good to acknowledge our own guilt. Britain has contributed to the racial divisions which have torn mankind apart in this century. Ask any of our political leaders to confront this problem and they'll run a mile.

Paul Robeson was one of the finest human beings I've ever known. He was profoundly ashamed of one episode in his life. In the 1930s, when he was living in London, he was talked into doing a movie. It was about a noble young native chief and an even nobler British governor. It was shot in bits and pieces. When he saw the finished product, Paul was devastated.

It was pernicious racism. Good noble savage. Bad noble savage. Wise, strong-minded, English pukka sahib, who is fair, and treats natives, of all ages, as children. The racial paternalism was deeply offensive and poisonous.

He tried to buy the film to burn it, so that it could never be shown. What particularly appalled him was that some of his English friends thought there was nothing wrong with the movie. To them racism was the Ku Klux Klan.

There is more to racism than the crudities of overt fascism. In a sense that is more easily dealt with. After 1945 none but the evil or chronically ignorant could identify with the racism of the National Front or the British National Party.

But there are many levels of racism. One of my favourite television programmes is *Dad's Army*. Corporal Jones regularly regales his comrades with stories about how the fuzzy wuzzies didn't like cold English-steel bayonets stuck up their jacksies. His stories implied that the English Tommy did.

If Corporal Jones met a black man on the street we know he is more likely to give him a black pudding, no pun intended, from his butcher's shop, than a kick up the backside. But if Corporal Jones was a member of the Labour Party, and he might well have been, and this black man was nominated for selection as a Labour candidate, then Corporal Jones might not vote for him.

He might not say much, for he is, after all, a decent old cove who doesn't want to offend anyone. But a black councillor or MP wouldn't sound or feel right to him. It is difficult to come to terms with this kind of racism, for it is ingrained and quiet, and resides in people who are otherwise reasonable.

Was there overt racism in Govan Labour's selection procedures? Definitely not. It would not have been tolerated. But racism has many levels. As a member of the Labour Party in the Govan constituency I became aware that all who had approached me in support of Mike Watson, who is a very good man, were white, university graduates, Christians, comfortably middle-class and with settled careers. Comfortable is the word. And all of them good people.

They had a natural affinity with Mike, who was white, a university graduate, comfortably middle-class, and who thought he had a settled career in politics, until his constituency disappeared due to boundary changes. They identified with Mike's career predicament. They were veterans of the Vietnam marches, student politics of bygone decades, but their chat was no longer a call to arms, but a substitute for action.

They have cruelly been called the chattering classes, but there is an element of truth in it. Sarwar moved not in their circles, nor they in his. Professionally they are miles apart. Cash and Carry, even on the grand scale, is, for them a jumped-up Barras.

The chasm between such people and Sarwar is more cultural than political. The cultural in this context can have slight racial undertones trembling in the background.

Mohammed Sarwar's natural affinity is with current community activists. The richest man around, he wears his wealth well, undemonstratively, and he moves easily among the poor, which isn't surprising, for he knows about poverty, having sampled it first-hand, at its rawest, in the Third World.

Having said that, I'm not certain that Sarwar would be a better MP than Mike Watson, and I'm not certain he wouldn't. We mortals have to take decisions without the benefit of certitude, which is the prerogative of the gods.

One thing is certain, politics has to rise above the subjective if it's to see the way forward, and you can't do this without principles, which are our guiding stars. The electoral loyalty of Asians has given Labour more than 20 seats in the UK. But to treat an ethnic minority as voting fodder is a form of racism, and is unprincipled electoral opportunism. Sarwar should have been elected as Labour's standard bearer in Govan, not in spite of being an Asian, but because he is an Asian.

This was the only principle at stake in this selection ballot. Labour is concerned that there aren't more women Labour MPs and decided, rightly or wrongly, on all-women shortlists in certain constituencies, to "improve the gender balance".

There are no Asian Labour MPs at all. Is racial balance given no priority by the Labour Party? That is how it looks, and as a consequence Labour could now lose Govan. Without the Asian vote, it might also lose Hillhead. The realisation that there won't be a single Asian candidate standing for Labour at the next election is now known by Asians throughout the UK. If they say, enough is enough, then Labour could lose a lot more seats.

This mess was predictable and predicted, by myself, and others. Parliamentary seats were at stake, but much more important, a principle was at stake. A multi-racial society needs multi-racial political parties.

Labour's history and traditions are for the unity of peoples. It was a Labour government that dismantled the Empire. People from the former colonies know this, and look upon Labour as their party. Just as the Irish did, when driven by famine, in years past, to our shores.

I know current leaders of the party are not too keen on old Labour traditions and are getting shot of them, right, left and centre, but mostly left. Some of these traditions became what could be called our birthright.

I believe in the unity of all races and creeds for a better way of life and a more just society, this, part of my birthright as a Scot and a member of the Scottish Labour movement. Part of my reaction to the events of last week was shame. We had once again betrayed an important part of our heritage.

JOHN BUCHAN AND THE LEGACY OF RACISM

4 JANUARY 1996

THE Rev James C G Greig chides me for suggesting that John Buchan was an anti-Semite. In a letter to the *Herald* he wrote: "Some of Buchan's characters do express the suspicion of Jews that was current in the first half of this century".

Well, I suppose that's one way of putting it. In Buchan's novel, *The Three Hostages*, there are abundant references to Jews, niggers, dagos, orientals, and assorted foreigners, that often come from the hero/narrator Richard Hannay—a man who made his money in Africa, was a fervent colonial, man of the Empire, and proud of it.

Here he is describing a sleazy night club: "There were the sham Chinese decorations, the blaze of lights, the nigger band, the whole garish spectacle . . . Round the skirts of the hall was the usual rastaquouère crowd of men and women drinking liqueurs and champagne, and mixed with fat Jews and blue-black dagos the flushed faces of boys from barracks or college who imagined they were seeing life."

There you have it. Nice, white, upper-middle-class young Englishmen, officers and gentlemen all, from the playing fields of Eton, the battlefields of the Empire, the colleges of Oxford and Cambridge, being corrupted by a motley shower of niggers, blue-black dagos, and fat Jews.

Buchan's hero, the indefatigable Hannay, is in an antique shop searching for clues that will expose a dastardly plot to subvert the Empire. Here is how he describes it: "A dishevelled Jewess confronted me, wearing sham diamond earrings." He asks a question. "She made no answer, but fingered her earrings with her plump grubby hands."

So there you have it. Male Jews are fat. Female Jews are dishevelled, have plump grubby hands, and the gall to wear sham diamond earrings. British Christian women, of course, only wore real diamonds.

Sure, oft times I heard my mum say to dear old dad: "Don't waste yer time buyin' me sham diamonds. If I wore them, well, I'd be the talk o' the steamie. They wid say, 'Look at Bella Reid, wearin' sham diamonds. Her man must be skint.'"

Here is Hannay refusing to be provoked by the arch villain: "Then he spat in my face. That, I admit, tried me pretty high. It was such a filthy Kaffir trick that I had some trouble in taking it resignedly. But I managed it." Kaffir is an abusive racist term for a Black African.

Again you can read: "He has lived so long among cringing orientals that his head is swollen like a pumpkin." Jews are fat and grubby. Orientals cringe and have heads like pumpkins. And again, a statement by a friend of Hannay's called Sandy. These are his comments about Gandhi, advocate of passive resistance and lifelong enemy of violence: "He (Gandhi) is always in a technical sense mad—that is, his mind is tilted from its balance, and since we live by balance he is a wrecker, a crowbar in the machinery."

Here are some other quotes, rarely, if ever, qualified in any shape or form by the author: "Look at the Irish! They are the cleverest propagandists extant, and managed to persuade most people that they were a brave, generous, humorous, talented, warm-hearted race, cruelly yoked to a dull mercantile England, when God knows they were exactly the opposite."

One villain is "a Jew with a dyed beard." Fat, plump, grubby-handed, dyed beards, and a weakness for sham diamonds. See those Jews, you've got to watch them, at least Jews as perceived by Buchan. How about this; it could have come from Hitler's *Mein Kampf*? "Cruel, humourless, hard, utterly wanting in sense of proportion, but often full of a perverted poetry and drunk with rhetoric—a hideous, untamable breed had been engendered." Where was this hideous breed to be found? "You found it among the young Bolshevik Jews." So it says on page 27 of my copy of *The Three Hostages*.

On page 13 you can read: " 'Think of it,' he cried. 'All the places with names like spells—Bokhara, Samarkand, run by seedy little gangs of communist Jews.' " So you thought Lenin was born in Simbirsk in April 1870 and baptised in the local church of St Nicholas on April 16? So did I. So you thought Stalin spent his teens in a Georgian seminary, and was being trained as a priest? Funnily enough, so did I. But according to Buchan, they were "seedy" Jews.

When Buchan, by his standards, was being nice to Jews, the poison still dropped. Here is Hannay talking of Julius Victor, a Jewish millionaire: "I remember that Blenkiron, who didn't like his race, had once described him to me as 'the whitest Jew since the Apostle Paul'."

The Three Hostages was first published in 1924. Just about the time Hitler and his gang were setting up shop in Munich. Buchan was no upstart scribbler full of racial poison. He was 1st Baron Tweedsmuir. A Scot. A statesman. Tory politician. Governor-General of Canada, a big wheel in the English Establishment, full of racial poison.

He was steeped in Empire and the racism which it nurtured. This corrupted his thinking, and that of many others.

What I find surprising is that a Scottish clergyman should be a member of the John Buchan Society which seeks to popularise his works. In the name of God, why? Of course he was of his times, so is everyone, so was Mussolini. Buchan was part of a popular British culture that dealt extensively in racial stereotypes. Anti-Semitic jokes abounded. They weren't funny, but steps down a road that led to Auschwitz.

We are not yet free of this influence. We can still hear the language of Buchan's books. The legacy of empire is all around. Institutionalised racism, unawareness of the needs or sensitivities of ethnic communities, is rampant. There isn't a Scottish Asian MP. The longer this goes on the more difficult it is to explain, except as an aversion to Asian candidates, on the part of the parties.

"SPEW OUT THE LUKE WARM!"

12 JANUARY 1996

YOU can't defend the indefensible. The ballot for the selection of Labour's parliamentary candidate for the Govan constituency comes into that category. To call it a shambles would be exceedingly kind; a shambles, after all, is an unintended cock-up. Some things happened in Govan which were intentional, offensive to the democratic spirit, and that was the real worry.

It was always going to be better if Labour sorted this out itself and within the party. Not by some window-dressing exercise but with a thorough-going investigation of all the many alleged irregularities, which, if only one is true, invalidates a ballot won by a single vote.

This investigation will now take place under the probing light of public scrutiny, and this is how it should be. The Labour Party isn't a secret society but the most likely party of government following the next election.

In such a party justice has to be done, it has to be seen to be done. The public have a right to know how a future MP is selected.

An MP is a law-maker. His selection must be within the law. His selection must be within procedures that are in conformity with accepted democratic norms.

One aspect of Labour procedures which emerged in Govan has shocked me and I'm a long-standing member of the party. Party officials, it seems, claim to have the authority to take away the right to vote of party members. These draconian powers are not bestowed on anyone, or any committee, by the party rules, and if they were, the offending clauses should be removed at once, if not before.

You can take away a person's membership, suspend someone from membership, under the rules, and logically this would mean they have no rights within the party, including the right to vote, for they would, by definition, be outwith the party. Now that logic I can follow.

But in a democracy you cannot say "We accept you as a member of the party; we accept you as a member of the local party; we accept your money in the form of dues, but we are taking away your right to vote." No way. And if Govan leads to the abandonment of such a practice then some good will come of it after all, and I mean good for the Labour Party.

In politics the most pernicious underminers of democracy are those whose response to a wrong or injustice, in a party which they might love, is to say, let's cover it up, it might harm the party.

If it's a party worth its salt you will do more damage by the concealment of wrong-doing than by its exposure. And implicit in this attitude is a contempt for the people. It's like saying, "There is something we know that is bad, but we can handle it, but we had better keep it from the people, for they can't." That's how the Politburo of the old Soviet Communist Party thought, and what a fine mess they got in.

In recent weeks we have had in the *Herald* a debate about latent and institutionalised racism in Scotland, including within the Labour Party, arising from events in Govan. People have told me they have discovered layers of racism in themselves which they had not realised were there. That has flowed from this debate and that's got to be good.

The honesty and openness of the exchanges can only be good and healthy for Scotland, which I want to see as the most open, the most open-minded, and the most tolerant wee country in the world.

You won't get that when so-called elites talk to other elites, with the people shut out. I'm fed up with philosophers who talk and write only for other philosophers. Sociologists who gabble on in an incomprehensible jargon about the problems of the sub-class without touching in the slightest the lives of these poor people they purport to serve.

I've rejoiced in our letters page even when I've been getting dokey. People must talk. Speak up for themselves. Speak up for others. We need a speak-up society where people feel they have something to say, and can say it, and others are listening. People who feel they can change things, and they could, if only enough spoke out. Silent pain evokes no sympathy, as Nye Bevan used to say, and he was right.

If things are wrong, holler. Some members of the Govan Labour Party did that, and an injustice might therefore be rectified, but the powder is being kept dry, just in case. In addition it might help bring some better understanding of our Asian friends, and their difficulties in adapting to institutions which emanate from a different culture. Because it was a public debate it might bring some wider public good, and who says it's over?

My favourite biblical text is, "I would spew out the lukewarm." My interpretation of this text is, "We need warmth in our hearts and fire in our bellies." Just think of this—our country is full of bloody terrible problems.

Twenty years ago the level of unemployment that prevails today would have provoked a revolution. The employed would have and actually did march in support of the unemployed when the numbers without work were only a fraction of what they are today. But today we accept it without a murmur. Now you can call that many things, but it sure ain't progress.

Today the employed slink past the homeless as if they weren't there. Warm homes beckon where they might erase from their minds all thoughts of the poor buggers on the streets. And the poor buggers might be teenagers whose benefits were abolished by this Government.

The Labour movement, in my opinion, should be the conscience of the nation. It works best when its own house is cleansed and when we acknowledge that sometimes in our attitude to others we fall beneath that level of compassion that should spring naturally from our socialist principles. But we cannot love justice without hating injustice. And you must fight injustice even in your own party, even more in your own party.

THE RIGHT TO ECONOMIC FREEDOM

8 FEBRUARY 1996

SOME fools seem to suggest that nations are products of whim or whimsy. As if, when it comes to nationality, we have an option, a subjective choice on the matter. This really is a load of codswallop.

I'm a Scot, proud to be so, but had no choice. My birth, the geography of my birth, my lineage, my heritage, my nationality, were settled as I was born. It was the same for you, and everyone.

A nation cannot be decreed into existence or out of existence by kings, queens, political leaders, or anyone else. A nation evolves historically, and though all are different, there are common criteria.

A nation is a territorial entity. Settled boundaries consolidate nationhood. A common language is a feature of most nations; not necessarily exclusive to one nation. Brazil and Portugal, for example, share the same language but are different nations.

Territory and a common language do not themselves make a nation. There has to be an internal economic bond. A nation also has what I can only call a spiritual dimension. A common and specific historical experience, shared conditions of life, and many other subtleties, come together in a common cultural experience that produces a national culture. A nation is all these things and other things I haven't thought of, or don't yet know about.

Nations having evolved historically become indestructible. Ethnic cleansing and genocide are diabolical and massive barbarities but have never succeeded in their objective. Despite Hitler the Jewish nation is stronger than ever. Nations earmarked for destruction by numerous despots are alive and kicking, the despots gone, if not forgotten.

In the Treaty of Union it was decreed that henceforth there would be neither an England nor a Scotland, but Great Britain. Nearly 300 years later one of the major issues at the next General Election will be the constitutional relationship between England and Scotland.

Instead of trying to will nations out of existence we should be glorying in their indestructibility and coming to terms with their great potential for good. Genuine peace is peace between nations, not the denial of nationhood.

The people of all nations, big and small, have an absolute right of self-determination. The two most destructive wars in human history took place this century and one of the factors leading to the bloodshed was the denial of national self-determination.

A love of all that's good in one's own nation generates respect and a love of all that's good in other nations. This provides the logical basis of genuine internationalism.

I've always been suspicious of cosmopolitanism which would reduce all of us to a kind of spurious nothingness with no national identity or specific roots. Cosmopolitanism has also been the cloak of big nations seeking the domination of other nations.

You would think Germans would have learned the lesson of their nation's awful recent past. In my experience the majority of ordinary Germans have done just that, but their leaders were and are a different kettle of fish. The only one I've trusted was Willi Brandt.

Helmut Kohl, the current chancellor, is no Brandt. He has the overweening ambition of an essentially shallow man. Last week he lectured Europe with a text that argued the days of the nation state were over. This from the man whose hasty and premature recognition of the breakaway nation state of Croatia, from what had been Yugoslavia, helped plunge a large chunk of the Balkans into murderous civil war, is an arrogance too far. Particularly as Croatia in 1939-44 became the prime acolyte of the Nazis in their onslaught against other peoples in that region.

His insensitivity is boundless. Germany has tried twice in the past 80 years to put an end to other nation states in Europe by military might, and to unite the continent under the hegemony of the German nation state. Is Kohl dreaming of the same objective through an economically monolithic Europe dominated by German economic power?

My views on this issue are not comparable or compatible with the Tory Little Englander Eurosceptics. I'm for a single market, for we have nowhere else to go. There is no going back to Commonwealth Preferences. These disappeared when we signed the Treaty of Rome.

In general, Maastricht is an inevitable step along the road to European economic union, but such a union cannot preclude national sovereignty in the economic sphere, and for very compelling reasons.

In any inhabited area of this planet there will be disparate levels of economic development. One of the major difficulties in tackling the post-war economic problems of the UK was that the level of economic activity in the South-east of England was greater than in Scotland, Wales, and the North of England.

The economy in the South-east would overheat. British Governments would slam on the brakes to counter the overheating. But the Scottish economy, far from being overheated, was still cold,

81

not having recovered from the last recession. The application of brakes to meet the needs of the South-east plunged our economy still further into decline.

If this is true of the UK then it's going to be true, in spades, for the European Union.

Nations must have rights to protect their economies. The destruction of a nation's economy is more deadly to the future of a nation than almost anything else. I believe these profoundly important matters can be resolved and a balance struck, but not by Britain kowtowing to everything that comes from Brussels and Bonn, or by Britain resisting legitimate progressions towards the coming together of the peoples and countries of Europe.

In Britain the debate on this issue is ludicrous. There is no sense coming from the increasingly Europhobic Conservative Party. Labour, as with everything else, is afraid to define policies on Europe lest it offends someone, anyone. The SNP, against London rule, seems happy to accept more stringent Brussels rule. The Lib-Dems view Brussels as sacrosanct. Thus doth party electoral obsession make cowards of them all.

CHOKED BY OUR OWN GREED

29 FEBRUARY 1996

AN AMERICAN singer of yesteryear, whose household name I can't recall, had a hit with a song that went, "Shrimp boats are a coming, their sails are in sight." The opening "shrimp" and "their sails are in sight" was a lyric potentially fraught with danger, particularly if the singer had swallowed a few haufs and was inclined to rush his words.

This reminds me of the old football scribe who enthused in print about a marvellous goal and ended his purple passage, "He then shit from all of 25 yards. It went screaming into the net. The goalie could only look and wonder." I bet he did.

For a small fishing town in America the shrimp boats were no longer "a coming", they weren't even "a going". The shrimps on which the local economy depended had disappeared. Local marine biologists sought an explanation. Some young scientists found the answer, more than a thousand miles away.

A factory in New York was dumping toxic effluent into the river. This effluent was carried by tides and currents down the east coast of America and attacked the sea flora which nurtured the early life of the plankton-like creatures which were the staple food of the shrimps in the waters fished by the men from this small town.

It was a classic example of the complex and often delicate food chain which sustains all life in this planet. Break one link in the chain and we might rue the consequences. Break many links and we might die from the consequences. Man's dominion over his fellow creatures should never be arrogantly discharged. We are part of nature's overall equation, not above or beyond it.

Real progress comes not from challenging the laws of nature but from understanding them and using them to our advantage. The whole science of agronomy was based on understanding the laws that governed the development of plant life. We wanted to fly. We learned to fly not by breaking the law of gravity but by devising the science of aeronautics based on the use of natural laws.

The human species can do anything within the laws of nature. When we try to work outwith these laws we are in danger, even if we don't yet know the essence of the dangers. We have used more and more chemical fertilisers, successful in terms of land productivity, but we don't know what's happening in the longer term.

Don't let experts tell you that they know. If you have enough money you can get experts to corroborate anything. When the causal link between cigarette smoking and cancer was overwhelming, scientists working for the tobacco industry still swore there was no proven link.

In the past century, if the needs of British industry required, let's say, 5% of the working class to be literate and mathematically aware, then a government expert would prove that only 5% of the working class would benefit from higher education. If this moved to 10% then the same experts, or a new generation of experts in the service of the State, would be trundled out to prove that only 10% of the working class would benefit from higher education. They would "prove" anything the government wanted proved.

Such intellectual prostitutes keep cropping up throughout history and always in the service of those who govern directly or indirectly. But we also give too much respect to honest experts, for they too are often wrong, honestly wrong. You will have experiences of your own, where experts were wrong and your acumen or instinct was correct. Here are two examples from my own experience.

As a councillor in Clydebank I was opposed to high-rise flats. Good guys, architects, and town planners of some considerable standing told me I was wrong and that high-rise developments were the only answer to the problems of housing in the conurbations of countries like the United Kingdom.

I still had my doubts and in my inaugural speech as rector of Glasgow University I referred to high-rise flats as "filing cabinets for human beings". Apart from that the weight of their expert opinion muted my public criticism. Today no high flats are being built. They weren't a solution and created a lot of new problems.

Twenty-five years ago I was in 10 Downing Street with fellow shop stewards from Upper Clyde Shipbuilders for talks with the then Prime Minister, Mr Edward Heath. On the basis of briefings from his experts, he told us that rivers like the Clyde had no future for they could not physically accommodate the size of ships that were needed in this modern age. He spoke of tankers and bulk carriers of half a million and even one million tonnes.

In response I made three points. First, more than 98% of the world's ports could not handle vessels in excess of 50,000 tons. Secondly, bulk carriers and tankers were only economical if the payload in terms of cargo was right. In a recession the giant tankers would be the first to be mothballed and the last to come out of mothballs. Thirdly, million-ton tankers would be a floating nightmare. Such a vessel spilling its crude oil would be an ecological disaster that couldn't or shouldn't be contemplated.

There is no talk today of leviathan tankers. Heath's experts were wrong. The shop stewards were right. If you want more proof cast your eye to what is happening in and around Milford Haven. The oil spillage from the *Sea Empress* threatens an area of glorious beauty. That such a disaster has not yet taken place in the Minch is a miracle.

Such matters can't be left to the good people of Greenpeace and Friends of the Earth. It's our business. It could also be our lives. Medical science is now expressing alarm at the very low sperm count among our young men. Scientists point to the chemicals in our food chain as a possible cause.

The fundamental danger to our ecology stems from a belief widespread in the West that they must enjoy a greater and still greater consumption of earthly goods, and that this is how we must measure progress. This is a mad concept. A sufficiency for all is technologically possible, only our primitive sociology stands in the way. But the present manic consumption so prevalent in what used to be called the Christian world, if unchecked, will ultimately endanger the human species. We will be choked by our own greed.

WORSHIPPING THE GOD
OF MAMMON

28 MARCH 1996

RUMMAGING through newspapers of the past few weeks it's clear that overall the Scottish press showed good judgment and good taste in their handling of the horror of Dunblane; the letters pages were a different matter. Some Christians used a monstrous and tragic happening once again to contemplate aloud into their theological navels.

One group wailed: "How could our God let this happen?" Another group bellowed: "God Almighty didn't let it happen, and couldn't have stopped it happening, because He made us free agents." But surely almightiness has no limit. Another group told us: "God's heart was broken." His heart must have broken a million times from Herod to Hitler, not forgetting Ethiopia and Rwanda, at atrocities committed by men they told us their God had made in His own image.

I'll be surprised if there is a God. I will be chuffed, dead chuffed, if God turns out to be Jesus, the joiner from Galilee, for he seemed a good guy when he was hanging about Jerusalem 2000 years ago. But this doesn't make it any easier to take the theological self-obsessiveness and spiritual egocentricity which seems to be the stock response of some of his avowed followers to heartbreaking tragedies such as Dunblane. It sidetracks concern for the only people that matter in the short term, the damaged, the bereaved, and the grief-stricken families.

The wringing of hands, the beating of breasts, the baring of souls from those whose only concern seems to be "what does this mean for me and my God" is selfishly self-centred. The rest of us put it differently. "What does this mean for the families of the dead, the survivors, the local community?" Then we might look at the wider social implications.

To explain barbarities in terms of intrinsic evil lets everyone else off the hook. It evokes images of evil spirits, witchcraft, the devil. If someone was born with an evil spirit, or genetically programmed to be evil, then nothing can be done about it.

If we can identify the evil ones we could incarcerate them before they do anything terrible, though how you would prove that they were evil in the absence of actual wrongdoing is difficult to envisage.

What we do know about the man in Dunblane is that he was profoundly sick in the mind and had access to lethal weapons.

We could do something about improving diagnostic research and the creation of diagnostic facilities that might enable us to identify such mental sickness before it is too late. This would cost money. We can certainly change the gun laws and make it impossible for such a man ever to have a legal right to own a gun.

We could have a look at the culture of violence in our society. There is, in my opinion, a particular problem of vindicatory violence. In a movie the violence of a baddie, an unpleasant anti-social character with whom viewers are less likely to identify, is less damaging than the violence of a goodie, a violent hero cop or

88

vigilante who obviously enjoys blowing the heads off those he perceives to be hoodlums, with the suggestion that he likes doing it anyway.

Our society, in political terms, now sings songs of praise for the strong and encourages them to act as if the good Lord gave them two hands to grab everything for themselves. It has made greed respectable. It has dismantled provision for the protection of the weak and defenceless, such as the councils set up by Winston Churchill to establish a basic minimum wage. All of this has made our society less compassionate and more cruel. And to be cruel is very much a form of violence.

Think of this. In the world today two men now dominate professional boxing which, with the help of television moguls, is now a billion-pound operation. One is an ex-convict found guilty of pistol-whipping a man to death. The other is an ex-convict found guilty of rape. Now tell me, what kind of message does this send to our youth?

That you should be able to walk our streets free from fear and feeling unthreatened, costs money, as does virtually everything we do. It cannot be individually purchased. It can only come through a public service funded by public expenditure. But in Britain public spending has become a dirty word.

To restore care for those who need care, costs money. To bring hope to the unemployed, costs money. To develop clinics that might be able to identify those likely to be psychopathic killers, costs money. During the past 20 years, tax cuts have given millions to those who already had millions. Tax cuts were funded by cuts in public expenditure. This led to decline and crises in our public services.

At the General Election, the Tories will campaign as the party of low taxation, Labour as the party of still lower taxation, which means that neither can tackle and resolve the pressing major social problems that beset our country. Talk of funding increased public spending from economic growth is hogwash. Whether there is growth in the British economy will be largely determined by what happens in the global market-place.

What it boils down to is this. In modern Britain mammon is god. Other countries had BSE and slaughtered and burnt infected herds. The British Government argued "where is the proof that it does infect human beings?" instead of "where is the proof that it doesn't?"

We eat beef. There must be an assumption that infected meat might infect us. Why then did our Government take a different attitude to other governments? It was all about costs. Farmers would have to be compensated. Our Government was obsessed with keeping down the PSBR (public sector borrowing requirement) so as to lower taxes for the super-rich. It took a chance it had no right to take.

The worship of Mammon is the madman's disease. This was Christ's message. If so-called Christians can't grasp this then for Christ's sake belt up, go to church in good suits, play at being pious, but please don't do it in the name of Christ.

WHO OWNS THE
SCOTTISH LABOUR MOVEMENT?

11 APRIL 1996

WILLIE McILVANNEY comes from the kind of family which
became the rock on which was built the Scottish Labour movement. He knows the working men and women that made Labour
great. His best writings are of those people, who were and are the
salt of the earth.

Willie feels that they have been betrayed by New Labour, and
he's right. New Labour's principles are old Tory principles. Blair's
economic thinking is more right wing than Kenneth Clarke's. Last
week I wrote of the dangers to democracy of further concentration
in the ownership and control of the media as exemplified by
Rupert Murdoch's News International, particularly cross-media
ownership, which embraces both newspapers and television. This
week it emerged that Blair's office wants to scrap or ease the limits
which restrict the further expansion of such media empires. Limits
made law by John Major's Government.

Political pundits in assessing Major's poor parliamentary

performances have insufficiently taken into account the unique problem he faces. He is under attack by a leader of the Labour Party who is further to the right than he is. After 17 years in which taxes were substantially reduced for the rich and high earners, Tories are attacked by Blair for not making more tax cuts.

The Tories punish unemployed youth and withdraw benefits. New Labour, not to be outdone as fiscal hardmen, promise to do the same thing under another name. The Tories attack social security scroungers and say nothing of the greater sums of money left uncollected by the very poor who know not their entitlements, and aren't told. New Labour respond by attacking beggars for begging.

Michael Howard, who to me is the most obnoxious Home Secretary in living memory, under the guise of combating terrorism, undermines important civil liberties. Jack Straw, Shadow Home Secretary, scourge of the beggars, high priest of the campaign to exorcise Clause 4, and all things socialist, not to be outdone by Howard, set out to prove that he is as anti-civil libertarian as any Tory, and succeeded.

The authoritarian tendency in New Labour was there from the start. When Labour Euro MPs opposed Blair's ditching of Clause 4 he abused them in terms identical to those used by Lenin in his pamphlet *Left Wing Communism, an infantile disorder*.

The Labour leader's office, staffed by his appointees and answerable only to him, now runs the Labour Party. The democratic institutions of the party have been sidelined. The NEC's new role is to rubber stamp the leader's pronouncements. His henchmen demand obedience and compliance.

Arms are twisted. Trade union leaders and MPs are threatened and cajoled. "Shut up for the greater good of the party", is the message. And who decides what is for the greater good of the party? The party leader's office, of course.

A senior BBC executive, Peter Horrocks, editor of *Newsnight*, writes in the April issue of *Parliamentary Review*: "Labour's internal machine has an iron grip. As a broadcaster and a believer in open political discussion, one deplores such authoritarianism. Faced with polls we can't rely on and politicians who are prepared to be controlled like puppets, what do we provide for our audiences?"

Horrocks claims that 95% of Labour back-benchers will not speak out openly on big stories without the prior approval of Labour's media centre, which is controlled from Blair's office. A spokesman from Blair's office said: "The message from this article is that the Labour Party is more organised, more effective, and better disciplined than the Conservative Party, which is something Peter Horrocks admits, as a media professional, he admires."

This response is disturbing. It acknowledges the substance of Horrocks' criticism and takes pride in how they silence critics from within while manipulating the news that goes to the outside world. Insert the world "iron" in front of disciplined and it could be a quote from Stalin's magnum opus *The Foundations of Leninism*.

Joy Johnson, who left a much more highly paid job at the BBC to be campaigns and communications director for the Labour Party, told the party conference: "We won't win by spin. We will win by getting our policies right." This angered Blair's spin doctors. They sidelined Joy. She was isolated in an office, left with nothing to do. She resigned.

One of Blair's henchmen at a Labour Party conference came into the press room and had a punch at a *Guardian* journalist who hadn't done what he was told. The nice-man, nice-men images, are for public consumption. These henchmen are not nice men but well-dressed hooligans. And that is the simple truth.

Labour were winning before Blair became leader. Labour will win because the people are sick to the back teeth with the Tories. Blair is not a reformer. In the late Seventies and early Eighties I was involved in the campaign for Labour Party democracy, advocating one person one vote, and in a book called *Manifesto* urged the democratisation of the trade unions by the trade unions. I saw neither head nor hair of Tony Blair.

In the early to mid-Eighties Labour was dominated by sooper-dooper ultra-leftist revolutionary sloganisers many of whom are now in the Shadow Cabinet. I wrote and spoke against this tendency which was making Labour unelectable. I saw neither head nor hair of Tony Blair. He was among the sooper-dooper revolutionaries.

Ten years later substantially the same people are at it again only this time they are sooper-dooper ultra-rightist counter revolutionary sloganisers. Such convulsive swings, in a short space of time, from one extreme to another, are not a sign of intellectual maturity.

The Labour movement was here before Tony Blair was a gleam in his Tory father's eye. It will be here when he has departed the scene. The Labour movement represents those who sell their labour, the needy and defenceless, and for everyone who believes that a society based on co-operation is morally superior to one based on exploitation and confrontation. Dear Willie McIlvanney, the Labour movement doesn't belong to the likes of Blair, it belongs to us, and millions like us. We should take it back, and not turn our back and leave it in their hands.

THE PROPHET OF SOUL-SELLING

30 MAY 1996

THEY SAT, in the Savoy, after the delights of lunch. Well heeled, well fed, well pleased. Fat cats one and all. Men in suits. After-shave scented the place like a whore's boudoir. The facial gloss of the seriously rich glistened, as they listened to words that told them what they wanted to hear.

Words that told them to heed not the plight of the poor for they will always be with us. For it is written that those who have, will have more, and those who have not, will have less, and anyway the have nots should belt up. Ungrateful gits.

The rich in spirit, old armagnac spirit, sang the praises of him who had come to show them the way. A New Labour prophet. His message! What doth it profit a man if he doesn't fill his own pockets at every opportunity. Verily I say unto you, harder will it be for a camel to go through the eye of a needle than for a poor man to enter the gates of Heaven, for Heaven like the Savoy belongs to the rich. Or words to that effect.

His vision, he acknowledged, would: "inevitably lead to

inequalities in income". He, of course, wouldn't suffer. The poor would suffer. His audience would benefit. A cross they were prepared to bear with fortitude. The prophet's words were a remarkable validation of inequality and its enshrinement, as a desirable and necessary objective, in the economic strategy of a government to come.

Even Mrs Thatcher never put it that crudely. She, warrior queen image, an' a', an' a', feared the backlash. The churches might start quoting what Christ really said. Once you acknowledge inequality, not as an unacceptable or unwelcome fact of social reality, which you will try to end, but as something devoutly to be desired, then you are left with no moral base for the fight against inequality, in any aspect of life.

Once rendered respectable, inequality can't be contained. It will, in such a circumstance, race through the political, social, racial and religious life of a nation or state. Slavery was not the product of subjective bloody-mindedness. The defeated in tribal wars previously slaughtered were allowed to live, as slaves. The product of their labour, in excess of the slave's subsistence, could in aggregate, amass riches for slave owners. Ancient Greece, the cradle of Western democracy was a slave society. So was Rome. These societies also sought to validate inequality.

Economics unconstrained by moral considerations is a fairly accurate definition of slavery, and the modern concept of an untrammelled market. We are either the slaves of economics or economics are tools in the service of humanity. Man, as a species, either subordinates himself to economics or subordinates economics to his needs, and aspirations.

We either club together or club each other, the choice that faces us as we approach a new millennium. Yet here we have men, at a lunch for the haves, preaching the merits of inequality in human affairs. It's like a scene from the Life and Times of Caligula.

You're probably saying to yourself, come on Jimmy, name the reactionary. Okay. Mr Peter Mandelson, Labour MP for Hartlepool. Mandelson also attacked demands for a "minimum wage of over £4 per hour" at this gathering of mega-earners, multi-millionaires, millionaires, and apprentice millionaires. They roared approval. Let's dwell on this for a little while.

Here are some guys earning, let's say, £250,000 per annum. They have cashed share options of a million quid or more, now secreted in a personal or family investment fund. There will be more share options to come. Plus a golden pension, and a mass of other perks. Yet without blushing or without any sense of shame, they rubbish as excessive, and ruinous to the economy, the suggestion that workers should get £4 an hour. And a Labour MP eggs them on.

This isn't the isolated opinion of a maverick MP but the official voice of New Labour. Mandelson speaks for Tony Blair. The Shadow Cabinet has agreed on amendments to Government legislation. These amendments would end or ease the limits on cross-media ownership, and clear the way for Rupert Murdoch and others to extend their media empires.

Right-wing Tories will support New Labour because these amendments embody the de-regulatory principles of Thatcherism. John Major and his government will be defending the people's interests against encroaching monopoly control of media moguls. On the other side, an unholy alliance of New Labour and right-wing Tory MPs, fighting the Thatcherite cause.

In the last election Labour had a much applauded party political broadcast in which Neil Kinnock told how he, son of a poor railwayman, had been the first Kinnock ever to go to university. Higher education had been made accessible to the children of the poor, through Labour Governments, the broadcast implied.

John Major's Government froze student grants and brought in a system of student loans. Last week New Labour went further and said it would abolish student grants altogether. Neil was lucky. Under New Labour he might not have got to Yoony.

On a raft of issues New Labour is now further to the Right than the Tories. Clare Short said she wouldn't mind paying more tax to help the old and the sick, and was forced to recant her sin, like Galileo at the Inquisition. Mandelson argues for institutionalised inequality and there isn't a cheep from the Leader's office. Blair accepts the essentials of Thatcherism. He thinks more highly of her, than do Major or Heseltine.

The dominance of the market, which Blair proclaims, prevailed for more than a century and led to wars and devastating slumps. The dominance of humanity by the market is essentially de-humanising. In this concept of society, everything is a commodity and everyone has a price tag.

Care for the elderly and the sick is made a commodity. Hospitals no longer have patients, but clients and customers. The owner of a brothel for paedophiles can argue he is simply catering for market forces. Governments wedded to this concept will sell armaments to whoever has the money to buy, and then lie to conceal the sales. It's a corrupting philosophy. New Labour hasn't modernised Old Labour, it has sold its soul, as if it was an expendable commodity. I want it back, before the election.

BITE IS WORSE
THAN THE BARK

13 JUNE 1996

ONCE upon a time, Tory Party Conferences had annual ritualised debates, some called them orgies, about law and order, hanging and flogging. Television cameras scanned the faces of women delegates looking upwards, rapturously, to the rostrum, as speaker after speaker urged serious damage be done to the bodies of assorted miscreants, such as juvenile delinquents and shop stewards.

The women quivered with excitement that seemed orgasmic. They obviously found the notion of bodily damage unto others an aphrodisiac of sorts.

A Tory councillor in Glasgow once argued for the re-introduction of flogging, offering to do the flogging herself. I suggested she might also like to dress for the part in black leather thigh-hugging boots, matching mini skirt, suspender belt, bra and peaked black cap.

I do look askance at enthusiasts of flogging. I'm against killing.

It can become a habit. The British State used to employ hangmen, vocational psychopaths, who hanged non-psychopaths such as the innocent Timothy Evans, on our bloody behalf. It was a waste of time. Wrongdoers are still wrongdoing after centuries of horrendous punishments.

Once on the merry-go-round of escalating punishments it's difficult to get off. Introduce flogging for a crime and the numbers committing the crime increase. What next? You go further. Lock criminals in stocks at street corners, where they can be pelted with rotten fruit and excrement by Tory women councillors in black thigh-hugging boots etc, etc?

That doesn't deter. Human bodies could be dismembered on automated racks or manually operated racks by volunteer Tory women councillors in black suspender belts etc. That doesn't work. We then force them to listen to Robson and Jerome or watch Cilla? That fails. Disembowelling? Or as the old lady from Govan said when a man was found guilty of multiple murders, "Hingin's too good fur him. Whit he needs is a good kick up the arse."

I knew a lad at school who jumped into the cabin of a lorry and drove it away. More the foolhardiness of incipient youth than a sign of an embryonic criminal mind. He was flogged. Afterwards he couldn't lie on his back, had to sleep on his stomach, became sullen and withdrawn. His high spirits had flown. Strange men had held him down as another flogged him. The boy was damaged, more in mind than body. The last I heard he was doing time in Peterhead.

In deterring crime, the severity of punishment is irrelevant. The certainty or near certainty of being caught is very relevant. More than half the prison population in Britain shouldn't be there and wouldn't be in prison elsewhere in Western Europe. The money to be spent building more prisons should be spent putting more policemen on the streets.

The lust of "An eye for an eye and a tooth for a tooth" can only end in a land of the toothless blind where a single-toothed one-eyed man is king. Human judgment is fallible; a killing, including a state killing, is irrevocable. Fallible judgment and an irrevocable sentence are morally incompatible. I'm not a bleeding heart, but prefer bleeding hearts to bloodthirsty minds. I'm for people going to prison who deserve to be there, but don't want to torture them while they're locked up. We know that prison, itself, does nothing to tackle the social causes of crime.

In a television programme I once stood on the boundary between Drumchapel and Bearsden and explained that those living in Drumchapel lived 10 years less than those living in Bearsden. Those convicted of murder get a life sentence and will generally be freed after 10 years. Children born in Drumchapel therefore have the equivalent of a life sentence imposed on them as compared with their peers in Bearsden, before they've even drawn a breath.

My mother had seven children. Where we lived kids were dropping like flies. She was obsessively protective about our health. When there wasn't enough to eat she went without, and gave what there was to us. Despite her sacrifices, three of my sisters died in infancy. As a child, I remember my mother sometimes cried for her lost babies. As the years passed she stopped crying, but I knew she hadn't forgotten. Neither did I.

Glasgow's slums were disease-ridden. Germs were in the air we breathed. Life on the means test meant that malnutrition was rife. Many who survived had rickets and stunted growth. The poisoned dwarfs of battlefield fame. The disease, the deaths, and the crime which emanated from the slums had their roots in poverty. They still do.

I bet more people from Bearsden have been found guilty of company embezzlement than people from Drumchapel. It would be nonsense to conclude from this that people from Bearsden are genetically more inclined to embezzlement than folk from Drumchapel. They are more likely to embezzle because they are more likely to be in positions where they could.

On the other hand those from Drumchapel are more likely to do a bit of breaking and entering which also has nothing to do with their genetic propensities and a helluva lot to do with prevailing social and economic conditions. This is not a justification of embezzlement, or attacks on property, but an insistence that crime, the nature of crime, is often determined by class and social circumstances.

The problems of ill-health and premature deaths are often class-based and stem from poverty and deprivation in all their degrading and debilitating manifestations. If, as is now being argued, the problems of health and crime have nothing to do with poverty, those who are not poor are absolved of responsibility. Like Pontius Pilate they wash their hands. The poor mother is then held responsible for the premature death of her poor child. Crime has no objective social base and is therefore caused exclusively by personal bloody-mindedness, of people who, coincidentally, just happen to be poor.

So build more prisons, close more hospitals. Assuage the irrational fears and prejudices of middle England. Grovel for their votes. The mad bitches who once bayed for blood at Tory conferences and were then constrained for another year have been let loose by Michael Howard, wooed by Jack Straw and are now in heat. They should be re-caged before it's too late.

LORD PROTECT US FROM
MEN OF DESTINY

4 JULY 1996

THAT the end justifies the means is a flawed proposition. If the means are bad they debase the end, even if the end was originally well intended. History is littered with examples of how bad means corrupt good ends.

Labour party members have accepted the abandonment of Labour principles and values, as electoral ploys, because they so desperately want to see an end to Tory rule. Blair has promised to deliver this. He could in the formal sense. The Conservative Party might be out of office. But will it be an end to Tory rule in an ideological sense, in terms of content. That is something else.

Blair has got the Tories flummoxed for bizarre reasons. John Major, as leader of Britain's right-wing party, has to contend with a Labour leader who, in essence, is as far right as he is and, on some important issues, further to the right. Last week Lady Thatcher opened an exhibition at the Imperial War Museum on "Conflict Since 1945". She told a group of brass hats: "I'm not a

Tory any more—I'm a Thatcherite." She praised Tony Blair for being in her mould. "I'm sure he would press the button," she said, "when he is in power."

Blair's economics differ not a jot from Thatcher's. His social nostrums are Thatcherite. There is abundant evidence to suggest that Labour is being re-made in the image of Blair, who is fundamentally a Conservative. People keep telling me he has no principles; he has. He has Tory principles. He's in the wrong party.

You can't seek to destroy a party's soul and leave the party as an organisational entity unchanged. Labour's democracy has been ravaged. The Shadow Cabinet now rubber-stamps the directives which flow from the leader's cabal. The parliamentary party is expected to rubber-stamp every policy change that emanates from the same cabal. The party's NEC ditto.

Unions who will foot the bill for the election are already marginalised, held at arm's length, as if in bad odour. It's bad enough biting the hand that feeds you, but crapping on it as well? The national conference is also to be marginalised, stripped of power. It will be a theatre for hurrah, hurrah speeches of leaders whose status in the party hierarchy will be discerned by where they sit, on the platform, in relation to the leader.

The manifesto for the General Election is to go to a postal vote of party members. There will be no amendments. You can vote for or against. If a majority vote against, the party will have no manifesto for the election, and no time to formulate another. It's blackmail in the guise of grass-roots democracy.

The leader and his cabal rigidly control the party. He flies in and sorts out troublesome natives. As the Prime Minister he will run his Cabinet and Government along similar lines. There is already talk of powers to ban the re-selection of MPs who are "disloyal". If political differences are treated as acts of disloyalty, can the use of words like treachery and treason be far behind? What next? The ice-pick? We don't need a crystal ball to know where these means end. We can read the books.

Blair's arrogance might be his downfall. He sees himself as a man of destiny, and Lord protect us from men of destiny. We in Scotland saw his imperious style of leadership at work last week. It was an eye-opener for some. Labour's policies for a Scottish parliament with fund-raising powers had been settled. Agreed by party conferences. The NEC. The Scottish EC. It was drawn up by all parties to the Scottish Constitutional Convention. A vote for Labour or the Liberal Democrats would be treated as a mandate for the implementation of this agreed policy.

The Tories in Scotland had made no measurable impact by their tartan tax campaign. There was no negative factor operating in Scotland that required any change of direction. There were problems in England. Blair decided early last week to assuage the feelings in the South by leaving the Scots in a lurch. We got the referendum scam.

There was a substantial inbuilt majority on the Scottish Executive against this policy somersault. The Blair cabal got to work. Union bosses in London were dragooned into action. Bill Morris of the TGWU was phoned by Blair. Morris left the decision to his Scottish members. Other union bosses didn't. They told union delegates on the Executive to toe Blair's line.

Party officials in London phoned members last thing at night, first thing in the morning. Wednesday, Thursday, Friday. Cajoling, threatening. It was a severe exercise in arm-twisting. At the meeting, Blair, by now aware that he had gone an arrogance too far, apologised for the lack of consultation. His main argument once again was on the electoral consequences if the Scottish Executive dared snub him. In other words, let me away with murder or you'll let the Tories in.

The resolution before the meeting reaffirmed the policy of the party; expressed concern that Shadow Cabinet members had sought to change this policy; insisted, "They do not have such authority." Despite the arm-twisting the motion was defeated by only 16 votes to 12 with three abstentions.

That night on BBC, ITV, all radio stations, it was reported that Blair had been supported on the Scottish Executive by 20 votes to four. There had been another handwritten motion moved after the main vote regretting the manner in which the announcement of the referendum had been made.

Because the vote to reaffirm party policy had just been lost by the numbers quoted, this gave general support to a referendum; members of the Executive welcomed Blair's offer to consult on the questions to be asked on the ballot form, and expected "that the Scottish Executive will be closely involved . . ."

Many opposed to Blair's U-turn voted for this resolution on the grounds that it gave them a chance to try to influence the presentation of the question or questions. The media were only informed of the 20-4 vote, which was interpreted as massive enthusiastic support for Blair. Next day George Robertson ruled out talks about the ballot questions. This isn't party management but media manipulation. British broadcasting was sold a pup. The Executive's views were misrepresented. Labour can win without this kind of nonsense.

THE HEARTLESS SOCIETY

11 JULY 1996

LAST SUNDAY in a newspaper magazine there was a picture of a fully-dressed young man, face exposed as he smooched the bare left shoulder of a young woman. She wore a fur coat, nothing else. Her left hand hung submissively. Her bare left leg, shod in a black, high-heeled shoe, pressed between the young man's legs. Her leg exposed to the waist, on which his right hand rested. Her body draped in a compliance which reeked of indifference.

Her head is over his left shoulder. No face shows. No personality. No person. This is not a woman. This is packaged sex. The marketing of the perambulating vagina. Women, it implies, are for fucking. The F word is a term of abuse or disgust. Not to "give a fuck" is not to care at all. To "fuck around" is to treat someone inconsiderately or behave selfishly. To tell someone to "fuck off" is an emphatic expression of dismissal and contempt. Fuck is the very antithesis of love and affection.

In our society sex is viewed as a commodity. Despite claims to the contrary women are still economically and socially inferior.

Female sexuality is much more a commodity than male sexuality. Many men look upon girls and women as sexual commodities, sexual playthings, taken up, discarded, sold, or sold out.

Last week television news carried a story of how the breeding of puppies has become a seedy business in Britain. Bitches and puppies are kept in the most squalid conditions. Bitches forced to have litter after litter till their insides collapse. The business comes to a head at Christmas time. Get the wee cuddly puppies in the shops. The beseeching eyes that melt the heart. The cash registers ring more than the yuletide bells. Many pups die miserably and prematurely.

A young lady from the RSPCA said: "We mustn't allow puppies to be treated as commodities." But we live in a society that treats everything as a commodity. Water, the essence of life, has been made private property in England and Wales. Where the domestic use of water was metered, people flushed their toilets once a day or less, washed and bathed less frequently. They feared the bills that were to come.

No so long ago it was generally agreed that mineral resources found under the soil or under our offshore waters were either God-given or nature-bestowed, and belonged to people as a whole, by right.

Gas which belonged to us is now the private property of a few. This immediately unleashed a tidal wave of sleaze and fat cats—£180bn from North Sea royalties has gone to the British Exchequer and used in part to pay the tax concessions of the very rich. In Britain, the most energy and fuel-rich country in Western Europe, pensioners die each year of hypothermia.

On Tuesday, Edward Heath was 80. He and I had a bit of a rammy when his Government tried to close the shipyards on the Upper Clyde. I argued that major economic decisions couldn't or shouldn't be taken abstracted from their social consequences, at least not in a civilised society. These and other moral arguments had an impact. One Cabinet member told me that John Davies,

Minister of Trade and Industry in Heath's Government, had warned that he would resign unless they got "Jimmy Reid off my back". He agreed, it seems, with much of the substance of our arguments.

Davies had left shipbuilding policy to a junior Minister called Nicholas Ridley. Ridley, a Thatcherite before the term was coined, hated Upper Clyde Shipbuilders because it was publicly owned. He had drawn up a confidential document which sought in his own words, "to butcher Upper Clyde and sell off the pieces". Davies wanted rid of Ridley. Heath hawked him around the other Ministries. None would have him. He was considered a right-wing extremist. Ridley became a key Minister in Thatcher's Government.

Harold Macmillan in his final speech to Parliament equated privatisation with "selling off the family silver". In other words, flogging the assets of the people. I didn't agree with Macmillan or Heath on many things, but you could live with them and even find some areas of agreement. They had lived through the inter-war years when the untrammelled market prevailed. A system with an inbuilt tendency towards under-consumption and relative over-production. This led to the phenomenon unknown before in human history. Periodic slumps and recessions which reduced millions to penury and starvation, in the midst of plenty.

John Maynard Keynes argued that governments had the moral and legal duty to intervene and seek to regulate the economy, in the long-term interests of business and the well-being of the people as a whole. Thatcher rejected Keynes in favour of the market, red in tooth and claw. We now live in a human jungle, of her making. This was regression, not progression.

Instead of Heath and Macmillan we had a new breed of Conservative. The crudities of Tebbit, Portillo, and their likes. Thatcherism has torn the heart out of civic society in Britain. The losers are everywhere. In the new ghettos, begging on the streets. Packing our prisons. Britain is dirtier, seedier, more lawless, less caring.

Our problems are many, but at root is a moral void that comes from placing a price tag on everything. I therefore awaited with interest the debate in the House of Lords on morality, opened by the Archbishop of Canterbury, Dr George Carey. It was a disgrace. He demanded schools comply with the law requiring daily Christian worship. Thatcher no doubt got her daily whack of worship at school, and look what she's like.

Morality isn't an abstraction. It's about how you treat others. Don't accept my word, Dr Carey, listen to Christ, your gaffer. Christ kicked over the tables of the money changers, our religious leaders are so "respectable" they can't kick over the traces, even a wee bit, for the least of men and for the least of women and for their children. Human beings are not commodities. That should be the starting point of any moral awakening. The heart, meaning our informed and compassionate concern for others, has a part to play in all human deliberations. Robert Burns put it this way.

> Nae treasures nor pleasures,
> Could make us happy lang;
> The heart aye's the part aye,
> That makes us right or wrang.

JIMMY MAXTON: A HERO
AT THE HEART OF THE MYTH

22 JULY 1996

MYTHS have grains of truth. We can't dream without reference to the material world and our experience within that world. Psychiatrists take dreams seriously. In them, they assert, lie clues to experiences, embedded in the subconscious, that helped make us what we are.

Folklore is inspired by collectively remembered events. It has more truth than myths. But fanciful folklore can become myth and just as easily cloud our knowledge of the past, leading to wrong conclusions about the future.

According to Scottish folklore, during and following the 1914-18 war, Clydeside was in a revolutionary ferment. The revolution didn't happen because of the timidity and treachery of Labour leaders. John Maclean tried to organise the revolution but gloriously failed and died, broken in health by the rigours of revolutionary activism.

There are many grains of truth in this. But it's still a myth. And

111

myths are like cataracts on the mind's eye. If allowed to grow they impair vision. If left unchecked they can blind us to the truth. Myths should be excised so that a truer vision of the past might lighten the way ahead.

John Maclean was a great man who yearned for a socialist revolution that would end the misery and degradation of chronic poverty that he saw around him in the slums of Glasgow. In every outbreak of social discontent he saw a portent of impending revolution. The Soviet Revolution of 1917 seemed to confirm this prognosis. Lenin argued that Czarist Russia was ripe for revolution. It was, but for a bourgeois or capitalist revolution, not socialist revolution, as time was to show.

Marx argued that the socialist revolution could only come when capitalism had more or less realised its full potential and had exhausted all possibilities of continued development. He suggested that capitalism, to ensure its own dominance, had to end feudal rule in all guises. To do this it had to assume the mantle of democracy and arraign itself against feudal autocracy. The capitalists wanted democracy only for themselves. But the middle classes and the rapidly burgeoning working class would demand their right to a place in the democratic sun. They too wanted the vote.

This fight for the franchise was the basis of all the reform movements in Britain from the end of the eighteenth century, through the nineteenth century, and into the twentieth, culminating in the victory of the suffragettes. The leaders of the Chartists saw the vote as a means by which workers and their families would have a say in determining their own destinies. As the working class became a majority it opened up the possibility of a working-class majority in Parliament.

Marx had stated in the 1880s that in advanced capitalist democracies like Britain and America it was possible to conceive transition from capitalism to socialism, through a democratic parliamentary process, without recourse to civil war. Lenin claimed that Russia could go from feudalism to socialism, missing out capitalism. Marx believed this was impossible, and any attempt to try it would end in grief. Marx was demonstrably right.

This is now obvious to all except a few surviving dogma-ridden Leninists. But it was not clear in the years following 1917. Lenin and Trotsky were convinced that the Soviet revolution was doomed without similar revolutions in other European countries. They sought to precipitate such revolutions by establishing Soviet-type parties throughout the continent.

Maclean would have no truck with a Soviet-type party here. He was for an independent Scottish Socialist Republic. Lenin wanted a British revolution that, given Britain's then global strength, would guarantee his own. A revolution in Scotland wouldn't quite suffice. Maclean believed a Soviet-type revolution in Scotland was nigh. He burnt himself out for a revolution that didn't come.

The struggles he thought were harbingers of revolution were actually demands for changes within the system. A shorter working week. Higher wages. Immediate relief for the poor and unemployed. The fight against rent increases by private landlords. These were expressions of class militancy, not revolutionary ardour.

People followed Maclean onto the streets on issues. They didn't follow him to the ballot box to vote for revolution. He stood for Parliament and was defeated, more than once. If workers won't vote for you at the ballot box, how can you expect them to risk life and limb by joining you on the barricades? Such an expectation is not of this world.

Maclean was a great man, mass leader, brilliant lecturer on Marxian economics. My mother was a Maclean. Her father was from Mull, as was John's. When I was a babe in arms she would tell me stories of this man who stood up for the poor in the slums of the Gorbals. I inherited her reverence for him. He literally sacrificed his life for socialism and the working class. His devotion was exemplary, his analysis was flawed.

I go over this ground not for the hell of it, for it gives me no pleasure, but to remind myself, and hopefully others, of men who were great, unsung heroes of those times, and who have relevant things to say to us in our times. In the General Election of 1922, Scotland returned 30 Labour MPs. Not all Labour MPs were or are socialists, as you will have gathered. But 10 of these new MPs, way back then, were from Clydeside, and were socialists, and became known as the Red Clydesiders.

They were a disparate and talented bunch. They believed in the need for a socialist revolution through a combination of a mass movement outwith Parliament, with the efforts of socialists inside Parliament. Revolution to them meant fundamental change, not civil war. Where people had the right to vote there was no justification for violence in pursuance of political aims. To them evolution and revolution were not conflicting propositions but a duality, like two sides of the same coin.

Nature is full of evolutionary, quantitative, almost imperceptible changes that at a certain stage become a qualitative transformation. You heat water, it gets warmer and warmer, then at a certain stage turns to steam. In life the evolutionary and revolutionary are part of the same process.

The Clydesiders saw change as a process. Some narrow revolutionaries are actually cop-out merchants. They want a revolution now or nothing. They get nothing and go back to the beer till the revolution comes. To fight here and now for everything that is possible for your cause, but realise the ultimate goal might be years ahead, calls for a higher level of commitment.

But of all the Red Clydesiders the one who merits most study is Jimmy Maxton. Tomorrow is the 50th anniversary of his death. Like many of the other greats he was a member of the Independent Labour Party, that had its autonomy with the Labour Party. The ILPers saw themselves as the keepers of the socialist faith.

Maxton was a spellbinding orator. A skill often viewed by non-orators as the triumph of form over content. Technique over substance. This applies to demagogues, not orators. Orators communicate because they have something to say that matters, whether you agree with them or not. Most are highly intelligent, well-read, original in thought and its expression. They also have what we now call bottle. This applies across the political spectrum: from Nye Bevan to Lloyd George, Winston Churchill, Willie Gallagher, and most definitely Jimmy Maxton.

Born in 1885, Jimmy died in 1946. MP for Bridgeton for 24 years. A teacher sacked for his socialist beliefs. A conscientious objector during the First World War. Jailed for sedition. A full-time organiser for the ILP during the arguments and fights about Lenin. The Russian Revolution. Should we follow the Soviets? A trenchant critic of Labour's leadership during the Thirties when they surrendered all principles and became the toast of high society in London.

He held no government office. Seemed not to want one. As you probably know by now, I believe that's the only kind of politician who should be trusted with power. To him politics was about people. In his book you judged the extent to which a society was civilised by how it looked after the weak and defenceless, the old and the young, the sick in mind and body. He didn't only rail about injustices but advocated specific solutions. Along with Wheatley he drew up an alternative programme based on the concept of Socialism in Our Time.

Where others were interested in office without knowing what they would do with it, he was preoccupied with principles and their application, and what might work or not work. His disregard for office made him appear unreal in contra-distinction to careerists around him in Parliament.

He could move people to tears. He could be moved to tears. He was no "dessicated calculating machine", as Bevan once said of Herbert Morrison. In human calculations emotions should have a part to play. They played a big part in Maxton's calculations. He was a better man for it.

115

THE EMPIRE THAT IS DEAD

1 AUGUST 1996

"ALL empires die of indigestion," said Napoleon. They do. They bite off more than they can chew, swallow territories their colonial systems can't digest, and die. The only empire worth a damn was the Glasgow Empire and it died of television. That apart, empires stink. The Roman Empire spread not science and plumbing, but slavery and surrender to the rule of Emperors. It also crucified dissidents, including a woodworker from Galilee whose death caused a bit of a stir.

The real cross-fertilisation of ideas came from migrants and traders, going about their business, while colonising armies plundered and raped. At school we were told the British Empire was different. Its concern was with bringing Christianity and civilisation to the natives. We were urged to give pennies to our teachers who would pass them on to starving black babies in India and Africa.

Through movies, our window on the world, we knew of Sabu, a young lad from India who could drive an elephant like nobody's business. He looked healthier and better-fed in his jungle than we did in ours. He had an elephant, and I didn't have a bike.

What was beyond our comprehension was African poverty. Kids in Govan knew something about the world. The docks were in our midst. My grandfather was a docker. My dad worked in the docks for years. My sister lived up a close in Govan Road. Her windows overlooked the docks. Ships from all over the world came to our doorstep. Those from Africa were full of iron ore, copper, all sort of minerals and valuable raw materials. Africa was an Eldorado, it was said, teeming with gold and diamonds. How come kids were starving?

In my teens I learned that Africa had the biggest potential iron-ore reserves in the world, the biggest per capita reserves. The continent was abundant with raw materials and natural wealth. Colonialism built railways, often single-track, that ran to mines and centres where cash crops were stored, then to ports where these treasures were put on ships and taken away.

In Mauritania there was an 18-mile-long mountain of rich high-grade iron-ore deposits. A four-nation consortium of companies from Britain, France, Italy, and West Germany was formed to exploit this resource. They built a railway line to a newly developed port. The ore was relatively easy to quarry. "It just has to be blasted, tipped down chutes, gobbled in eight-ton gulps by mechanical shovels, tipped into hundred-ton trucks . . ." wrote Ritchie Calder in the *New Statesman*, December 26, 1959. It would then be taken down to the sea where ships waited to take it to places like Govan.

The manager of the project, M Jean Painsard, told the world: "When we have finished, there will be no landscape." He could have added the railway will crumble in disuse. The port will crumble when the ore runs out. Africa will have been drained of another mineral resource worth billions, and African children will still be starving.

They couldn't tell us this truth, so they told us lies. Rudyard

Kipling put it this way:

> "Take up the White Man's burden—
> Send forth the best ye breed—
> Go, bind your sons to exile
> To serve your captive's need;
> To wait in heavy harness
> On fluttered folk and wild—
> Your new-caught, sullen people,
> Half devil and half child."

But truth will out. Britain's rulers never wanted the empire to end. In a joint declaration issued on August 14, 1941, Franklin D Roosevelt and Winston Churchill set out eight principles as guides to the post-war world we were all supposed to be fighting for. These included, "Respect the right of all peoples to choose the form of government under which they will live."

Anti-colonialists asked if this applied to Britain's colonies. On September 9, 1941, Prime Minister Churchill issued an official declaration that specifically excluded the British Empire from the terms of the Charter. "At the Atlantic meeting we had in mind primarily the restoration of the sovereignty, self government and national life of the states of the nations of Europe . . ."

On February 21, 1946, Ernest Bevin, Labour Foreign Secretary, told the House of Commons: "I am not prepared to sacrifice the British Empire because I know that if the British Empire fell . . . it would mean the standard of life of our constituents would fall considerably." All talk of the white man's burden had now been dropped. Naked self-interest was proclaimed.

Bevin was wrong in one aspect. The poor in Britain were not beneficiaries of empire. At its height the children of the poor were dying like flies in cities like Glasgow. Empire distorts the economies of the colonised. It also distorts the economy of the colonisers. In the 1880s Britain was the workshop of the world. Exporting goods to every corner of the globe. The zeal of empire building put an end to that. Profits made in Britain were invested in the colonies in pursuit of fabulous profits made from exploiting the mineral resources of subject lands and the cheap labour of subject peoples.

This starved British manufacturing industries of capital investment which over decades led to widespread obsolescence in our manufacturing industries. Britain was exporting capital at the expense of goods. The outcome, the industrial dereliction we see around us in the central belt of Scotland.

The post-war world called for a decisive break with the past. The empire was finished. A new world and a new role for Britain beckoned. But one way or another those who ruled Britain wanted to cling to the past. Instead of making the best out of no longer being a superpower, they sought global influence through hanging on to the shirt tails of the new superpower, America. The kith and kin of Anglo-Saxon blood ties got laldy. Churchill boasted that through his mother he was half-American. By this time Winston was mostly half-drunk. Britain pleaded for a "special relationship".

Our politicians became Atlanticists. In 1945 Britain could have led Europe but preferred to be Uncle Sam's poodle. Today Britain dithers. England clings to imperial illusions. Tory Eurosceptics are reincarnated Empire loyalists. Loyal to an empire that is dead. Both Major or Blair duck and dive trying to say nothing about Europe for fear of falling foul of English chauvinism. Serious matters have to be resolved but there is no debate, only soundbites. At times I wish that Scotland was an independent nation.

A GENERATION BORN TO FAIL

8 AUGUST 1996

WHEN scientists speak about matters of public concern it's important to know who pays their wages. Scientists working for tobacco
firms assured us that links between cigarettes and cancer were not
proven. This opinion, delivered in the measured tones of dispas-
sionate science, was just what addicts wanted to hear. Those
reassured continued to smoke. Some died.

These scientists weren't liars. They were employed not to un-
cover evidence that smoking was deadly but to look for evidence
that might undermine the argument of those who believed there
were causal links between smoking and cancer. It was argued that
the burden of proof lay with the anti-smoking lobby. That the duty
of the defence, as in adversarial law, was to combat the case for the
prosecution, wherever and whenever possible, and let justice be
done.

Science, however, is not a university debating society. Science
seeks the objective laws that govern life and matter. Science is part
of human society. Matters deriving from the social circumstances

120

that surround the scientist intrude into his work. Economics play merry hell with his scientific impartiality. Economics, as a science, is about the production and distribution of wealth. The economist lives in a world in which the struggle of men for possession of wealth helps shape history, makes and remakes society. Any suggestion that economists are uninfluenced by this struggle is absurd.

If there had been financial gain to be made by challenging the law of gravity, Newton's theory would have been rubbished by those with a vested interest in its non-acceptance.

Think of any economic issue that's been in the news recently. Television news will have interviewed an economist from the staff of some City finance house. Nobody else would be there to balance his views. He's considered impartial. Imagine they brought on an economist working for the TUC, with nobody to balance his views. It couldn't happen. He wouldn't be considered impartial.

The market is now presumed sacrosanct and impartial. The so-called economic laws garnered from the study of market forces are equated with laws of nature and given the same authority. Yet these "laws" are simply deductions based on an abstract concept of a society sometimes loosely based on reality. No wonder economists are often wrong.

It's the world of Adam Smith, who died in 1790 when there were few big companies, no giant companies, no monopolies, no global companies, no multinationals, no massive consortia. There is no free market today. No completely unrigged competition. Labour is far from mobile, geographically or technologically. Norman Tebbit told the unemployed, "Get on yer bikes." To go where? To London to live on the streets?

It's deemed all right to direct labour through market forces, but to direct capital, as an alternative, is deemed an infringement of civil liberties. Capital has no feelings and is inanimate. People have feelings, belong to families and communities. Our politicians have more respect for capital than people, and that, as accountants say, is the bottom line.

This destroys families and communities and creates widespread alienation. People feel excluded because they are excluded. It is now widely believed that the rule of law in Britain is in danger of breaking down. In some areas it already has. Taxi drivers have told me that there are parts of Glasgow into which they will not go. Doctors are fearful of making house calls in certain areas. The provision of burglar alarms is now big business. Law and order has been made into a political football.

Michael Howard and Jack Straw pose as macho men and try to talk like Dirty Harry. Unlumbered by analyses, causes aren't sought. Without knowing causes you can't find cures. Law and order can't be upheld by the vigour and toughness of law enforcement agencies alone. Law and order have to be underpinned by a social consensus based on a belief that life can be better. Society must at least give people hope of a better life. Why should people respect the rules of a society which won't give them even the right to hope?

Yet today in our society youngsters are being brought up in homes where the father has been unemployed for years. The family has lived on social security payments based on subsistence. Youngsters leave school and are unemployed. By their twenties they are considered unemployable. In the course of time they will marry; if lucky, get a council house. It won't be much good, for the best have been sold off. They will live the rest of their lives on social security handouts; bring up a family born to fail. While all around is evidence of abundance in a world of conspicuous consumption.

Things already grim will get grimmer. All talk is of cutbacks on welfare spending. These victims of our social system are called the underclass, by middle-class smart asses. They don't work because society has denied them that right, but they're working-class, and know it. There are millions of them living in dreadful urban ghettos. They're a big minority with no political clout. Some are too demoralised to vote. When they do they vote Labour, through habit rather than conviction. Their plight will not feature in the General Election. The emphasis will be on middle England.

In any society, if a large minority is left without hope, then for them the laws of that society are stripped of that moral authority in which respect for the law is rooted. Law and order can then become unsustainable.

Last week I was sent a glossy magazine, *New Labour New Life for Britain*. There is no mention of full employment. It gives five priority pledges about what New Labour will do in government, including "Fast-track punishment for persistent young offenders by halving the time from arrest to sentencing". There you have it. New Labour will punish miscreant kids twice as fast as the Tories. Kids who don't go to grant-aided schools, children of the ghettos. It's their own fault. They should have been born to well-heeled lawyers and live in places like Islington.

STONES, BONES
AND THE PEOPLE'S DESTINY

5 SEPTEMBER 1996

I NEVER did go inside the Lenin Mausoleum. Whatever was in there wasn't Lenin but a stuffed skin of sorts. It smacked of medieval religion and its obsession with body parts of long-dead saints and martyrs. An obsession which led to parishes claiming custodianship of so many bits and pieces that some saints seemed indeed miraculously endowed, with multiple ears, hands, testicles etc.

I couldn't care less about the dug-up heart of Robert the Bruce, for it isn't his heart. If it was his heart it would be inside his chest, pumping away. When it stopped pumping Bruce was dead, and his heart was a piece of useless tissue. And that was 600 years ago. Today it must be a piece of useless disintegrated tissue.

Poets invoked the heart as the source of emotion and affection, but it was only, at best, a metaphor. A metaphor that serves us well. But in reality it's a pump, as mechanical and unfeeling as those produced by Weirs of Cathcart. If it were otherwise then heart transplant patients would come out the operation more or less emotional, more or less affectionate and loving. And they don't. They're their same old selves.

I also don't give a toss about the Stone of Destiny. Where it's dumped doesn't matter. My preference is for the depths of the North Sea. When it was pinched, me and my mates, teenage socialists and nationalists, thought it was a prank by middle-class students. For us it had no serious political significance.

I still feel that way. An ugly stone on which we are told Scotland's feudal kings were crowned. Big deal. With few exceptions they were as disgusting a shower of cruel, grasping, treacherous illegitimates as you were ever likely to meet in a gallery of horrors. The majority did only harm to Scotland. At the first offer one ran for it, down south, to be king of England, where the living was easy, for feudal kings.

Just about the same time as the stone was pinched from Westminster Abbey I learned from some members of the Iona Community the words of a hymn which I've never forgotten, which is saying something, for I often forget the words of songs. It goes: "When wilt thou save the people, O Lord of mercy when, The people Lord the people, Not crowns or thrones but men."

Hereditary monarchs, owing to incestuous breeding, were often mute. This is no exaggeration. Walter Bagehot, widely respected nineteenth-century English writer and political philosopher, opined: "It has been said, not truly, but with a possible approximation to truth, that in 1802 every hereditary monarch was insane."

It was well-intentioned, but nonetheless a political gimmick, when the Stone of Destiny was pinched. It will be a political gimmick when it's returned. Oh that the Scottish people would tell John Major to keep that worthless piece of masonry and even tell him where he could keep it. Give us instead what is ours by right, the right to govern ourselves. When the history of these times is written there will be no mention of that tissue which is claimed to be the heart of Bruce or of a stone that has little to do with our destiny.

History has always been about a lot more than the pedigree of kings and queens. Or the whims and acrobatics of swashbuckling individuals who changed, so it is implied, the course of history by a parry and thrust of the rapier. Monod, the French historian, put it this way: "Historians are too much in the habit of paying attention only to the brilliant, clamorous, and ephemeral manifestations of human activity, to great events and great men, instead of depicting the great and slow changes of economic conditions and social institutions which constitute the really interesting and intransient part of human development." That, I believe, is profoundly true.

Nobody invents something if its time hasn't come. There has to be a build-up of information based on previous experience, trial, error, hypotheses, more trials, more conclusions. The great innovator is the beneficiary of the accumulated knowledge of others who went before. Every breakthrough is a social as well as an individual achievement.

To highlight the individual and not the collective dimension is to distort history. The greats are portrayed as the makers of history, the people as mere spectators. It wasn't like that at all. Women got the vote in this century because enough of them fought for it. It's been the same throughout history. Things change for the better only when people make them change and when the time is ripe.

A stone can't determine our destiny, nor the bits and bobs of long-dead kings. It's up to ourselves. That's the real lesson of history. There are no messiahs in secular life. Leaders have to be called to account, not the other way round. Scottish Labour is in a fankle because it's loyal to a leader who isn't loyal to Scottish Labour.

Last weekend, at the Party's Scottish executive, people were outrageously pressured. Phoned repeatedly. Threatened. Cajoled. Bribed. The leader's will had to prevail. The leader's acolytes were told not to budge. Ordinary members sought a compromise, but there can be no solution in semantics to a serious difference of opinion. It ended in a farce.

Two Executive meetings ago a vote for Labour at the General Election was a mandate for a Scottish parliament. Then the Executive voted for a two-question referendum, in addition to a vote at the General Election. Then it met to determine whether it was still in favour of two questions or one, and voted for three, in addition to the General Election.

With more meetings before the election, who knows what will happen. A weekly referendum?

It's the politics of the absurd. Labour is now a laughing stock.

When people start laughing at a political party it's in real trouble. Labour's Scottish policy is beyond comprehension unless the aim is to sabotage any chance of meaningful self-government. This nonsense will cost the party dearly. Membership. Influence. Votes. Its political partner in the Constitutional Convention, the Lib-Dems, might also suffer by association. The SNP will be laughing all the way to the polls.

The moral is clear. Unquestioning obedience is for sheepdogs, robots, the servile. The man o' independent mind, He looks an' laughs at a' that.

TONY BLAIR—TORY RADICAL

13 SEPTEMBER 1996

CHAIRMAN MAO'S thoughts were encapsulated with highlighted homilies in a wee red book. The thoughts of Tony Blair are encapsulated with highlighted homilies in this bigger book. Tony ranges over ministerial portfolios, diagnosing and prescribing at great length his cures.

I finished reading the book last Monday. On late television news that night I saw Tony entering a hall in Aberdeen. His arms raised to the heavens, like Michael Jackson, milking applause. He started clapping too. Oh dear.

New Labour. New cult of personality. New leader knows everything. Knows what Scotland wants better than the Scots. Dictates referendums, detailed questions, full stops and commas. The book is a collection of speeches and comments covering economics, foreign policy, crime and punishment, Stanley Matthews, family values, and anthropological asides. There is nothing wrong with a man ranging far and wide in his interests, but implicit in the rhetoric is that his is the only authoritative voice of New Labour, on all matters.

128

In that sense he is a New Labour Thatcher, which explains why he often expresses his admiration for her "strengths". As Prime Minister, with the power that now resides in that office, he and his courtiers will brook no opposition from within the party. Such rule by an individual always ends in government by whim.

This is particularly so when the individual boasts of his contempt for the theories of others. He writes: "I was brought up to form my views on the basis of what I saw around me, what I read, what I learned from friends and colleagues—in other words, to study reality rather than theory." But Tony's book is full of theories, his theories.

Now this wouldn't matter if it were just a loose formulation, but he comes back to this theme time and again. In his parliamentary maiden speech he says: "I am not a socialist through reading a textbook that had caught my intellectual fancy." What's wrong with reading textbooks? All students read textbooks that specialise on their subject.

In another chapter he writes disparagingly of "dry academic theory or student Marxism". Well I know nothing about student Marxists; Jack Straw, his Shadow Home Secretary, does. He was one. But again you will note his contempt for theory. He can't mention the word without a derogatory prefix. He apparently doesn't know that human progress has been illumined by theories.

Homo sapiens studied and studies reality and evolves theories to explain the processes by which things happen. A theory is then tested. If it works it is added to the treasure house of human knowledge. If it doesn't it is either rejected and we start again, or modified so that it might work. Blair dogmatically confuses theory with dogma.

He explains elsewhere how he approves of the assertion: "If socialism without a moral doctrine is impossible, then a socialism without an empirical theory can become a mere fantasy." Why are empirical theories OK but political, economic, and philosophical theories are not OK? This kind of narrow practicalism led to a lack

129

of political perspective which damaged the Labour movement. By the mid-Sixties Labour knew not where it was going. Lack of theory was crippling the party. The profile of the working class was changing. Labour, in the absence of theoretical analysis and steeped in the culture of the male manual industrial worker, couldn't respond.

The British economy was in difficulty funding the Welfare State. Labour had no answers. Thatcher had: back to nineteenth-century laissez-faire capitalism. That was a bigger disaster. If it hadn't been for North Sea oil revenues the British economy would by now have been close to economic collapse.

Blair points out that the 1945 Labour Government "built a durable post-war settlement that forced the Tories to move on to our ground". That is what he is now doing in reverse. He has moved on to the ground occupied by Thatcherite Toryism. That is not a "settlement" Labour can accept.

A Labour government that tries to do so will fragment or destroy the Labour Party. There is an alternative. Adapting Labour's socialist theories to current reality. In rejecting this, Tony isn't left without theories. He is left with Thatcherite theories. He claims to be a radical new thinker, as did Maggie. He's a Tory radical thinker. And it's writ large in this book.

NEW LABOUR'S VISION THING

2 OCTOBER 1996

WITHIN the little group which runs New Labour there is no horny-handed son of the proletariat. John Prescott, ex-ship's steward, is therefore at times pushed into service as a token prole, to show that, really, New Labour hasn't sold the jerseys. He is primed before a broadcast. Given some New Labour mantras to mouth. John has also acquired a range of facial expressions, à la Les Dawson, including the leaning-forward, let-me-tell-you-something-in-private, expression.

It was the latter he used in a recent programme. Leaning forward, he told us, "Tony has vision." So, John, has Mystic Meg. So had Thatcher. So, for that matter, had Hitler. The value of a vision lies in its worthiness and the realisability of what is being visualised. New Labour, beneath the froth, is Thatcherism with a new face.

It has accepted the socio-economic system constructed in the United Kingdom over the past 17 years. A system that seeks to identify every social relationship in terms of crude cash payments.

131

A philosophy that is ruining the health service. New Labour's critique is that the Tories are incompetent. Rubbish. They have achieved their objectives with great competence. They dismantled all restraints on the activities of the very rich and enabled them to become very much richer. They did so at the expense of the very poor.

This was done through deregulation and by enormously reducing the taxes paid by the very rich. They sold public assets at giveaway prices, putting more billions into their pockets. This was primarily not new wealth but a redistribution of existing wealth. During this period our manufacturing base was decimated. Public spending for public works or the public good became four letter words. This led to crisis in the health service and in welfare provisions. Pensions were seriously eroded. Education was also plunged into crisis. The housing market collapsed. Homelessness spread. The social fabric of our society was torn apart. Lawlessness became rife.

High-flown and meaningless generalisations are of no use in confronting this social malaise. Gordon Brown's speech at Labour's conference was a peroration from start to finish.

There was reference to a classless Britain but it didn't amount to much. New Labour seems to perceive class as a purely cultural phenomenon. The Tories are labelled imprudent and incompetent, which, even if true, is the least of their sins.

New Labour promises to be more prudent and competent in the management of the prevailing system. New Labour will manage this system better than the Tories. At least that is what they are saying.

New Labour has eschewed any redistributive aspirations. There will be no tax increases. The tax burden is already too high, says Blair. That's true but the burden of tax has been shifted from income to indirect taxation, what used to be called purchase tax. The pensioner pays the same tax for a particular commodity as does the billionaire.

New Labour says that it will fund its programme, whatever that is, from economic growth and savings from pruning the bureaucracy in, for example, the NHS. But neither a New Labour government nor any other British government can determine whether this country's economy will be in crisis or in boom. There is a global market economy that is as likely to be in recession as anything else, when New Labour comes to power. Britain's growth would once again be on hold. Getting rid of the managers/accountants in the health service, and good riddance, won't even begin to look at the problems. It's the same with pensions. New Labour gives no specific commitment. It can't, not without taking back some of the billions given to the mega-rich by the Tories, and this it has pledged not to do.

The concentration of wealth in our country is now greater than ever before. Apart from anything else this is now of such a proportion that it is incompatible with democracy. Wealth is power. Super-wealth is super-power. The super-wealthy can buy newspapers and television companies. They have political clout in a million different ways. Tony Blair defers to Rupert Murdoch, who isn't even a British citizen, but has plenty of shekels. This gives him an authority to which a Prime Minister in waiting must submit.

Blair speaks of change which leaves this power intact, as if the interests of the super-wealthy cannot ever be in conflict with the country's interests. In all the talk about the low paid, one thing isn't mentioned. If there weren't low-paying employers there wouldn't be low-paid workers.

Blair talks as if there is no objective or potential conflict of interest between employers and employees. I've spent a big chunk of my life negotiating on behalf of workers with managing directors and chief executives. Most of them I got to know personally. Some became lifelong friends. But across the table my job was to get the best possible deal for the workers. Theirs to get the best possible deal for the shareholders. If we forced an increase that

133

could make the company uncompetitive it might also turn out to be our passport to the Labour Exchange. Sensible recognition of both the conflicts and commonality of interests between employers and employees is the only basis for good, lasting industrial relations. Middle England appears not to understand this. Instead of rectifying their ignorance Tony Blair panders to it.

I watched new members of New Labour being interviewed on television at Blackpool. It was depressing. They seemed to have come off a conveyor belt. All were without regional accents. Spiffingly petty bourgeois. Not a rebel in sight either in dress or manner. Young conformists who talked of change that has no substance. But then so does Blair.

Programmatically the Liberal Democrats are further to the left than New Labour, so is the SNP. On an important issue, the limiting of cross-media ownership, New Labour is further to the right than the Tories. On the management of the economy New Labour and the Tories are indistinguishable.

The Tories have no chance of winning the General Election and are now fighting among themselves for the post-election leadership of the party. In such circumstances the super-rich in Britain will welcome a New Labour government. They have nothing to fear from such a government. Where this leaves the poor and the health service is another matter.

NO PRINCIPLE
LEFT UNTURNED

30 OCTOBER 1996

WHEN she deemed my expectations to be excessive, my mother would say: "You canny hiv yer cake and eat it." Sage advice, I suggest, for Tony Blair, who has made a big political thing of his religious beliefs. He has done this to a greater extent than any other party leader in living memory. He waves his brand of Christianity like a political banner. Big trouble was inevitable.

More than half the people of this country are not meaningfully religious. I've been at church weddings where 80% of those attending were definitely not religious, including the parents of the bride and/or bridegroom, and sometimes even the bride and groom as well. The same can be true of funerals. The less than half of the remaining populace, who might be termed believers, are made up of Christians, Muslims, Jews, Hindus, Sikhs, etc. All these groups have internal groupings that sometimes hate one another with unyielding ferocity. They are, by no means, homogenous.

That is why politics should be secular. The various churches and religions might want to add or subtract something from the political agenda, that is their right, but party politics and religion must be kept apart, lest the political arena becomes a religious and sectarian battlefield, and that would be dangerous in the extreme. Yet the religious beliefs of party leaders have now become an electoral issue. The party leaders have made it so.

What can they argue about? Certainly not about macro-economics. New Labour and the Tories agree that market forces must prevail. They can't argue about micro-economics either. New Labour swears to the City of London that when it comes to things like supply-side economics it will be even more prudent and orthodox than the Tories. On taxation both swear they will further reduce income tax. There is no real difference between the parties on economic policy and economic policy determines most other policies. In other words, New Labour and the Tories now share a common ideology.

You would think this would lead to less confrontational electioneering but you would be wrong. The most minuscule of differences can generate the most acerbic bile. Look at our Wee Frees glaring at one another, over what others perceive as a teeny-weeny theological divide, with a hatred even greater than they have for Catholics. In politics when you have serious principled differences with an opponent you argue about principles. If you have no principled differences, and given our two-party adversarial system, you are left with personal abuse and abstractions.

The debates in the House of Commons over the past year have been about challenge and counter-challenge, about who would be most competent in running the existing set-up. Millions of children in Britain are now living below the poverty line. Social breakdown is widespread as the gap between the poor and the rich gets ever greater. There is no cosmetic solution to our social ills. We need real change. This the political parties do not offer.

Given there is no difference of ideology they are resorting to theology and abstract moralising. "Mirror, mirror on the wall, who is the most Christian of them all?" "Me, me," they say. I don't think this is going down well with Christians, but what about the others, the non-Christian majority? What are they to make of this?

Tony Blair, in particular, is digging himself into a hole. He believes that socialists will vote for him because they have nowhere else to go. The working class will vote for him through the inertia of tradition and because it also has nowhere else to go. He has gone for the support of the Big Boys in the City, and has got it, because they have nothing to fear from him, and he could do them a lot of favours.

He has even made a play for unreconstructed Thatcherite Tories, posing as the rightful son and political heir of Maggie. But his main target was always Middle England. Generally seen as WASPs. White Anglo Saxon Protestants. Anglican Protestantism, soft on Catholics, whom he presumed were on his side anyway. This was the rainbow convergence of votes that would sweep him to power. No principle was to be left unturned in pursuit of power.

Blair claims he is personally opposed to abortion. He's entitled to his opinion. I think the law should be left as it is, and so do the majority in this country, of all religious persuasions and none. But it transpires that Blair has voted 27 times in the abortion lobby and only once in the anti-abortion lobby. Cardinal Winning has therefore every right to challenge Blair on this issue.

He can't have his cake and eat it. He can't parade his religiosity, make claim to the moral leadership of the country, and not expect people to scrutinise what he is actually doing, as opposed to what he is saying. There is widespread unease that he has no principles or that they are expendable in the search for votes. That despite what he says he is really amoral and very much in the mould of American political leaders who are as cynical as hell and also speak the same gobbledegook of high-falutin' generalities that mean absolutely nothing.

I do not believe there is such a thing as Christian socialism. There are Christians who have become socialists through the teachings of Christ, as they interpret them, and also through their experience of life. That's different. The historic Christ has influenced many people. He was a Jew and is revered among Muslims as an Islamic prophet. He belongs to the world. It is, anyway, dangerous to delineate socialism in religious terms.

What is also troubling is the number of aggressive atheists of a few years ago that are now popping up as members of the Christian Socialist movement. Maybe they are genuine converts. Given the present climate, they could just as easily be political careerists on the make.

We should be apprehensive of politicians who claim their policies are derived from God. It doesn't leave much room for argument.

VOTING BY NUMBERS

6 NOVEMBER 1996

LABOUR'S ballot on Clause 4 was presented as a massive victory for the New Order. We were told that 90% of the members voted for the change. I asked the party headquarters in London how many members had voted. The information wasn't available. In most ballots the information most readily available is the total number of votes cast. I rang a week later. It was the same. These facts were not being revealed.

The public had the right to know. Members of the Labour Party had an absolute right to know, so you would have thought. I pursued it as a party member. So did others. The information was not divulged, top secret, it seemed. I concluded that fewer than 50% had voted which could not be acknowledged for it made nonsense of the assertion that the ballot was a ringing endorsement of New Labour's abandonment of socialism.

We now know that fewer than 40% voted for this fundamental change in Labour's constitution, and that, after all the arm-twisting and hype, many members considered the ballot a sham, and didn't vote. Yet the spin doctors made this ballot out to be the greatest thing since sliced bread. We got trumpet fanfares, tales of New Labour triumphant, but were not allowed to read the small print that would expose the charade. The media were manipulated. The public deceived. Labour's membership dumped on. Clever stuff but the clever stuff of con-men, not honest intellects.

This cat was let out the bag as New Labour announced the outcome of its latest ballot on the party's election manifesto. Again the fanfares and tales of New Labour triumphant. The spin doctors as usual were spin doctoring. This time we got the figures because more than 50% were recorded as having voted. They couldn't still keep secret the total numbers who had voted on Clause 4 and therefore we learned long after the event that only 40% of the membership had bothered to vote in that ballot.

But the conduct of this latest ballot has raised more serious doubts about whether New Labour's leadership can be trusted with the inner democracy of the party. Two weeks ago the Shadow Cabinet had been told that only 30% had voted. The credibility of the leadership was at stake. At least 50% had to be counted as having voted.

About 10 or 11 days ago I received a phone call. A young lady claiming to be speaking on behalf of the Labour Party asked if I had voted in the manifesto ballot, and had my wife voted? We had. She apologised and said she should have been informed of this, then hung up. Why should she have known? The counting of the votes was in the hands of an independent organisation to ensure, among other things, the confidentiality of the ballot. In a democracy people have the right to vote but they also have the right not to vote if that is how they feel.

Those who handle ballots have a right to tell others how many have voted. They have no right to tell who has or hasn't voted. How did they know our telephone number? It's ex-directory.

Other members of the party got phone calls. A couple from Barnet in London, Labour members for many years, were phoned.

The gentleman answered and was told, "We know you have voted but your wife hasn't." He wanted to know how they knew. He protests that the names, addresses, and telephone numbers of thousands of Labour Party members have been given to a commercial enterprise.

A political party has a right, in a general sense, to urge members to vote. It has no right to badger individuals, has no right to know whether they have voted or not in what is supposed to be a secret ballot.

Things then moved from bad to worse. Members started getting frantic phone calls telling them, "We know, you haven't voted. You can now vote via a free telephone number."

This was unprecedented. I was an activist in the engineering union that was then the most democratic in the country. Every office and position was subject to periodic election and re-election, some annually. We were always involved in a ballot. As a political activist I've been involved in ballots for public office and party posts. I've been involved in more ballots than Jack Straw's had hot dinners. I've never ever heard of a ballot which started with one means of voting and changed halfway through to some other form of voting.

It gets worse. The leadership were struggling to get 50%. Party members who still hadn't voted received an open postcard. I have one in front of me. It's got the party member's name and address on the front page. Lower down it reads on the same page: "YOUR personal voting number is . . . Please quote this number when making the call." What call? All is explained inside. "A message from Rt Hon John Prescott MP." "Dear Member, We recently sent you a summary of *New Labour, New Life for Britain*, our pre-manifesto programme. Conference has endorsed it. Now is your chance to pledge your support for our election programme and boost Labour's campaign. If you have not yet voted, please post your ballot papers today. Or vote by phone-call 0800-212556 . . ."

You will note the even-handedness. Vote Yes and ". . . boost

141

Labour's campaign." The implication is clear, vote No, and you're a bastard. Then at the bottom, "(PS. Thanks to the *New Statesman*, I am able to write to you without using party funds.)" The *New Statesman* was bought earlier this year by Geoffrey Robinson, multi-millionaire right-wing Labour MP. The open post-card also contained an offer to deliver the *New Statesman* at below quarter-price. "Plus you will receive a free copy of Tony Blair's book, *New Britain: My Vision of a Young Country*, worth £9." What? No Christmas hampers? No Green Shield stamps?

There is an arrogant authoritarianism about all of this. Yesterday's *Financial Times* said that the Labour leadership was struggling to get 50% to vote and had modified the rules to allow free telephone voting. This rings true. But who has the right to modify the rules. Who took the decision? Were they legally entitled to do so? If a trade union had changed its method of balloting, midstream, because its leadership wasn't happy with how things were going and had initiated telephone voting, a ballot-rigger's paradise, they would have been kicked from pillar to post, and doing most of the kicking would have been the leaders of New Labour.

ON DIFFERENT
RIGHTS AND WRONGS

13 NOVEMBER 1996

BRITAIN'S workers work longer for less wages than workers in other European countries. Our Government says to transnational companies, "Come and take advantage of our low-paid workers. You can work them round the clock for we have no legal restraints on working hours. They also have fewer holiday entitlements than workers elsewhere in Europe.

"There are still a lot unemployed. We are currently reducing and taking away their unemployment benefits. In desperation they will accept whatever you're prepared to throw at them in the way of wages. Don't worry about the trade unions, we've sorted them out, tied them up in repressive laws, made them less free than all other trade unions in the western world.

"We have broken those who might have fought, and corrupted the rest. You can't lose. We have moved the political agenda so far to the right that the so-called centre ground could easily be an ideological campsite for Genghis Khan. Please come, be our guest, make a killing on the profit fields of Britain. If you know of another country, not counting places like Bangladesh, that has lower wages than Britain, let us know, we'll sort it out by battering the poor some more."

In the early 1920s, workers in Scotland went on strike for a 40-hour week. Nearly 75 years later the British Government tries to defy the rest of Europe by insisting that British workers must be allowed to work more than 48 hours a week. By civilised standards we are heading back to the nineteenth century instead of forward to the Millennium. More and more children work today in Britain, for peanuts. The European Union, as an elementary act of social justice, seeks to establish a basic minimum wage. All other countries agree. Britain opts out.

Our civil rights are daily under attack as the Home Secretary and the Shadow Home Secretary fight it out to see who is toughest on crime. Our prisons are already crammed. Most prisoners shouldn't be there, wouldn't be in other European countries. Laws are now being proposed that are dangerous in the extreme, for victims. Learned judges are appalled. Crime has become a political football. This won't solve the problem, for the problem of crime is immensely more complex than punishment and retribution.

The causes of crime are overwhelmingly social. Things are now getting out of hand. I don't think that Parliament should be allowed to legislate new laws in the run-up to a General Election.

Politicians fear being accused of being soft on crime. This leads to all sorts of contradiction and absurdity. The Prime Minister is happy to have a free vote in the House of Commons about the caning of children in schools but no free vote on the banning of handguns. Debate in the chamber is an unedifying spectacle in which the unethical are being hounded by the unprincipled.

Yet it seems to be one of life's cast-iron certainties that the unethical and the unprincipled at some stage try to clamber aboard a moral high-horse. In this respect our current crop of party leaders are, if anything, worse than their predecessors. This has created a most unhealthy atmosphere.

Recently the BBC banned from our radios a play about Christ portrayed as a man from Galway. It was a comedy, a satire, of sorts. The language was apparently a bit rich. I can't be more explicit, the Beeb will not let me or you hear the play. I do remember Billy Connolly's wonderful sketch of Christ as a bloke from the Gallowgate in Glasgow having supper with his apostle mates in the Saracen Head pub, or "Sarry Heid" as the locals call it.

Would this be banned by the Beeb today? Where the hell are we going? Westminster Council is banning some movie. Presumably they saw it before they banned it and won't allow others to see it because it's corrupting. If it would corrupt us, why hasn't it corrupted the councillors of Westminster, who did see it? Were they already corrupt? I don't like pornography, it's boring. I don't like violence. But blanket censorship isn't the answer. It opens the door to authoritarianism.

Many of the finest works of art were banned because they told truths about life that the rulers didn't want us to hear, see, or read. People are not corrupted by the truth, but by untruths. Emile Zola was a moralist who wrote about society with great compassion, including its cruelties and crudities. Some wanted to ban his novels. His books survived and enrich us to this day.

The parents of Dunblane have been inspiring. Trauma often leads to paralysis of the will. Their trauma became a catalyst for collective action for socially good ends, and not in some vague or amorphous sense, but precisely aimed at changing the law on handguns. That's a positive ban. A child's right to live is greater than anyone's right to own a gun. If these parents had gone home, pulled the curtains on the world, their grief would have taken root. Instead they pulled together, helped each other, and today their loss has not been in vain.

It's how we should live our lives and not just in response to tragedy. But we live in a society that has been atomised. One against another. We are biologically and psychologically unsuited to such a way of life. The headmaster of Dunblane Primary was honoured last week for his courage and the way he conducted himself through those many months. He richly deserved the honour. Afterwards he said that he wanted to teach the difference between right and wrong. That's not as easy as it sounds.

In Shaw's *Major Barbara*, Undershaft is quizzing his son Stephen about what he wants to do in life. It appears he isn't really good at anything. Stephen then volunteers the information, "I know the difference between right and wrong". Undershaft (hugely tickled): "You don't say so! What! No capacity for business, no knowledge of law, no sympathy with art, no pretension to philosophy; only a simple knowlege of the secret that has puzzled all the philosophers, baffled all the lawyers, muddled all the men of business, and ruined most of the artists: the secret of right and wrong."

Shaw was at it a bit but there is truth in his words. What is right and wrong has to be specific. I believe it's wrong how the unemployed and low-paid are treated in this country. It's obscene. Couldn't we all get together and do something about that? What an example that would set our children.

THE HUMILITY OF KNOWLEDGE

20 NOVEMBER 1996

I RARELY use the word evil. It has too many devilish connotations. I'm happy to entertain the notion of God as something worth considering, but the idea of a supernatural ogre, a kind of horned and cloven-footed Jack Nicholson, is too ridiculous to waste good thinking time on. Belief in a devil is also a cop-out. If things bad are the work of a devil why seek other causes? Blast the devil instead.

I long ago concluded that the avoidable tragedies of human history were made by men convinced they were acting for God or as agents of history, genuinely seeking good as they saw it. Please, somebody, save us from the "goodness" of the closed mind.

The Crusaders, aliens in the Holy Land, slaughtered Christ's cousins, all for the glory of Christ. Muslims have been slaughtering other Muslims for some time now, all for the glory of Allah. A young Jewish fanatic killed the elected Prime Minister of Israel, then was allowed to vote for the candidate of his choice, who won, and is damn near to destroying the Middle East peace process. It will take a century or more to repair the damage done by religious and ethnic fanatics in what was Yugoslavia. Tribalism wreaks havoc in Africa.

You may think that these events merit the title evil, and in a pejorative sense they do. But that doesn't help us much. Damn them properly. Call them what they are, unreasonable. They are without reason, and reason is the homo sapiens' greatest asset.

The more we know, the more we know we don't know, isn't an acknowledgement of ignorance but the humility of knowledge. Human beings are part of the great ecological equation. Our dominance on this planet has made us appear god-like in our relations with other forms of life. We now know that if we destroy flora and fauna without regard to consequences then we can upset the ecological balance that sustains our species. We must be more modest about our place in the world for we are a part and not apart from nature and its laws. Our future and the future of this planet depends on us recognising that we break the laws of nature at our peril. The real challenge is to understand nature and its laws, not so that we can break them, but to use them intelligently for our common benefit.

Part of our problem is that in the past 100 years we have acquired more information and knowledge than we can handle. Man has had to specialise in ever-decreasing areas. Today millions are burrowing away, working in laboratories, experimenting, shedding more and more information about the nature of matter. Applaud their labours, but there is a snag.

There is no other scientist from another discipline looking over their shoulders and saying: "Hold on chaps, feeding the brains of dead sheep to cows isn't natural. It might be terribly wrong." The economist looks at the statistics which argue that such a practice makes the cow produce more milk or beef, and gives it his ringing endorsement. There is no philosopher asking probing questions about what they are doing.

Where are the philosophers? In the mists of academia, speculating about things abstruse. Scientists speak a gobbledegook which excludes the layman. Our practitioners in the humanities battle about such things as deconstructionalism. Academics rush into print, not because they have something to say but because they have to say something, in print, for the curriculum vitae and consequential career enhancement.

Add to this the separation of the sciences and the humanities in higher education, the insistent calls for more vocational training at an ever-earlier age, and it's no wonder we are in a mess. Every science graduate should be grounded in the humanities, every graduate in the humanities should be versed in the methodology of science. Many of the scientists and artists that I have known were polymaths. Men and women of letters and of culture. In the best traditions of Greece, the Renaissance, and the Enlightenment. Da Vinci to Einstein. This doesn't seem to be the case any more.

There are exceptions. Richard Dawkins is one. Some years ago I read his book *The Selfish Gene*. The opening sentence reads: "The chimpanzee and the human share about 99.5% of their evolutionary history, yet most human thinkers regard the chimp as a malformed, irrelevant oddity, while seeing themselves as stepping stones to the Almighty." I was hooked. The foreword was written by a colleague but the language was a portent of things to come in the book.

A fool makes the complex more complicated. The wise will make it less so, and more comprehensible to the non-specialist, by concentrating on essence and using analogies from everyday life. Dawkins does this because he believes that scientific knowledge belongs to the people, not some tiny elite.

His argument is that the gene is the only replicator of life in our universe. The gene, the DNA molecule, is the replicating entity which prevails on our planet. Our genes and DNA are factories for making human beings. The gene is not concerned about the species but about the replication of its own gene. Hence, the selfish gene. Humans can accept this for all other living creatures but not for themselves. I believe human beings are manifestly exceptional but need to be reminded that this exceptionality doesn't place us beyond the laws of nature. That's why I warmed to Dawkins.

He is branded as a political reactionary because he doesn't believe in the biological altruism of the human species. He does believe "that a new kind of replicator has recently emerged on this planet". He calls it "the soup of human culture". "Among animals, man is uniquely dominated by culture, influences learned and handed down. Some would say that culture is so important that genes, whether selfish or not, are virtually irrelevant to the understanding of human nature." Makes sense to me.

In his most recent lecture Dawkins berated paranormal obsessions on television and widespread interest in astrology. If the location of stars influence things on Earth such as which horse wins the Cheltenham Gold Cup, the punters would have been on to it by now and the bookies would be skint. They're not.

150

A FORMULA FOR DISASTER

4 DECEMBER 1996

TO ASSUME that those who don't agree with your primary beliefs are bad and have no case worth answering, is unreasonable and a form of fanaticism. It means you only really converse with those who think like yourself. You then start arguing about marginal differences and then more minutely marginal differences until you disappear up your own dogma. There are Tories I like very much. They are friends. We argue sometimes like hell. None is Thatcherite, which is a blessing. A few were but have moved with the hindsight of experience.

Michael Foot, whom I know and revere, and Aneurin Bevan, whom I didn't know but revered, were friends of Lord Beaverbrook. Regular dining guests at his country home. On one such occasion Beaverbrook chided Bevan about his liking for Bollinger champagne and Nye opined, "I'm a Bollinger bolshie," suggesting that nothing was too good for the workers.

In the late Fifties and Sixties I was in London. Most of the giants of the Labour left from the Thirties and Forties were still very

151

much alive. I was privileged to meet and know them, including James Cameron, Wilf McCartney, Claude Cockburn, Harry Pollitt, Foot, and others. The consensus was that Beaverbrook was a bourgeois maverick. He employed lefties including Foot and even the *Daily Worker* cartoonist "Gabriel" when he resigned from the Communist Party in 1956. Though an Empire loyalist Beaverbrook didn't feel at ease with the British establishment, but then neither did Churchill.

Maybe it had something to do with their North American family ties. Anyway they were outside the fold, only brought within during the darkest days of 1940 when things were desperate and Hitler was knocking on the door. Nobody questioned their intelligence or abilities but there were big question marks about Beaverbrook's character. His vindictiveness was legendary. He waged through his newspapers unremitting personal vendettas. It had often nothing to do with politics but stemmed from petty jealousies, presumed slights, or unfathomable dislikes.

He had a hit list of those who were to be given no credit for anything they might do, and be besmirched at all other times. It was a relentless campaign of character assassination. Lord Louis Mountbatten was pursued with malevolence because one of Beaverbrook's mistresses rather fancied him. This came to light in *Secret Lives* on Channel 4 last Monday.

But Mountbatten also incurred Beaverbrook's wrath for negotiating the transfer of power from the British Raj.

John Strachey and Manny Shinwell, Ministers in the 1945-51 Labour governments, were also hounded by Beaverbrook. Both were Jewish and Beaverbrook was an anti-Semite. His apologists deny this and quote as evidence that he had a beautiful Jewish mistress, a refugee from the Nazis. So what? Many white racists in South Africa had black mistresses. In the demented mind of the racist such a relationship might even bring added pleasure.

Beaverbrook could be charming, witty, generous, and pathological, maniacally intolerant, very cruel even to his nearest, and paranoid. Symptoms of serious psychological disorders were evident. This is bad in itself but he controlled mass circulation newspapers in Britain. He laid down the law to his editors. They pandered to his whims. This in a country that boasted of its free press. Now it's true that in Britain we are all free to own newspapers. All we need is a few hundred million quid. The right to own a newspaper and all the influence and political clout this entails therefore exists only for a minuscule few, whose enormous wealth sets them apart from the rest of us. Such wealth and the power it bestows tend to corrupt not only the owners of such wealth but those who do their bidding.

The value of a vote is undermined if information is doctored or slanted or withheld from the voter in accordance with the political dictates of newspaper owners. Labour believed it lost the last election because the *Sun* in England filched for the Tories more than a million working-class votes. The *Sun* was originally the *Daily Herald*, founded by the Labour movement to give expression to the principles of Labour. It was bought by Rupert Murdoch, an Australian turned American who turned it into a populist, jingoist, right-wing, land of hope and glory, last night at the proms, anti-Labour tabloid.

Since the last election Labour has pandered to Murdoch instead of demanding the re-regulation of the media. His control of BSkyB and numerous newspaper titles is incompatible with democracy. It isn't a matter of left or right but of protecting the voter from an unacceptable concentration of unregulated multi-media power.

Such power over the rest of us should not be for sale to the highest bidder. There are values that should be above price tags. If everything has a price then everyone has a price, including politicians. This cash register culture has dominated British politics for too long. It is the primary source of the moral decay that is eating away at our society.

ITV's *World in Action* commissioned a poll on the class system in Britain. The findings were interesting. One woman explained

153

how she and her husband had built up a business and now enjoyed a very good lifestyle. She said the two main parties were catering for the needs of people like herself; that there was not much difference between them in that respect. But she was extremely worried that no party was addressing the problems of the millions who had lost out. I could have kissed her.

My argument all along is that Labour should appeal to all that's best in the middle class by tackling the deep-rooted poverty of the many millions who have plunged into the lower depths during the Thatcher years. Labour shouldn't try to compete with the Tories in appealing to the narrow, selfish economic interests of the self-centred greedy. They'll not vote Labour anyway. Nor should they. The hostility to the Tories now so manifest is largely a disgust at the brutal economics of Thatcherism. As this poll showed, the victims, mired in their poverty, felt New Labour had abandoned them, and they might not vote at all. Among the middle class many want something done about poverty. They know that a large minority without hope is a formula for disaster that could engulf us all.

Labour should stop insulting people by pandering to all that's bad in their midst. Appeal instead to all that's good, in all classes, and win with dignity.

COME CLEAN, SPEAK OUT,
OR DEMOCRACY WITHERS

22 JANUARY 1997

MOONS ago when there was a sheen on my hair, a gleam in my eye, and mischief afoot in my mind, I had a brilliant idea; to write an anthology of public lavatory prose. My interest was not in lavatorial humour, well, not overly so, but in the intellectual profundity of much of the writing.

For example, Steve Benbow, who led an English folk group in the Thirties and was exceptional for the time, he could actually play the guitar, told me of a priceless piece above a urinal at the gents toilet in London's Charing Cross tube station. It read, "F*** the Halle Orchestra". What depths must the ensemble-playing have sunk to to evoke such disenchantment? And what priceless economy of language.

Billy Connolly told me that in a New York lavatory he was advised from scribblings on the wall that, "just because you're paranoid doesn't mean they're not after you". Sure now, Harold Wilson was a bit paranoid.

British seamen went on strike because their wages and conditions were lousy. Harold thought that it was a conspiracy to bring down his Government by "a tight-knit group of politically motivated men". I knew these men and most were motivated by a very strong desire to finish meetings before the pubs closed. Later, when Harold warned that MI5 was trying to bring down his Government, people laughed, but this time Harold was right. The Security Service was dominated by extreme right-wing nutters who were tapping Ministerial phones all over London. They considered a Labour Government subversive.

As history shows, any government or group who want to change society are considered subversive by those who want to keep things as they are. Those who benefit most from things as they are become fanatically convinced that things could not possibly be better. To them, those that advocate change are enemies to be spied upon and kept in their place, like maybe a cell. Suffragettes were deemed public enemies hellbent on subverting the realm, as were the pioneers of the Labour movement.

I knew a chief constable in Scotland who had been in Special Branch during the Thirties and Forties. For years he tailed an old friend of mine. They got to know and to like one another. My friend would tell his tail, "Look, I'm going to Newcastle tomorrow. Eight-thirty train. Let's have breakfast on the way up. Whose turn is it to pay?"

This police officer came to know that my old friend was no danger to British democracy. In fact he only wanted to extend the democratic principle into the realms of economics. For this he was branded a subversive. During the UCS work-in my phone was tapped. I guess the same was true of Jimmy Airlie and the other lads.

The telephones of leading trade unionists will still be tapped along with Labour MPs and a host of others considered a nuisance by the establishment because they don't accept the prevailing orthodoxies and have the courage to say so. The real traitors to

Britain, Burgess, Maclean, Blunt, and Philby, got away with it because they were part of the establishment. That won't have changed either.

This phone tapping and invasion of privacy wasn't sanctioned by law. It just happened. The perpetrators were not accountable. They were a law unto themselves. Theoretically the Security Service is now supposed to seek prior approval of the Home Secretary for phone tapping etc, but in practice, let's say, ah hae ma doots.

What is not in doubt is that the police were doing these things for years without legal authority. The Government's Bill now before Parliament intends to give that authority. Unfettered powers to break into private property and homes to instal electronic surveillance and do this without prior authority from any judicial agency. Such police powers exist nowhere else in the democratic world. Such powers have been part and parcel of every authoritarian state.

We averted this civil libertarian catastrophe only through the intervention of the House of Lords. Why was this not fought tooth and nail in the Commons? Because the Government and the Opposition are engaged in a desperate battle to appear tough guys against crime. They think this posture is a vote-winner.

The summation of their loony ideas would be a world of young offenders walking our streets with electronic tags fastened to their ankles. Television cameras in every street, watching. Curfews on children. Legally enforced homework. Longer prison sentences for every crime. No parole. Begging made a crime. A regime of Zero Tolerance. The biggest prison population in Europe. It beggars belief.

Labour promised to help the Government get its Police Bill through Parliament. Then came the reaction. In a democracy crime can't be fought by abandoning precious democratic norms. People felt revulsion that basic rights were being jeopardised as party leaders scrambled for the low ground. New Labour changed its tune. A cross-party upsurge in the Lords ended in defeat for the Government.

157

There's a lesson here. Silence in the face of injustice, or the denial of principles you believe in, is a coward's castle. For Labour MPs and trade union leaders to remain silent until after the election is simply no longer tenable. Gordon Brown has given an absolute commitment to hold public spending, for the first two years of a Labour Government, within the limits outlined by Kenneth Clarke in his autumn Budget. It is an absurd commitment.

Everyone knows that these expenditure figures were a product of inventive accountancy and aimed at helping the Tory electoral cause. These figures will be exceeded or held only by the most severe cuts in public services. There is no doubt that money is being wasted in funding the management of the internal market within the NHS. But such money won't even look at the burgeoning crisis of chronic under-funding which will bring the health service close to collapse within two years.

A Labour Government could not preside over the decimation of the NHS without destroying the Labour Party. Come clean now. Trust the people. Tell them the truth. Win with a mandate for change and not for the continuance of discredited Thatcherism.

SPAM, HORSE MEAT, AND AN ELECTION WITHOUT CHOICE

5 FEBRUARY 1997

SOMEBODY famous, whose name I can't recall, said: "Tell me what you eat and I'll tell you what you are." I've read many learned articles by those who tell us we are what we eat, which if true means the dung beetle certainly drew the short straw. For years I must have been Mr Pastry. A chieftain of the pudding race. All that's in the past. The witchdoctors posing as medical scientists decreed that my days of sweetie pie guzzling were over, so, I've been living mainly on things from the sea.

I've been munching molluscs, keeping body and sole together, quite nicely, thank you. It hasn't done any harm except that once in a while I sometimes drink like a fish. I also from time to time find myself outside a baker's shop ogling the pastries and bouncing my pouting lips off the window. As Shakespeare more or less said, "All the world's an aquarium and we are but little fish caught in the tides of destiny." Maybe so, William, but it's still a bit worrying, I'm getting rather fond of plankton.

There are mysterious stories from the last war about the metabolic mayhem of humans eating strange food. Stories that Mulder and Scully of television's *X Files* should investigate. The participants in these mysteries were not exactly paranormal, more paralytic, particularly at the weekends. Let me tell you of one case. During the war a young couple from Govan who were besottedly in love got married. He worked in Rolls-Royce, Hillington. They got a house in what was to become Penilee, a garden suburb of Govan. In those days it was known as Spam Valley.

It was a time of strict food rationing. Spam was the staple diet. Hard to describe. American I think. It did fill a space. The young couple were full of the joys of married life. The young man was also full of spam. He was getting it for breakfast, dinner, and tea. One evening he told his beloved: "If I get any more spam I will develop psychopathic tendencies and blooter unto death our gaffer whose brother is a butcher and provides him with sausages, black puddings, and succulent steaks. He tells us in detail the delights that await him at home. He even shows us his pieces at the teabreak before getting tore in."

You understand this was the gist of his sentiments. He actually said: "Any mair spam an' Ah'll hing for that wee b****rd of a gaffer." The young wife was beside herself with worry, searching high and low for some meat for her man. She stumbled on a shop that sold unlimited amounts of horse meat. The proprietor explained that cooked properly her husband wouldn't know the difference between horse flesh and prime beef.

He didn't. He got horse steak fried, grilled, braised, stewed, casseroled, marinated, au vin, minced, and curried. He was as happy as Larry, though to tell the truth the only Larry I've known was a miserable sod. Time passed and the young man suddenly realised he was taking much longer to shave. His chin was getting longer and longer. His ears were more pointed. The loving young wife had also noticed. She told him about the horse meat. "We eat salads without becoming rabbits," her husband jokingly pointed out, cuddling and coaxing away her fears. But he did go to the doctor.

The doctor examined him thoroughly, called in his partner for a second opinion. They muttered quietly to one another and eventually arrived at some kind of diagnosis. His doctor sat down at his desk and started writing. The young husband asked: "Is that a prescription?" "No," said the doctor." "It's a medical certificate for defecating in the street."

I've known of this since early childhood. I heard my father tell grown-ups all about it at a party in our house. The insensitive listeners laughed. I later asked my dad what had happened to the young man. He had run away, or should I say galloped. He might have been afraid of his family being made homeless for Glasgow Corporation had a rule which forbade the keeping of horses in council flats, even in Penilee. Nobody has heard of him since.

Some years later my dad was walking down Copeland Road and passing a stationary coal lorry. These were pulled through the streets by big, strapping horses. The coalman would shout his wares. "Coal!" A woman would open her window and tell whether she wanted one bag or two. The man would hoist a bag on his shoulder, take it up the stairs, and dump it in her bunker. This day my dad heard his name being called. There was nobody about, only the horse. He heard it again. It was the horse. The horse said: "It's me, Charlie." It was the young loving husband.

Well as you will appreciate my dad was dumbfounded. This was Charlie whom he had known and liked, and here he was a coal horse. "How's life?" he asked. "Bloody murder," Charlie growled. "This coalman is a beast. He has me at it all day. Trudging the streets, pulling load after load. Back to the stables at night. A cold draughty place in winter and a hothouse in summer. All I get to eat is some straw washed down with a pail of water. It's so bad I sometimes pine for spam." "Why don't you talk to the boss man?" said my dad. "Are you kidding?" said Charlie. "If he knew I could speak, he would have me shouting 'Coal'!"

161

You can bet there is no reference to this case in the files of the Southern General Hospital or anywhere else in Scotland. There are things we are clearly not allowed to know about this mystery and other more inexplicable mysteries. What will change if Gordon Brown is Chancellor instead of Kenneth Clarke? Now there's a real mystery. New Labour's windfall tax will raise an as yet unknown sum from an as yet unknown group of privatised public utilities. No-one has defined public utilities in this context. Does it include British Gas and BA? We don't know. That's another mystery.

New Labour accuses the Tories of high taxation. That's the biggest mystery of all. In the past 18 years taxation of the rich has plummeted. Both parties agree not to alter the existing levels of income tax. Neither party in government will therefore be able to solve the looming crises in the NHS, local government services, and state pensions.

The rationale of an election without choice is a mystery wrapped in sound bites. I tell you, most seriously, Govan's talking horse made more sense.

TIME TO FACE A DEBT
WE ALL OWE

14 FEBRUARY 1997

THE ONLY argument in favour of local government is that it counter-balances the centrality and remoteness of national government. And that, as they say, is one helluva good argument. Local councils had responsibility for a whole range of services that catered for individual needs, individual families, local commerce, and business within a community of which they were an integral part.

Local councils and councillors had probably more actual impact on our lives than Parliament and MPs. We had near at hand the elected representatives charged with providing and administering the services that mattered most in our everyday lives. The near at hand can more easily be scratched and, in the context of democratic accountability, such proximity should never be underrated.

During the Thatcher years the powers of government exercised from Westminster were dangerously centralised. Parliament was more rigidly controlled by Cabinet, Cabinet most rigidly controlled

163

by the Prime Minister. She became a de facto president without the checks on presidential power inherent in a democratic presidential system.

In the United States, apart from Congress and Senate, individual states and even lower divisions of local government have constitutionally sacrosanct powers that no president can touch. In Britain the Greater London Council was Labour-controlled. Not to the Prime Minister's liking. She abolished it. With a stroke of the pen, as it were, London became the only capital city in the world without geographical/political integrity.

The rest of local government was viewed as a conveyor belt for Westminster diktats. Councillors were expected to do as they were told. That they were elected, had an electoral mandate of their own, was totally ignored. They were treated like non-elected civil servants; forced under legal duress to implement policies contrary to those that people voted for in the local elections that made them councillors. There was no attempt at reconciliation. Given the prevailing ethos, that was deemed a weakness. Everyone had to be fought, made to submit. The widespread reaction to such politics is encapsulated in one incontrovertible fact: in Scotland today not a single local authority is Tory.

The Government's declared strategic objective was to cut public expenditure as a percentage of the Gross Domestic Product. Public expenditure became dirty words. Cut back public expenditure year after year and you must cut public services. At the same time taxes were cut. Public utilities were sold to pay for tax cuts. Then came the deregulation of the City, known as the Big Bang. Yuppies. Essex Man. And through it all the loss of a significant portion of Britain's manufacturing capacity.

Unemployment soared. The Government that set out to cut public expenditure had to increase the public sector borrowing requirement to pay unemployment benefits. Public expenditure actually rose. The next move was to cut unemployment and welfare benefits. To let the real value of pensions decline by ending their linkage to earnings. Millions were pushed down into the poverty trap. Social problems consequently, and horrifyingly, escalated.

Caught in the eye of the storm were the local authorities, overwhelmingly, but not exclusively, Labour-controlled. They had to carry the can. For well over a decade they have ducked and dived trying to cushion their communities from the worst effects of Government policies. Year after year, more and more cuts until the system began to break down. That's what we face today.

To explain this as town hall factional in-fighting within Labour groups is absurd; it also insults our intelligence. Scottish local authorities are confronted by a chronic crisis that's not of their making.

The cuts, no matter how they're dressed up, are imposed, as were all the others in past years, from Westminster. The difference this time is that the cuts now being called for might just break the camel's back.

Glasgow is arguably the worst-case scenario. The Government yet again re-organised Scottish local government without consultation. It looks upon local authorities as enemy encampments. If you can't beat them at the polls, demoralise them through fiscal skulduggery; that seems to be the aim.

The plight of Glasgow brings to mind the crisis in New York some years ago, when that city faced imminent bankruptcy. This can't happen here. British law requires local authorities to produce an annual budget, without a deficit, no matter what it entails. For this year it could entail for Glasgow massive cuts in a whole range of public services, 2000 redundancies, and a substantial increase in council tax. This on top of all that's gone before.

The situation is grim. Glasgow was part of Strathclyde Region, which had a population of approximately 2.5 million. It had about one million households registered to pay council tax. The tax is based on the valuation of the house. Valuation is organised into eight bands. Band A is the lowest value category and then it proceeds up to the highest valuation Band H. Because of Strathclyde's social mix the average valuation was Band D, the same average for Scotland and the UK as a whole. Strathclyde Regional Council was responsible for 70% of public services, including the high-spending services of social work, education, and roads.

The new Glasgow City Council has a population of 618,000 of which 280,000 households should pay council tax. Of that number more than 50% are eligible for council tax rebates. The average valuation of households in Glasgow is Band B—among the lowest in the United Kingdom. Glasgow is the hub of a much bigger conurbation. For 150,000 come in and go out of the city each day. This is equivalent to one quarter of the population. They come for work and play, to shop and use the cultural facilities that only a city can sustain. Some 64% of the professional and management staff in Glasgow's business and commercial world live outside the city boundaries. They make no direct contribution at all to Glasgow's costs. They did when there was a Strathclyde Region.

The maintenance of an infrastructure that serves a much wider community is a substantial added cost. Let me give one example. The Mitchell Library is reckoned to be Europe's largest civic reference library. It is fully computerised. It's wonderful and that opinion stems from direct personal experience. The library is used by thousands from all over Scotland. It costs Glasgow City Council £3.5m a year. Glasgow could close the library, sell the building, save millions, but that would be an act of cultural and intellectual vandalism. Is cutting home-help services for the sick and disabled less reprehensible? That's the kind of dilemma facing councillors.

Along with the raft of parliamentary legislation that came with the late and unlamented poll tax was a change concerning the business rate. This rate had previously been set by local authorities. There was a snag. The more deprived areas generally paid higher rates because they had greater social problems to cope with. Raising both domestic and business rates was the only means available for doing this.

If the more deprived areas raised the business rate too much there was always the danger that some businesses would move to lower rated, and, by definition, more affluent areas, thus further compounding the problems of the deprived areas. It was a vicious circle.

The local business rate was replaced by a unified business rate linked to inflation. Nobody is seriously arguing for a return to the old system, but the way the UBR is being applied is, to put it mildly, bizarre. This year Glasgow will collect about £210m in business rates from within the city. The money is put into a Scottish Office pool for distribution that takes little recognition of the city's real needs. Glasgow will get back about £160m.

The rest, about £50m, is distributed to other local authorities in Scotland, including Perth and Kinross, the richest area in the whole of Scotland; Aberdeenshire, which isn't far behind; East Renfrewshire, wi' Newton Mearns and Eastwood; an' a' an' a'. It would take some perverse notion of social justice to justify this.

Glasgow is facing a deficit of £80m. If it got that £50m the rest might be manageable without further cuts and redundancies. Next Wednesday a deputation from the city council and Glasgow MPs will meet George Kynoch, the Scottish Minister of State for Local Government, to press Glasgow's case. The £50m should be refunded. The Glasgow business community should make its voice heard. So should those from outside who are beneficiaries of the city's bounty. It would be one way of acknowledging that debt.

In a matter of weeks there will be a General Election. It's generally assumed there will be a change of government. Whatever the outcome there can be no continuation of the status quo in relation to local government.

It must be properly funded or the system will be reduced to a shambles and the most vulnerable will again suffer the most.

THE DELUSIONS OF MYTHOLOGY

19 FEBRUARY 1997

MYTHS are harmless when we know they're myths. Redundant religions provide harmless myths that become a source of allusions, not illusions. Where would Shakespeare be without ancient Greek and Roman mythology? When stuck for a word or two the Stratford-on-Avon man gave his fans an earful of mything links.

Hamlet commends the noble looks of his dead dad: "See what grace was seated on this brow, Hyperion's curls, the front of Jove himself, An eye like Mars, to threaten and command, A station like the herald Mercury, New lighted on a Heaven kissing hill . . ." Poets went further and gave us laldy, with reams and reams of mythology. Earfuls of Jupiter by Jove.

Talking of earfuls, a teacher once tried to persuade me that a major war was started because someone cut off the ear of a bloke called Jenkins. I was having none of it. If a Brit got his ear chopped off in a foreign clime a diplomatic letter of protest might be sent, but no way would nations go to war over an ear, unless looking for an excuse, a pretext for getting the jaikets aff.

168

The war of Jenkins's ear was a harmful myth. The war was about something else. Probably something to do with crude power and economics. Thousands, according to this teacher, lost their lives over an ear. I had this mental picture of a very startled Jenkins running around shouting, "Hold on chaps it's only an ear. I might even have cut it off shaving and didn't notice. Please pack it in."

Anyway what's the fuss? In Govan there was a bloke called "Cut the Lugs". He answered to this moniker. "How's it gaun, Cut the Lugs?" "No bad." Whenever someone got up his humph he cut off his ear with an open razor. Punters were knockin' about Govan with no ears. They stuck out like sore thumbs. Bunnets slipped down over their eyes. You could hear them muttering: "These fogs are getting worse." But when someone got an ear cut off in Govan, the Prime Minister didn't say. "Enough is enough, we'll go to war with Germany."

Such cause and effect is too daft to swallow. The same applies to the First World War. A teacher tried to tell me that it started because some anarchists had assassinated an Archduke on the streets of Sarajevo and this led to the slaughter of millions at the Somme and other places. Maybe they had only tried to cut off the Archduke's ears, à la Jenkins, but in their zeal had gone too far, was my observation. I was told this was a frivolous comment. No more frivolous than trying to explain the objective causes of war in terms of a missing ear or the killing of an Archduke. These myths obscure real causes and we need the truth if we are to come up with answers.

We're now enmeshed in a General Election influenced by a myth from the last General Election. In 1992 Labour was winning, so it goes, when, with a few days left to polling day, John Smith, Shadow Chancellor, brought out a Shadow Budget with proposed modest tax increases. This, it is claimed, gave victory to the Tories. Rubbish!

Labour lost the election when the Tories ditched Mrs Thatcher.

All the excesses since 1979 had been attributed to her. Major was perceived as less ideologically dogmatic. The prospect of a Major government was assiduously sold to the public as essentially a new, kinder, government.

The Tories were helped by a Labour critique that centred almost exclusively on Thatcher and not Thatcherism. Remember the marches, people screaming, "Maggie, Maggie, Maggie, Out, Out, Out". I asked at the time, what if the Tories obliged and got rid of Maggie? Where did that leave them? With no critique at all?

I am no fan of Mrs Thatcher, as you will have gathered, but the utter personalisation of modern politics trivialises political debate. The demonising of Maggie obscured the underlying philosophy which all Tory Ministers had served. When it came to the crunch the demonising of Thatcher helped the Tories, not Labour.

This is nothing new. Hitler was demonised. This let millions of Germans off the hook. Today there is still no definitive analysis of the causes and root elements of German fascism, that would blow the gaff. Instead we got the big bad man scenario. Italian fascism was, of course, Mussolini's fault. Soviet communism was betrayed by Stalin who was not only bad but mad, argue apologists of Lenin. The Soviet elite who governed like Tsars in the name of Lenin, under Stalin, still govern as gangster Tsars in the name of the market. Behind every scapegoat lurk many more big bad men.

The scapegoating of John Smith for losing Labour the last election has meant an election in 1997 in which the main parties swear they will not raise income tax. Britain now has a stack of millionaires. Ten a penny. They are products less of the production of new wealth than the re-distribution of existing wealth. For nearly 20 years this process has impoverished the poor and enriched the rich.

Look around. Social, welfare, and health services cannot cope. Local government services in disarray through a surfeit of cuts. The prison system in crisis. The judiciary under stress. The fabric of civil life under threat. There's no solution to these very serious problems without re-allocating resources, which means those who can afford to pay more tax should be asked to do so. What's the point of having more and more money if it means that you and your family have to live in a human jungle where nobody's safe?

A young woman, relatively highly paid, told me that she would vote for whatever party wanted her to pay the most tax. She doesn't believe in the honesty of those politicians who say that Britain's problems can be solved without her doing so. There are many like her, young and old, who believe in righting wrongs before they get out of hand and degenerate into a violent mess. They reject the present Government because it failed to ditch Thatcherism as well as Thatcher. They are not too well pleased with New Labour, which badly needs a clearly defined anti-Thatcherite agenda that reflects this desire for change. Change that this time will have to be real and not cosmetic.

SOMETHING IN THE AIR

26 MARCH 1997

IN THE LATE summer of 1939, a group of women standing at the close of a Glasgow tenement were chatting away. My mum among them. She must have been a mite depressed at the time for she said: "It will get worse before it gets better." Next day Hitler invaded Poland and the Second World War had started. In 1944 she told neighbours rather wistfully: "I think we should go to a beach and raise merry hell." Next day the allied armies landed in Normandy, raised merry hell, and that was the beginning of the end of Hitler's Third Reich. She forecast a landslide victory for Labour in 1945. Churchill got gubbed, Attlee became Prime Minister.

An academic from Gilmorehill led a safari into darkest Govan to investigate the mystic powers of this seer from the South Side, ma maw. When asked how she knew Labour was going to win in a canter she explained: "It was in the atmosphere." In Govan they could have saved time and money by weighing Labour votes, and so the atmosphere that informed my mum was Govan's atmosphere. Clean and pure as the driven snaw, but red. Red driven snaw.

She invariably backed a horse in the Derby. It always had a name like My Love. They won, much to the chagrin of my old man who was a serious student of form. She had sixpence each way. He had quids on the nose. One year we were huddled round the wireless listening to the commentary on the Derby. In the last two furlongs mum and dad's horses were battling it out. She was calling home her horse. Dad, the eternal sceptic, turned to her and said: "I'll gie ye a fiver if you call home mine." She dismissed the offer. Her horse won.

I don't believe in mystics or mystiques but have a certain prescience. For example, at the start of this season I predicted Rangers or Celtic would win the premier league, Coca-Cola Cup, and Scottish Cup. Rangers won the Coca-Cola Cup. Rangers will win the premier league, Celtic will be second. Celtic are in the semi-finals of the Scottish Cup. No big deal, you might say, predicting the dominance of these two clubs. No deal at all.

In life a great deal is determined by economics, a fact which is the main source of my prescience. Rangers and Celtic have benefited to the tune of millions from technology that has made the game a very marketable global product. The game in Scotland should be a non-contest between these two clubs and the rest. Like a competition about gross profits between a corner shop and Tesco. I predict in season 1997/98, Rangers or Celtic will win the premier league, and the following season, ad nauseam, ad infinitum.

Jock Stein's achievement in the Sixties and Seventies was most remarkable because a team from Greater Glasgow beat Europe and were a match for any club team in the world. Now look at a contemporary team list of Celtic or Rangers. It reads like a minute of those attending a meeting of the United Nations Security Council. The best players are now global mercenaries, so are managers. Finance directors rule the roost, as it must be when clubs are quoted on the Stock Exchange. Only fans are non-mercenary and retain a sense of romance about the game. How long will that last?

Politics is also about economics. Since 1993 I've known the Tories would lose the next election. Recessions from the Sixties onwards decimated the communities of industrial workers and left unscathed the nouveau middle class of the Midlands and South-east England. These jokers believed they were fireproof. Unemployment, evictions, repossession of households were for the Jocks, Scousers, Geordies, and Taffs, not for them.

In the recession that followed 1992 there were not enough Jocks, Scousers, Geordies, and Taffs left in manufacturing industry that would make any difference if thrown on the scrap heap, so it started to bite among the new Tories in Thatcher's heartlands. The housing market collapsed, Essex men and women found themselves on the dole. Houses repossessed, people made homeless. "Hold on," they wailed, "this is not supposed to happen to us. We're Thatcher's children." That was when I knew for certain the Tories had had it. John Smith was Labour's leader and opinion polls were starting to tilt decisively in favour of Labour. Now was the time for Labour to tell everyone that while market forces were essential mechanisms of an enterprise economy, they couldn't be left to determine everything. Market forces on their own have no heart, no soul. They reduce everything to crude, callous, cash payments.

The sleaze of recent years is the product of a society which asserts that everything and everyone has a price. We then get the best politicians money can buy and brown paper bags of £50 notes are handed over furtively as between traders in dubious goods, passing in the night. To place the odium on MPs as individuals, is a cop-out. As was the blaming of individual traders for the series of corruptions, insider dealings, and hijacking of funds, that damaged the City of London's reputation in the world's financial markets. The Tories deregulated the City. Restraints that protected the public interest were dismantled. Markets would sort out things, was the credo, and we got Maxwell. Billions were made from the undervalued sale of public assets, and we got fat cats. Cause and effect. The election is being fought on effects without a cause in sight. It won't work beyond polling day.

After May 1 the phoney war will be over, the real political battle will commence. One year from now Glasgow City Labour group will meet to decide the council budget. As things stand councillors will have to impose higher council taxes, more cuts in services, more job cuts. There will be no Tory government to blame, for it will have gone, in its place a New Labour Government.

It's impossible for a Labour government to apply Thatcherite economics. The Labour movement, those who voted for change, won't wear it. That's the nub. If there is more of the same there will be uproar. And the Labour Party isn't the private fiefdom of Tony Blair, as will be shown in the next few years. That's why I'm voting Labour.

MPs GRIPPED BY SILENCE

2 APRIL 1997

YOU may recall reading the following: "It is going to be a crazy election. In a contest of principles things can become torrid. In a contest of no principles things can become horrid. Personal abuse and dirty tricks will abound, masterminded by party managers and spin doctors. The election will be an inglorious exercise in dishonesty." These words are mine and appeared in the *Herald*, January 29, 1997. I quote them to remind you that my expectations for this election were low, very low.

In the third week of the actual campaign it can be recorded that the election has fully lived down to my expectations, only more so. It has been vile and remorselessly putrid. To think that this is not the work of the party managers would be fancifully unfair. Give them their due. They're in control. That New Labour's campaign managers didn't know of the "revelations" concerning two Scottish Tories, before publication in a tabloid, is so inconceivable as to be risible.

Two families shattered. One man driven almost unto death.

Matters not germane to politics raised to try to influence voters. We now have a General Election enmeshed in pubic hairs not public affairs. Tabloids tasting blood will turn on them that fed them, and that's for sure.

It has obviously escaped some people's notice, but years ago this country decided that being a homosexual wasn't against the law. What consenting adults do in private was considered to be their business and not ours. Yet a prominent Tory politician has been driven from public life because of a past homosexual indiscretion. I'm rather in favour of driving Tories from public office, not for what they do in bed, but for what they do out of bed to the sick, the poor, and the pensioners.

Let us also be clear, the Tories have by no means cornered the market on homosexuals. There are homosexuals in other parties. As you read this hacks will again be perusing their names. All they need is past lovers to finger them, for a big fee of course, and the hunt is on. It's appalling. There is an old saying, if you don't run they can't chase you.

I've known Mickey Hirst since 1974 when he stood as Tory candidate in East Dunbartonshire. I know him and his wife. Won a bottle of wine from him when I bet that the SNP would win the Govan by-election. Won another when I tipped Labour to win back Govan in the General Election. Politics apart they were a nice couple. We were both supporters of EIA, an organisation set up to sustain and encourage manufacturing industry in Scotland.

As a political opponent and without any personal animus towards him at all, let me say quite bluntly that Mickey Hirst was wrong to resign. He should have stood his ground. Matters concerning his private life were matters for him and his wife, and nobody else. His public life, in politics and business, was different. He could be held to account on that, and nothing else. He would have won support by taking such a stand. To run away wasn't really an option. Major might have sacked him but that would have put him in the frame as someone scared of homophobics as well as Europhobics.

Piers Merchant on the other hand has been assailed for being an over-enthusiastic heterosexual. Stitched up by the New Labour-supporting *Sun*, Piers might be a plonker but he has bottle. John Major and Heseltine wanted him to resign. He refused. We might not be able to send Piers to the local corner shop for a bottle of Irn Bru lest the burden of remembrance be too great for his mental capacities, but he is profoundly preferable to the photographer who lurked behind a bush to try to snap Piers groping the young tart who set him up, and that photographer's employers. All they got was a fotie of a kiss. Why didn't the swine bonk her? What a story that would have made. "Merchant Bonker and Soho Virgin." "A lark in the park."

Meanwhile the election flounders on. What about the single currency? No single currency, no single market. No single market, no inward investment that comes here to take advantage of the single market. There is, of course, more to it than that. Does a single currency need a central European bank? Does that mean a single interest rate for all member states and is this feasible? Will it mean a federal Europe? Would that be a bad thing?

Some very important decisions about Europe will have to be taken before the next General Election. Yet the main parties will not even define what conditions they believe would justify entry or non-entry. It's as if the electorate were all fools that had to be pandered to at elections, and then ignored. It is no longer a question of informing and winning minds but of winning votes and dis-informing minds. Shades of Orwell's *Nineteen Eighty-Four*. Things are said and done that don't make sense in any social or historical perspective.

In Monday's *Times* Tony Blair wrote about New Labour's proposals on trade unions. "The changes that we do propose would leave British law the most restrictive on trade unions in the Western world." Here is the leader of a party founded by trade unions to fight for the collective rights of workers boasting that his Government will have laws that are the "most restrictive on trade unions in the Western world".

Labour's election campaign is funded by trade unions. New Labour and Blair have been given millions by the unions to represent their interests in Parliament, yet here he is, before entering the portals of 10 Downing Street, boasting that under his Government trade unionists in Britain will be less free than anywhere else in the Western world. Arguably the least free in Europe since the collapse of Franco's Spain.

No protest from the TUC. Unions are mute as are trade union-sponsored Labour MPs. Vociferous left MPs seem gripped by the silence of the dead. Votes, any kind of votes, are what it's all about. Power is all that matters even if that power is to be used to make British workers less free than others. Trade unionists in this country should sue New Labour for taking their money under false pretences.

The Tories are beaten. They will claw back some support but not enough even to soften their fall from grace and power. The only danger to New Labour is that Mandelson and Blair get too clever by half and end up in a word spin-soundbite-fankle. Maybe it's time to send Mandelson back to his lair.

RUBBING SALT IN THE WOUNDS: BLAIR AND THE NATIONAL QUESTION

9 APRIL 1997

MARTIN BELL, a good man fallen among spin doctors, might regret getting involved in this election that looks like being the most corrupt of the century. I use corrupt because the word fits the intellectual squalor and downright dishonesty so rampant in this campaign. Sleaze was less apposite but as a one-syllable word sat more easily on a tabloid front page.

Tory MPs who took money for parliamentary questions were guilty of corruption. End of story. But corruption is not only about exchanging cash for illicit services, it also means dishonesty in a wider framework. The debasement and abandonment of principles and ideals in pursuit of power can be the most deadly form of corruption. Labour is now haemorrhaging from a multitude of ruptured principles.

There is a growing awareness of this within the Labour Party. On Saturday I was out on the hustings. Nowhere was there a poster or a leaflet with Blair's photograph to be seen. The party workers refused to take such material. Blair they reckon is a recruiting sergeant for the SNP. Every time he pays a visit Labour activists groan. One more time and Michael Forsyth might be safe and Alex Salmond can chalk up a few more seats.

Is Blair dense? No, but he is clever rather than intelligent, so is every conman. Some months ago I reviewed his book for the *Herald*, the thoughts of leader Blair sort of thing. The intellectual paucity of his arguments was manifest. He isn't thick but slick. A man on the make. Packaged by cynics. "Smile" they told him. He smiled. The smile grated on many. "Don't smile. Give them some gravitas." He didn't smile, tried to give us some gravitas. His handlers wanted to shepherd him through the election without exposing him to serious probing. They succeeded until he came to Scotland.

Subject to a bit of grilling where his minders couldn't help, his urbanity cracked, so did his language. In any context to compare a Scottish Parliament with an English parish council was insulting. He rubbed salt in the wound when he opined that sovereignty would still reside with him as an English MP. Then to top it all he declared that Labour members of a Scottish Parliament would not be allowed to raise taxes for five years even if the Scottish people gave them the power to do so.

In a sense it is irrelevant whether a Scottish Parliament does or does not raise taxes. It's the arrogance. The contempt for Scotland's Labour movement and Scottish people whom he clearly views as unthinking voting fodder. Like most clever dicks he has painted himself into a corner. If Labour members in a Scottish Parliament can't increase taxes for the next five years, why should Labour-controlled Scottish councils be allowed to raise council taxes? Or are Labour councillors in Glasgow to be told they cannot raise council taxes? If so then along with Gordon Brown's acceptance of the public spending limits in the last Tory Budget, this would mean massive cuts in services and mass redundancies.

If Labour councillors are allowed to raise council taxes and New Labour members of a Scottish Parliament aren't, then Labour members of a Scottish Parliament will have less authority than Scottish Labour councillors. This makes a laughing stock of the Scottish Constitutional Convention and all those good people who worked with Labour, in good faith, for a meaningful Scottish Parliament.

The truth, I believe, is that Blair hasn't a clue about the national question in Scotland. For John Smith, the establishment of a Scottish Parliament was unfinished business. A matter of principle. Blair was told a devolved Parliament was necessary to spike the electoral challenge of the SNP. The proposal, in his mind, was an electoral ploy. He had made no serious study of the matter.

Scotland is one of the oldest nations in the world. Proudly independent with its own culture in the widest anthropological sense of that word, its own law and institutions that were splendidly unique, and an intellectual, moral, philosophical, often iconoclastic tradition, that placed our nation among the innovative vanguard in most aspects of life and thought.

If there had been a democratic referendum among the Scots in 1707 the Treaty of Union would have been overwhelmingly rejected. Among royalty north and south of the Border there were those who aspired to a united kingdom. Given the numbers involved there was little doubt where this would lead.

When James VI of Scotland became King of England as well, he rode south with his courtiers, never to return except for a brief visit. The Treaty of Union meant our Parliament went south, too. There was no mechanism whereby the Scots could be protected in this unitary state against the sheer numbers of their much bigger neighbour. There is none today. Thatcherism proved that without such safeguards Scots could be disenfranchised. Over 18 years the Scots were governed by an alien philosophy that they had rejected time and time again.

New Labour has embraced Thatcherism. If Thatcherism was

alien to Scots under Thatcher, it will be no more palatable under Blair. There will be a Blair Government. Will Scottish Water be safe from privatisation? Even if he says yes can you trust him? He told us our railways would be publicly run. His spokesman swore that Britain's air traffic control was not for sale. He reneged on these things. Putting his right hand across his chest, he asks us to trust him. What a bloody cheek.

THE RISK BUSINESS

16 APRIL 1997

SLEAZE is one word you associate with this election. But trust and risk have been much to the fore. Why take any politician on trust? The person and/or his party should have past form of some kind on which a judgment can be made as to worthiness for office. If they haven't they shouldn't be standing. Their record and explicit commitments for the future should be the only basis on which they ask for our votes. Blind trust shouldn't be asked for or given.

The exclusion of risk makes the status quo permanent. The first man to try lighting a fire no doubt burned his fingers, but without taking that risk man would still be munching berries, living in forests alongside our cousins, the apes, who never got round to lighting a fire. Trust me, says Blair—don't risk trusting him, says Major.

The crassness is depressing. Major leads a party that has governed for 18 years. Eighteen years that have seen a massive transfer of wealth from the poor to the very rich through changes in taxation, car boot sales of public assets, the run-down of public services.

The price paid is a country that is less fair, less just, cruder, greedier, dirtier, seedier, with a rising crime rate and the largest prison population in Western Europe. This threatens the social infrastructure that makes society a community of communities. Another Tory government and the integrity of our communities might crumble beyond repair.

The only alternative is a Labour government. That is the real politics of this election. A Blair-led government might not be much of an option but it's the only one. From way back when John Smith became leader I've believed Labour would be swept to power by an anti-Tory surge. That's still the most likely outcome. But I've also been aware of the strong hostility to Blair and New Labour's abandonment of Labour principles. A hostility not picked up by the polls for it tends to be submerged in the overwhelming desire to get rid of the Tories. In Scotland people are going to vote Labour in spite of Blair.

Each week I am in touch with hundreds of people. Most are voting for New Labour but with a heavy heart and without enthusiasm. Some are not voting Labour for the first time. Some are abstaining. Some are voting Liberal Democrat because they don't believe politicians who claim they can solve the problems of Britain without raising taxes. Paddy Ashdown is getting lots of mileage from his penny tax increase, though it is seen more as a symbol than a serious alternative. Some are voting SNP. It might win some seats, but if New Labour botches it this time, particularly on devolution, its day will assuredly come.

New Labour isn't rooted in a set of beliefs or principles, recoils in horror at the word ideology. Rejects any suggestion that there is a class basis to its politics. Ideals, firmly held beliefs, class consciousness, social group bonding, firm up a party's roots and were the main strengths of both Tory and Labour parties. The Tories still adhere to their core beliefs. New Labour has abandoned its core beliefs and has embraced the ideology of right-wing Conservatism.

Times do change. Sooner or later everything changes. Ideologies can become outmoded. Or have to be modified in response to changing circumstances. Social classes change under the impact of new technologies. When technological change abounds we have what might be called an industrial or technological revolution.

A few weeks ago a man reminded me of an analogy he had heard me make about technology more than 25 years ago at Glasgow University. He quoted my words back to me. "If you view electricity only from the standpoint of the electric chair you would want to ban it. But electricity also brings light, warmth, and puts priceless energy at our disposal. Whether electricity kills or brings light is determined by how we use it and for what purpose." This, of course, applies to all technology. This is seen at its starkest in nuclear physics which can bring blessings or annihilation to the human race. The choice is ours.

Modern technology can produce an abundance sufficient to meet the material needs of all human beings alive today. Yet we sit in our homes watching millions starve to death in the Third World on our multi-option hi-tech TV sets. In Britain technology has further enriched the wealthy but between 30% and 40% of our people are living in or around the poverty line, despairing, demoralised, and increasingly alienated.

The problem is that we have the technology of the 21st century and the economics of the nineteenth century. The management of technology has been left to those who see it exclusively as a money-making exercise. For personal greed, not human need. Socialist and social democratic ideas had to be brought up to date. But the core values of socialism and social democracy were and are most relevant to today's world. The Blair modernisers ditched these values, ditched socialism, social democracy, even Keynesianism, and a market economy without something like Keynesianism, is Thatcherism.

In this century the Labour movement lifted working men and women from their knees, brought dignity, through trade unions, to workers in the workplace, brought the welfare state, the NHS, decent pensions, full employment, the concept of housing as a social service for the poor. Yet New Labour is ashamed of this past. Doesn't mention it. Doesn't point to it proudly as reasons for voting Labour. By betraying its past New Labour has lost the moral ascendancy. By ditching its principles it has lost its soul.

Don't trust Blair, trust the Labour movement. New Labour's economic strategy inherited from the Tories is unsustainable. It will mean even greater cuts in public services and all that entails. It's a vote loser in Scotland. The main struggle after May 1 will therefore be to change that strategy. I believe the avowal of such an aim is honest, for it's going to happen. It could also secure for Labour the votes of those who believe that Blair has gone too far, far too far, and want him reined in. A democratic party isn't a fan club, nor can its beliefs be replaced by smart-ass soundbites that try to be all things to all men. Principles, in a very real sense, are never out of date. But try telling that to a spin doctor.

A REAL LESSON BEHIND THE
LIES AND DIRTY TRICKS

30 APRIL 1997

THIS has been a wretched election. With no policy differences worth talking about, politicians talked about one another. The fight for office became personal, not ideological, fuelled by career ambitions unleavened by scruples. Sleaze, hypocrisy, lies, dirty tricks, jingoism, xenophobia, demon eyes, taxi-driving angels, messiahs, chickens, cult of personality, the destruction of personalities, sexual innuendos proliferated. Sitting MPs were bribed to give up their seats (watch the honours list). Leadership clones were parachuted in, like a second Arnhem. In one Scottish constituency the dirty tricks degenerated into obscenity. Individuals destroyed, families put through hell, with malicious intent.

Parties adopted a wait and see approach to the single currency on the grounds that there was a lot of information which would be available only in a year or two's time. That's not true: 98% of all information is available now, including that a single currency will be supervised by a central European bank which will not be accountable to, or controlled by, national governments, the European Commission, or European Parliament. It will be run by bankers and will set interest rates for the whole of Europe.

This formula, apart from being undemocratic, cannot take account of the different levels of economic development that prevail throughout the nations and regions of Europe. An interest rate trimmed to the needs of the German economy at any given time, or to the economies of Northern France, Northern Italy, and Southeast England could be disastrous for Scotland, Portugal, Southern Italy, Southern, Spain, South Wales, the North of England, and other parts of the EC which need economic growth and development, not the consolidation of under-development. The facts about the central bank were known to all parties before the election. At the end of the election voters are still none the wiser about their policies on this issue.

The disparity between the wealthy and the poor in Britain is now greater than at any time this century, some believe greater than at any time in the recorded history of these isles. Richard Branson owns more wealth than any feudal baron ever did and the disparity between Branson and someone living on the basic pension, it is argued, is greater than the disparity between a feudal baron and the lowliest serf. Yet the parties explicitly rejected any concept of narrowing this gap. They made it clear that any such egalitarian aim was not part of their agenda.

The further impoverishment of the poor in the past two decades helped create this enormous wealth at the top, and lies at the root of the social malaise that now grips our country. Poverty without hope is dispiriting. As things stand there will be no hope for the poor, whatever the outcome on Thursday. Just more poverty and hopelessness, drugs and crime, homelessness and prostitution, while awful political prats prattle on about moral high grounds and Christian values.

Those who tell us they can make Britain a more just and decent society, without some kind of redistribution of wealth through taxation and other fiscal means, are liars. This election has been full of lies. More to do with concealment than commitment. They want the Eurosceptics' vote without alienating Euro-enthusiasts. To be all things to all men. On May 2 the party that governs can no longer maintain that façade. It will have to take decisions. Take an attitude on the powers of a central bank. It probably has done so already but hasn't told the electorate. Instead we've been asked to buy a pig in a poke. Or trust him, or him, or him.

This election has done no good for the credibility of the democratic process. The manipulation of broadcasting has become intolerable. Politicians will not answer straight questions. They talk over and through insistent urgings to answer and get away with it. Punters are fed up with the lot of them: 15 million watched *EastEnders*, a David Dimbleby election special followed; 13 million switched off, or to another channel. News and current affairs coverage of election campaigns should be drastically curtailed.

As it is hardly any public meetings now take place. Spin doctors plan media productions where only the faithful and pliable are allowed to participate as living and reverential stage props. The Tories started all this with Saatchi and Saatchi. New Labour now out-spins them with Peter Mandelson, who looks the kind of bloke who has to get back to a stygian darkness before the sun rises. He has much more power than Tom Sawyer, Labour's General Secretary, who must, I suppose, be about somewhere.

There is no doubt where the priority lies on Thursday. Get rid of the Tories. They've turned the clock back to the social squalor of bygone eras in the midst of the greatest technological revolution the world has ever seen and with the advent of North Sea oil revenues that have literally been wasted. You can't get them out without putting Labour in. That's the only real alternative and the people know it. Labour in Scotland will hold on to its seats and win some from the Tories. The SNP might also win seats from the Tories. Lib Dems ditto. They might lose one or two as well. If there is tactical voting in certain key seats the Tories could be wiped out.

A New Labour Government can't adhere to the Thatcherite nostrums that Blair has espoused without bringing convulsions to the British Labour movement. In Scotland this could lead to a major political re-alignment, particularly if devolution is seriously delayed or diluted. A home rule left-of-centre Scottish Labour movement could then become the focal point of a home rule centre-left Scottish coalition with potential to transform the political landscape of our homeland.

Alex Salmond has played a blinder in this election but the SNP might not benefit from such developments. Nationalist zealots on the ground once again have antagonised the best of Scottish Labour and Scottish Liberalism by their intolerance of all other opinions honestly concerned with Scottish nationhood. In life, an all-or-nothing-at-all attitude invariably ends in nothing at all, and isolation from the social forces crucial if real change is to be achieved. The SNP's acceptance of rascals from the world of Old Labour hasn't helped them either. No Scottish political movement can be successful without the Labour movement. That's the lesson of this century.

BITTEN BY A DOGMA TOO FAR

7 MAY 1997

WHAT were you doing on May 1, 1997? I was working in Govan for the return of the Labour candidate. Later that day I went to a party with friends. It became a celebration. Next morning just after nine o'clock I was walking down a well-known Glasgow street in search of a taxi. I'd been up all night. People were beaming. The atmosphere was ebullient. Some called out: "Eh, Jimmy. We've got rid of them at last." The mood was festive. A few shook my hand as if it was New Year's Day. The taxi driver had just started his shift, bright-eyed and bushy-tailed, in obvious good spirits.

The celebrations continued at a more leisurely pace over Friday and Saturday, resumed full intensity on Sunday when the traditional May Day march turned into a festival. By Monday I had had enough. Celebrations are only tolerable when spaced out. When you think of it, a lifetime of continuous celebrations would be a horrible prospect, more punitive than a prison sentence and the lifetime would be shorter.

The fat lady, whoever she is, has sung. It's over. What really did happen and where do we go from here? That the Tories were soundly beaten could only have surprised someone who had lived the past two years in outer space. I have argued in the *Herald* that come the election the Tories would be out and Labour, as the only credible alternative, would be in. For me the issue was what Labour would or should do in government.

The vote was essentially a root and branch rejection of the past 18 years. The poll tax was a disaster. Britain's entry and then exit from the European Monetary Union was high farce and destroyed Tory claims that they were better managers of the economy. This debacle was caused by Thatcher's chauvinism. She went into the EMU with a ludicrously overpriced pound. The dealers were selling the pound faster than it could be propped up. Thatcher lived in a fantasy world of empire where Britain ruled or should be ruling the roost. The Falklands war was her apotheosis. The newsreel of her sticking out the top of a tank like General Patton in drag was risible. She believed in a strong pound as a virility symbol of England's greatness. We have a strong pound today and it's pricing our manufacturing industries out of export markets and threatening jobs.

Thatcherism is an ism whose time had gone before it came. Economic and social theories of the early eighteenth century had no place in the second half of the twentieth century. This contradiction created the social carnage and human debris that we see all around, and not just in Scotland. London is filthy. London is full of youngsters from Scotland and the provinces begging on the streets. The Underground was once very clean but is now incredibly dirty. The place is seedy. The City is seedy. Parliament is seedy. Seediness is everywhere.

People like paying less tax but not if it means being enveloped in public squalor. I've lived in London and know the place. I've friends in London who have more than a bob or two. In recent years they've been sickened by the cruelties that abound. It was visible, couldn't be missed. The privatisation of water in England didn't help the Tory cause. Water was nature's gift, to make it private property was like privatising the air we breathe. For many it was a dogma too far. All these interacting factors brought the Tories down and put Labour in power.

The enormous size of Labour's majority as a whole surprised many but reflects more the vagaries of our discredited electoral system than the popular vote. The Scottish results, including the Tory wipeout, were very much on the cards. I was told that Labour couldn't win Govan with a Paki candidate. But Govan's punters are made of better stuff. Now that it's all over we're back to what really matters. Labour's strategy in government. Keep your eyes on the economics. It determines virtually everything else.

The continuation of Thatcherite economics will mean a continuation of Thatcherite social policies. Economic priorities and social priorities are interlinked. Always have been, always will be. The first omens are not good.

Chancellor Gordon Brown has announced that he, i.e. the Government, is giving up its right to set interest rates and giving this right to the Bank of England. A monetary committee will be set up within the Bank to take on this responsibility. But the intent is clear. Interest rates are a very important economic lever. Hugh Dalton, Labour Chancellor in 1945, saw this lever as a responsibility exercised by government on behalf of the people as a whole.

Even Thatcher in her most monetarist and deregulatory days didn't dare do this. Bankers will now decide interest rates on the basis of monetarist criteria, which, by definition, excludes social objectives and social considerations. It further diminishes democratic control of the economy. We see all around us what happens when society doesn't even try to regulate markets. Markets then regulate society.

The other cause for alarm is the appointment of Frank Field as Minister in charge of welfare benefits. Frank wants to dismantle welfare services on the grounds that people don't want to meet the costs through taxes and should therefore be compelled to make their own private arrangements for pensions, and only those that can't should be paid a basic state pension.

Peter Lilley, influenced by Frank Field, floated this idea during the election and was clobbered by Labour. We should stick to universal benefits as a right. State pensions only for the very poor will be very poor indeed, and means-tested. Why pay the very rich a pension? So that the pension is seen as a right and not a handout. Then you can get it back from them through taxes. People have learned from the Thatcher years. Better to pay taxes and live in a decent society than not pay taxes and live in a jungle.

Labour is on good reforming ground in its constitutional policies. Reform the House of Lords, get rid of the hereditary peers. But it's Labour's plans for a Scottish parliament that excite me. This is of historic significance. The Scottish nation will have its own parliament. We didn't have one in 1707. That was a parliament for the nobility and for less than 1% of the population. There will be no going back. Once we have it we'll never let it go. All my life I've worked for the day when a Scottish parliament would meet in Edinburgh. I even wanted it to meet in Govan, but you can't win them all.

GETTING THE SNP
BACK ON BOARD

12 MAY 1997

IN WORKING out a strategy, members of a political party can take the approach that those who are not for us are against us, or take the counter approach that those who are not against us are for us. I favour the latter.

The first approach is politically sectarian and precludes working with allies who, while not prepared to go all the way with you, are happy to go part of the way and, who knows, may be converted somewhere along the way to your point of view.

To reject the concept of allies is not only churlish but foolhardy. It usually springs from a state of mind that envisages change as something abrupt and cataclysmic. It isn't.

Change is a much more complex phenomenon. It's a process that involves quantitative changes that lead to qualitative change. Evolution and revolution have always been interconnected. Revolutions come as a surprise only when there is insufficient cognition of the multiplicity of smaller changes that have taken place and their cumulative impact on society, which in turn makes social revolution inevitable.

The industrial revolution was the culmination of many quantitative progressions, over a century and more, in how goods and commodities were produced. The same is true of the current technological revolution.

Scotland as a nation is now in the throes of constitutional change; a change that's been brewing for years, from 1707 in fact. Scotland's Labour movement from its inception was committed to Scottish home rule. It's part of the Scottish liberal tradition. Scottish churches have favoured home rule. Strands of traditional Scottish Conservatism were for some kind of home rule. The concept of the Scottish nation controlling its domestic affairs through a Scottish parliament never did belong to any one party or narrow sector of the political spectrum.

Why then did we not get a Scottish parliament years ago? It's a good question, and the answer has a bearing on what we must do now. The support for home rule was never organised into a movement transcending the party-political divides that exist in every modern society. The Scottish Covenant just after the Second World War was the nearest approach we ever got to a coalition of Scots for a Scottish parliament.

There were also other political priorities that occupied minds. For example, the social devastation of the Thirties slump; the emergence of fascism; the war against fascism; the stupendous task of post-war reconstruction; and the advent of the Cold War. In 1948, when it lurched to the right, the Labour Party dropped its historic demand for a Scottish parliament.

The Fifties saw the movement for a Scottish parliament at a low ebb. But this changed in the Sixties. Things began to stir in the Scottish Labour movement. Discussions started about what was a nation. They established that Scotland was not only a nation but one of the oldest nations in Europe. We examined the rights of nations and specifically the right of the Scottish nation to govern itself. But nationhood cannot be viewed in the abstract. We explored the precise nature of the Scottish economy and drew up an economic strategy for Scotland. A programme of social renewal. All to take place under the aegis of a Scottish parliament.

The Scottish Trades Union Congress debated the national question and came down in favour of a Scottish parliament and all that entails. This became the policy of the Labour Party in Scotland and the UK. Other parts of Scottish politics had never abandoned their commitment to home rule and we envisaged the development of cross-party unity. This eventually did take place in the founding of the Scottish Constitutional Convention. And led to where we are today.

I was terribly disappointed when the SNP withdrew from the Convention. Even from the narrow standpoint of party interests, it would have been advisable to stay in. Imagine what a strong position it would have been in, if there, when Blair did a somersault on a referendum. But I believe there was another factor operating. That element within the SNP that always wants to go it alone. Independence or bust. Those who don't agree with them are traitors to Scotland or even quislings.

They claim that independence will be won when a majority of Scots in an election to a Westminster Parliament vote SNP. This is as near as dammit saying there will never be an independent Scotland. It would take a General Election in which the only issue for Scots would be independence and that a majority would then vote for that option. In every election there's a host of issues that concern people: jobs, education, the health service. At other times it might be whether war or peace. We know that people vote SNP who do not want independence; that there are people who vote Labour and Liberal Democrat who do. To wait for a one-issue General Election is going to be one helluva long wait.

A political strategy predicated on circumstances unlikely ever to occur is fantasy politics. Alex Salmond is one of the best political leaders in Scotland today. He is a social democrat, which puts him a mile or so to the left of Gordon Brown. But at grass-roots level some within his party burn bridges at an alarming rate. Expectations of electoral victory become inflated. When it doesn't materialise, voters are condemned as 90-minute patriots, opponents castigated as an homogeneous bunch of traitors. Potential allies are antagonised. Unthinking zealotry like this leads to isolation.

It will therefore be a very grave error if the SNP turns its back on the campaign for a yes, yes vote in the referendum on constitutional change. I didn't want a referendum. In fact, in light of the General Election, where the only party for the status quo was routed in Scotland, it's a piece of nonsense. Nonsense or not, it's going to take place. We don't have the luxury of washing our hands of it. In terms of the Scottish people that would be criminal irresponsibility.

We can have our own parliament at last. It will have considerable policy-making powers. It could have the power to raise or lower taxes, as every parliament should. It will be the sovereign right of a Scottish parliament's MPs to decide that, and not someone in London. That's the reality, whatever anyone says.

When that day comes, there really will be a new dawn for our nation. If we are able to run our own affairs to our satisfaction while still within the UK framework, then most will probably settle for that. But, if not, then independence will become a favoured option, for there can be no going back.

As a betting man, I know it's foolish to rush fences. That way you can come a cropper. I want us to get there and want the good folk in the SNP to be on board when we do. We should be organising now an all-Scottish campaign for a massive yes vote. To fail through disunity would be a disaster for our nation and people. Let's make it unthinkable.

COLD TURKEY FOR SINNERS

2 JULY 1997

SAM GOLDWYN wanted new clichés. One of the few wants he didn't get. It takes time for a cliché to mature. It's never an overnight success. So Sam had to make do with old clichés and very well he did. Diamonds are forever, so are clichés. Climb every mountain, ford every stream, follow every rainbow till you find your dream.

Rangers, we will be told yet again, "have a mountain to climb" (on an even playing field of course) if they're to go further in Europe. When it comes to clichés we don't do things by half. Football is a game of two halves. If at the end it's eachy peachy there might be extra time or a third half. Are these haufs quarter gills?

Clichés are rampant with contradictions. The best things in life are free. You can't buy love. Every man has his price. Money is the root of all evil. Who wants to be a millionaire? It's a landslide for the I do's. "Give it to me straight doctor. How do I stand?" "I've been wondering about that myself." TB or not TB. Better health than wealth. Do we have to choose? Is it just a coincidence that the poor are more prone to sickness? "Your money or your wife?" "I'm thinking." I think therefore I am.

Where does that leave Tory MPs?

We're the boys of the old brigade. Comrades in arms. Shoulder to shoulder. Bolder and bolder. Backs to the wall. Parry. Thrust. Touché. Touchy. Clobber them wi' oor claymores. Begad Scottie, you've gouged me groin. Severed my manhood. Shivered me timbers. It's a far, far better thing I do, nothing will become me more than a manner of my going, in the corner of a field that forever will be England. For England and King Harry.

"What's it all about Harry?" Hong Kong. King Kong. Gie's a song. Rule Britannia, marmalade and jam, three Chinese crackers up your backside, bang, bang, bang. Someone's gonna hear about this in Whitehall. Button your lip, Buster. The dog that didn't bark has laryngitis. Up yours, Sherlock. Play it again, Sam. Play what, you humphy tone-deaf lisping bletherin' boozing bogie bampot? The fatman should have bumped you off in the 'Falcon.

I ask you very confidentially, ain't she sweet. Nope. She's as ugly as sin. Ugly as those bricklayers masquerading as women playing tennis at Wimbledon. Overheard from the centre court stand during the downpour: "Know something, Daphne. I knew there was something wrong when he asked for a loan of my brassière."

The surge of the waves breaking on the sands glittered with the reflected timeless glory of the sun. They lay in each other's arms, like Burt Lancaster and Deborah Kerr in that picture, what was it called, *From Here to Maternity*. They both felt a warmth spreading over their loins. Would the Earth move? Nah, it was just the tide coming in, and time and tide wait for no man. They went to a bar. "Let's be merry for tomorrow we might die," said the soldier. The girl trying to cheer him up started singing,

"Always look on the bright side of life."

Better to remain quiet and be thought a fool than to speak and remove all doubts, from the ashtray of life, as we approach the millennium. Time to stand up and be counted, to put our money where our mouths are. This will be the dawn of a new day. The day of a new dawn. Both Hong and Kong have gone from our Empah. The Empah has gone. But we still have Commanders and Members of the Empah. Why don't the Italians have MREs. Members of the Roman Empah? They say it's because there is no Roman Empah. Poor excuse. Machiavelli must have been an Englishman from Surrey.

Tyson's bite is worse than his bark, not worse than battering opponents senseless as he once did frequently. Nobody complained, as if the brain was less important than an ear? But Tyson might have started a new sport. Professional biting with professional biters and world biting championships. Right and left bites to the head. A foul if you bite below the belt. Can't someone bite the heid off Don King? I would pay to see that. I know a lady councillor who could bite the ears off both Tyson and King. Any day.

"Whether they give or refuse, women are glad to be asked." I imagine it would depend on who's doing the asking. But then being married I know nothing about women. More to the point, this priceless prose was penned by Ovid. Can a man called Ovid be taken seriously? It sounds like soap powder or a pungent deodorant. Imagine the sales pitch. "Ovid makes your armpits charm pits." The road to hell is paved with good intentions, as Einstein should have said. Scratch my back and I'll stab yours, reasoned Brutus, establishing a tradition that has become an integral part of our political culture. A watched pot never boils. Wanna bet? What you don't know can't hurt you. How do you know?

The next leader of the Conservative Party, it is rumoured, after Hague that is, will be Annie Moss, a hard-bitten bitch, being groomed by Lady Thatcher, who now prefers to be known as Magi, the plural of magus, meaning sorcerer. She has always thought of herself as plural and a bit of a sorceress. Remember

"We are now a grandparent"? As to her own future, Magi exclusively told this column: "I want nothing of God but eternity and a Heaven to throne in." Heaven will surely not be big enough for her and God. My money is on you know who. He has seen off devils before, and she has too many ironies in the fire, too many hostages to fortune, etc.

But who are we to judge? Sins, like drugs, are addictive yet you don't hear people pitying the poor sin addict. They don't give him substitute sin to help him cope with withdrawal cravings. It's cold turkey for sinners. Let those without sin cast the first aspersion. Talking of aspersions, I'd like to become a vegetarian. I love fruit and vegetables, but also fish, meats, and poultry. If there were no fish, meats, poultry, I would definitely be a vegetarian. Mankind is murdering the fauna, putting the skids under the flora as well. And who wants to be a starvationist? I've seen it in the Third World, and it doesn't work. But I looks at it this way - if God had wanted us to be vegetarians, he wouldn't have made butchers.

Today is B-Day. New Labour's first Budget. "It's the rich that gets the gravy, it's the poor that gets the blame, it's the same the whole world over . . . Ain't it all a bleeding shame?" Yep. And, as the good book says, Acts of the Apostles. 9:4: It is hard for thee to kick against the pricks. True, but that's no excuse for not trying.

SOCIAL VANDALISM
AND SOCIAL SECURITY

23 JULY 1997

IN THE 11-plus, or qually as it was known here, I got a pass mark
of 99%, was streamed for Oxbridge, and left school at 14 without
sitting for a single educational qualification. By no means was this
unusual. It happened to millions of working-class kids of my
generation. A few years ago I listened to Neil Kinnock's best ever
speech. He told how he was the first Kinnock ever to go to university. Ordinary working men and women, and the best elements of
the middle class, had come together in the Labour movement and
fought for equal educational opportunities for all young people as
of right, including free university education and student maintenance grants. This became reality during the lifetime of the 1945-50
Labour Government, later enabling young Mr Kinnock to go to
university.

Many members of the present Cabinet have been to university
with full grants and tuition fees paid by the rest of us, the tax-
payers, including people like myself who had been denied such an

opportunity when young. We were delighted that these young-sters had opportunities denied to us. It's called progress. What we couldn't envisage was a future Labour Government in favour of re-introducing tuition fees and the abolition of student grants. Such a reversion to the evils of the past was inconceivable.

Tony Blair had his fees paid and received a grant while at Oxford. Gordon Brown got the same treatment at Edinburgh. He was Rector there when I was Rector at Glasgow. If it had been proposed that students should pay tuition fees and get no grants, Gordon would have led a student revolt. I would have been with him, so would the workers in the shipyards, and elsewhere. Jack Straw was President of the National Union of Students on full grant. These Cabinet members were beneficiaries of a fair system which they now dismantle to the detriment of today's youth and those of tomorrow.

That isn't political reform but social vandalism. It is to be dressed up in means-testing arrangements purporting to help the children of the lower paid. Crap. The main victims will be the children of the poor whose lives are already damaged, their expectations al-ready diminished. Cultural deprivation can often be more insidiously destructive to the human personality than economic deprivation. To be stuck in a culture of failure from which there is no apparent escape creates the impression that you're born to fail. As if it was genetically pre-ordained. So to hell with it. Where's the drug pedlar? Where's the Giro? Get some booze. University's not for the likes of us. We're too stupid. Before you can say David Blunkett, we're back in the nineteenth century, with the techno-logical gadgetry of the 21st century, able to watch on satellite television civic society disintegrate on the streets.

The alarm bells are ringing for more than education. It is more than likely that single mothers will have their benefits cut and still have no job. The link between pensions and earnings will not be restored. There will be no amelioration of the poverty that pen-sioners endure. Pensioners who saved a few bob will be made to pay for their prescriptions. Save for old age and get hammered. Don't save for old age and get hammered.

Welfare to work will fail unless real jobs are created. The Chancellor has ceded to the Bank of England the right to determine interest rates. The rates have gone up three times since the election, another is in the pipeline. The value of the pound is soaring. Grand if you're holidaying abroad but disastrous for exports. It could cost more than 100,000 jobs. There will be more jobless by the end of the year. Youngsters caught up in the Chancellor's job/training schemes could be thrown back on the scrap heap as subsidies and training end, and there are still no new jobs.

Illusions about what really happened at the General Election are still rife. Labour polled marginally less than John Major's Conservative Party did in the previous election.

Tory voters in England could return to the fold at the next election. Labour made no ideological impact on them. Blair even made a pitch for the votes of unreconstructed Thatcherites, as Maggie's rightful heir. Labour's massive bedrock vote could be in danger if current policies continue. Those who voted Labour in hope of drawing a line under the Thatcher years look like having their expectations dashed. They might take their votes elsewhere, or not vote at all.

This is no far-fetched scenario. Better Labour Governments have failed because they accepted the status quo. Those who live by the status quo die by it. Today's prevailing socio-economic status quo was fashioned by Lady Thatcher. A Labour Government that tries to operate within its stifling confines is bound to fail.

But this scenario could be changed. Labour MPs could start to make their voices heard. Go on picket lines with BA cabin crews. Shout the House down in defence of students and pensioners. Insist Britain is rich but the riches are going to the wrong places and people. The concept of the welfare state with its promise of security for all, from cradle to grave, is more than ever valid. Pervasive insecurity is a corrosive phenomenon. It cripples the human spirit, clips the wings of the young, darkens already dreary prospects for the old, and gnaws away at the soul.

Without social security society is a jungle. Yet these two words have become dirty in Britain; equated with ne'er-do-wells and scroungers. To me social security is to be secure in your home, on the street, in the community, in or out of employment, in old age, in sickness and health. It means, for example, parents of handicapped children living secure in the knowledge that when they die society will look after their children with tender respect. Such social securities are things of beauty. Priceless rather than costly. They make us truly civilised.

AFTER THE RAT RACE: REBUILDING CONSENSUS

30 JULY 1997

WHEN the bell tolls in the Greenwich millennium tent to usher in the 21st century, the gap between rich and poor in Britain will be greater than at the beginning of the twentieth century. When I suggested about a year ago that this was the case some readers scoffed, but it's true. The progress made this century towards a more egalitarian society has been exaggerated. The reactionary rich, whose voice is always heard through their place-men in politics and the media, wanted to dampen down the clamour for more reforms and hopefully create a climate of opinion that might, at some later date, enable them to roll back whatever limited progress had been made.

That time came with Thatcher. The past 18 years have seen a massive redistribution of wealth in favour of the rich, and we're talking here in terms of many billions. It's an ongoing process that now has its own gathering momentum. That's why we can't properly fund state education, state pensions, and the National Health

Service. For two years I've argued that Labour in government had to reverse this process. If it didn't it would then have to continue the process, for inertia wasn't an option.

The Labour Government landed running, as they say, but it's where they're running to that concerns me. Labour is operating Thatcherite economic policies and thus promoting the inequality it was founded to end. This contradiction, if not resolved, will destroy the Labour Party. Fissures are already discernible.

I have no quarrel with those, including long-standing friends, who have rejected socialism or social democracy and make no bones about it. I can admire Tories like Bill Deedes though we hardly agree about anything except our right to disagree. I've known Charles Moore, the editor of the *Telegraph*, since he was editor of the *Spectator*. I like the bloke though he is a Tory traditionalist. The point is I don't mind Tories in the Tory Party but Tories in the Labour Party are subversives and get on my wick.

Prior to the General Election colleagues in the Labour Party were telling me not to rock the boat, to subdue my criticisms of New Labour until after the election. My estimation was that it might then be too late. I also believed the Tories couldn't possibly win and the real issue was what Labour would do in government.

The first defining act came when Labour's Chancellor ceded to the Bank of England the right to set interest rates. This went beyond anything Lady Thatcher dared do. Later this week we are likely to see the fourth hike in interest rates since the election. The pound is already absurdly over-valued. Manufacturing industries suffer. They cannot compete in export markets because the value of the pound has added 30% to their prices.

Some will go to the wall. During the Thatcher years our manufacturing capacity was decimated. It looks as if New Labour is going to finish the job. This would leave Britain with an unbalanced economy overwhelmingly dependent on service industries. Many companies in this sector, operating here, are branches of transnational companies. In the event of a world recession they could be closed down, virtually overnight, to protect core investments elsewhere. In Scotland, earlier this century, our economy was over-dependent on heavy industries. The first to suffer in recession and the last to recover when a boom beckoned.

Scotland bled. In vast areas of the central belt we now have all our eggs in another basket and are likely to suffer the same fate again, unless steps are taken to rectify this imbalance.

The boom/bust cycle is a product of unchecked market forces. The market ruled the world from 1850 to 1950 and we had monstrous slumps and booms. We also had two world wars not unconnected with the phenomenon of slumps that paralysed economies and brought in their wake political and social instability. Attempts were made to even out the cycles. To make slumps less severe and booms more cohesive. Keynesianism was born, and other attempts to regulate market forces. Roosevelt's New Deal was part of this scenario.

Britain's post-war consensus, which included Tories like Macmillan and Butler, was based on a mixed economy and the welfare state. By and large it worked albeit with insufficient changes in the distribution of wealth that left intact the British class system. This Keynesianism/Social Democratic model needed reform for the world had indeed changed. Instead of reform we got a reversion to the old world. Reaganomics and Thatcherism, the economics of nineteenth-century laissez-faire capitalism. You can read all about it in Dickens. The Reagan-Thatcher dominance in the West coincided with the collapse of communism in the East which was interpreted as the historic failure of socialism. I dispute that the Soviet model was in any significant sense socialist, but that's for another day.

The political dinosaurs of today are those who seek in the nineteenth century a panacea for the next. The pursuit of a just, modern society is best served by an expanding social wage that brings security and justice to all, free access to education and culture, more creative leisure time. A society in which the social wage can become more important in determining the real quality of our lives than the personal wage.

The dismantling of the welfare state has an exactly opposite effect with global implications.

Unchecked human greed will assuredly destroy this planet, the jewel of the cosmos. Look at the pictures that have come from satellites in outer space. Earth is verdant, and teeming with life. Compare this with the pictures of Mars. Other planets in our universe, in so far as we know, are too hot, too cold, too gaseous, too hostile, to sustain such a wondrous diversity of animal and plant life. For God's sake, is it to be sacrificed to our greed?

A Labour Government should at least make a start towards building a society that will reinstate the values of togetherness instead of the rat race. (Poor rats, what have they done to deserve such odium?) During the General Election I got pelters for saying that with a Labour Government the main political battle in Britain would shift to within the party itself.

This isn't a private matter. On the contrary it has to be public. It's a fight for Labour's soul but the outcome is too important to be left to us. Which side are you on?

ALEC KITSON: AN APPRECIATION

7 AUGUST 1997

ALEC KITSON was a devoted member of the Labour Party. He had no other political interest or affiliations. To work for the Labour movement was for him a vocation. The poverty he saw and endured as a child made him a socialist. He sought in his teens and early manhood a coherence of thought and action. He knew what he was against, that's the easy part for those who started life in the slums of pre-war Scotland.

But what are we for, not just in high blown terms, but in every day details? Alec was a thoughtful man. He really did believe that it wasn't enough to explain the world, but to change it. To make a better world where there could be no hiding place for poverty. The means of doing this in Britain, he believed, was through the Labour movement and Labour Party. He never departed from this belief.

I've been a close friend of Alec's for 37 years. I was a Communist in the Sixties and part of the Seventies and worked with him on many issues. Many outstanding trade union activists in the

Scotland of those years were members of the Communist Party. Even the most right-wing Labour diehard had to work with Communists. Alec was no right-wing diehard but a left-wing socialist and trade unionist. He had enormous respect for some Communists and little respect for others. During those years a few trade union leaders, members of the Labour Party, automatically supported anything the Soviet Union did. I know from research in Moscow over recent years that they were kept men.

Alec Kitson was not of that ilk. He was his own man. A dyed in the wool Labour man. McCarthysim didn't die with McCarthy. It was used throughout the Cold War against anyone who fought for the workers, spoke out for peace and disarmament, or supported liberation struggles in the colonial world. They were often branded fellow travellers and reds under the beds. Alec fought for all these things, and received the full treatment. This smear has been resurrected since his death last Saturday. It's a lie and slanders the memory of a decent man. One of the great figures in the post-war history of the Scottish and British Labour movements. This slander should be nailed. Generations to come deserve the truth.

As with most human beings the child maketh the man and his childhood experiences certainly made Alec Kitson. His father was a shale miner. He volunteered in the First World War. Fought in France and German East Africa. Contracted malaria, suffered from ill health for the rest of his life, worked as a grocer in East Calder and had to give it up owing to ill health. He died in 1949. At no time did he receive an army pension.

The family stayed in a tiny house in Kirknewton where Alec was born in 1921. His paternal grandfather, who had also been a shale miner from which the first commercial oil was made, sought to make a fortune abroad in the oil industry in the Persian Gulf and elsewhere. He returned penniless and was taken in by Alec's mum. Alec then stayed with his maternal grandfather David Grieg who lived down the stairs. He was an active Liberal who became a socialist and joined the Labour Party. A member of the National

Union of Railway Workers and secretary of his local branch. He was also a parish councillor and took young Alec to union meetings, local party meetings, and out on the hustings.

There is no doubt that Granda Grieg had a significant influence on Alec. He left school at 14, though winning a place at West Calder High.

The family was living in dire poverty. He went to work as a van boy at St Cuthbert's Co-op in Edinburgh for the equivalent of 47p a week and was paid off at 16 when his employer was legally bound to pay his insurance stamp. The transport manager must have spotted his potential for he offered him a job as milk boy. He had his own barrow that carried five or six hundred hundred-weights of full milk bottles. He worked seven days a week from 6am till 11am. He couldn't afford the fares, got an old bike and cycled to Edinburgh and back, 23 miles a day, 160 miles a week. He became a driver in 1938 and joined the Scottish Horse and Motormen's Association.

He became the union's youngest official in 1945 as collector in Leith and North Edinburgh. He met and married his beloved Ann McLeod in 1942, became the union's General Secretary in 1959. The union had fallen on bad times and Alec with his comrades put that right. They organised schools at the union's convalescent home in Ayr, training activists to look beyond immediate issues and learn to think strategically. It soon became a force in the Scottish Trade Union movement. Alec was elected to the General Council of the STUC, an organisation which he cherished. Through all these years he worked for the Labour Party in Edinburgh.

Then amalgamation with the TGWU in 1971 saw Alec become deputy General Secretary of the biggest union in the Western world. His home and heart remained in Scotland. He was a member of the British Labour Party's National Executive from 1968 until 1986, and chairman. He was in charge of the International Committee of the Party and helped, among many others, his comrades in South Africa during the dark and terrible days of apartheid.

Some events in the Sixties are worth recalling. It started over a drink, of an evening, at a Scottish Trade Union Congress. We were bemoaning the fact that the Scottish Labour movement was all at sea on the national question in Scotland. The Party had abandoned its Home Rule policy in 1948, leaving a vacuum that could only be partially filled by the SNP. Labour was simply reacting to the issue in terms of political expediency. A flutter of support for the SNP and it would pay some lip service to the question. If the SNP was doing badly the issue was quietly dropped.

This we considered an unprincipled approach. We had further discussions and agreed that we must try and redefine the underlying principles. We posed some questions to ourselves. Was Scotland a nation? And decided it was, one of the oldest in the world. Was the status quo tolerable? We reckoned no. What changes were needed, how could we give effect to them? It had to be dealt with objectively and not in the abstract. We had to deal with the social and economic realities including the problems of the Highlands and Islands.

I was to do some initial drafts but it was very much a collective input including George Middleton who was an expert on the Scottish economy, George Houston, a professor at Glasgow who helped on rural and agricultural issues, Mick McGahey, Hugh Wyper and others. Very much to the fore was Alec Kitson. We took our findings to the trade unions and they were widely debated.

The arguments for a Scottish parliament thus became the property of the Scottish trade unions. And then the property of the Labour Party. The ultimate goal was to make them the property of the Scottish people. Alec lived for the day when this would happen, but it was not to be. When that day comes it will be due in no small measure to Alec Kitson and his kind. Alec's wife Ann died suddenly, a few weeks ago. Now Alec has gone. My heartfelt sympathy goes to their daughters Irene and Joyce and grandchildren Nicky, Jonathan, and Lee. In the midst of our grief there is also gratitude for a life well lived in the service of others.

THE WEAKER SEX THE STRONGER

13 AUGUST 1997

IF THIS be summer can winter be far away? Oh to feel a chill in the air and wear once again an overcoat and thermal longjohns, a muffler, and even a hat to ensure that your body heat doesn't leak through your napper. Oh to see your breath vaporise as it collides with the icy air and to hear the frost crackle underfoot.

I've had more than a sufficiency of this bloody good weather. The clamminess clings to your body like heavy cobwebs in a long-disused cellar. There are a few minor benefits. The magpies are too clapped out with the heat to spout forth their hideous cackles. In the garden they sit in the trees and pant. I'm too knackered to pant and lie kind of comatose in a shaded corner where the dappled sunlight has filtered through the trees just to annoy me.

I wonder how Bess, my trusted hound in her fur coat, can cope with this weather. Rosie the cat has an even thicker coat, looks like a miniature black panther, swaggers like one, too, and seems able to switch off into a state of total inertia under the shade of a bush. Total sleep. Meanwhile, see me, I'm melting, and dreaming of a white Christmas. My family sit around the garden table sipping soft juices or white wine. Wife, daughters, grand-daughters, grand-mother, sister-in-law. It's like a feminist convention, except for me. The token male.

My women all seem very comfortable in this atrocious weather. They look very attractive. The few times I've ventured out there they all are in their flowery fineries. Short skirts and shorter pants. A reminder that I'm not too old. None of us is. Women, I insist, are the best opposite sex that men have got. The weaker sex is also the stronger. Women are nicer people than men. More honest in a philosophical sense. More down to earth and practical.

I admire women. They're the source of life. Man's contribution, by comparison, is piddling. A mere shot in the dark. Laddishness is often close to loutishness. The presence of women in a gathering of men is invariably a civilising influence. Yet woman doesn't belong on a pedestal. As an early suffragette put it: "Men put us up there (on a pedestal) to get us out of the way." Women are workmates, colleagues, pals, comrades, lovers, wives, mothers. You can't be all these things on top of a pedestal.

In recent weeks some particular women have entered my thoughts and sparked off this train of thought. I read an article on Naomi Mitchison in the *Herald*. Naomi was celebrating her 100th birthday. She has a small estate in Carradale on the Mull of Kintyre. A beautiful place well worth a visit. She is one helluva lady. She comes from a family of upper-middle-class non-conformists, freethinkers, radicals, probing intellectuals, socialists, and even a Marxist. Naomi married Frank Mitchison who became a law officer in Attlee's Government.

She's a novelist and had a somewhat polygamous approach to marriage. Years ago Mary Marquis, the statuesquely beautiful BBC Scotland newscaster, was in Carradale interviewing Naomi. She gave Mary a book inscribed on the flyleaf to myself. Mary delivered it to me. I still have it on my bookshelves. It was the biography of Bram Fischer, son of a very wealthy white South African family.

217

Bram couldn't stand apartheid, joined the ANC, and became a trusted and brave colleague of Mandela.

He went to prison with Nelson and died some years ago. It was men like Bram who by their example taught black Africans that not all whites were racist thugs. His fight against apartheid has given South Africa the possibility of building a genuine non-racial society.

About four weeks ago a gracious lady from Clydebank, who is 82 and walked all the way to London in the Thirties as the youngest member of the famous hunger march, gave me the autobiography of Nelson Mandela as a birthday present. I couldn't leave it down. Bram Fischer features prominently, as do many other heroes of our times. But Nelson Mandela, who spent more than 27 years in jail fighting for elementary rights for his people, emerges from this horrific experience without a shred of bitterness. The man is not just a hero, but an angel.

A couple of weeks back an angel from Kilmarnock celebrated her ninetieth birthday. Her name, Helen McIlvanney. As sharp as a needle, she emanates warmth and kindness. Her two sons, who can write a bit, worship their mammy, as does Betty who sings like a lintie. Working-class mothers of Helen's generation are the proverbial salt of the earth. They often went without food so that their children might eat. No wonder they're so loved.

I also met recently two younger women of immense strength of character. They are the daughters of Alec and Ann Kitson. They lost their mum and dad within a few weeks of each other. A shattering blow almost too awful to contemplate. Yet they conducted themselves throughout with great grace and dignity. There were obviously uncharted depths to their characters.

Everywhere I turn I meet women of all ages with talent and commitment who care for children, aged, the ill. They do things to help increasingly in areas where governments have reneged on their commitments. Women are realists and romantics. Doers and dreamers. Strong and vulnerable.

As I write, thousands of women are caring for parents who can no longer look after themselves. Wrecking their own lives that their parents might live out theirs with some dignity. The state doesn't give a damn. It exploits their fidelity knowing that they will suffer in silence.

I wish there were fewer statues of men of war and more of women.

> A Lady with a Lamp shall stand
>   in the great history of the land,
> A noble type of good,
> Heroic womanhood.

DESPITE THE EUPHEMISMS, THE POOR ARE STILL WITH US

20 AUGUST 1997

I'D had a hectic time and was looking forward to an unhectic weekend. Then that saucy jade called fate intervened, and I found myself up the creek, in a canoe, without a paddle. How did I get there? Easy. I sat in front of the telly and did something daft. I turned it on. I was actually looking forward to the usual dose of visual valium served regular as clockwork on Saturdays and Sundays on our five television channels, more if you have satellite.

So it proved to be except for one little thing, language. That precious and priceless phenomenon that distinguishes us from the beasts. Language that communicates our thoughts and gives them coherence. Language of love and sweet nothings that can weigh so significantly in the affairs of men and women. Language that can convey the most complex of conceptions. Language of the poets that tells truths with alluring clarity.

I really didn't want my mind stirred, not this weekend. Television Temazepam would do quite well. At first things looked promising. A movie of sorts starring a rather superficial-looking youth who ponced about kind of singing to a young lady who was nine tenths leg. He carried a guitar for no discernible reason. It hung across his midriff like a pelmet. He sang: "Tonight she'll hold me in her arms." To which the girl, playing coquettishly hard to get, responds: "I'd rather hold two hydrogen bombs."

As lyrics go this ain't exactly Oscar Hammerstein. It ain't exactly Ben Hammerstein, who used to be a pawnbroker in Glasgow, the Sam Goldwyn of the Sou'side, who could fracture the English language like a latter-day television football pundit. As movies go this movie went badly. It was an Elvis Presley extravaganza. Television was celebrating the anniversary of his demise, an event I hadn't noticed at the time, but it must have delighted music lovers in the know. I watched some of the other movies out of scientific curiosity, on the grounds that by some arithmetical law they couldn't all be that bad. They weren't. They were worse.

After a while I tried to avoid Elvis movies with something akin to desperation. The remote control was overheating. It was then I found myself in the middle of an Elvis documentary listening to a guy explaining that the name Elvis had supernatural connotations. "Elvis," he intoned, "God and Pepsi-Cola." The new holy trinity. He was dead serious. That's when I started giggling. When Joan put me to bed with a large malt I was still giggling. I would have been better off getting blootered.

It is said the first casualty of war is truth. It isn't. It's language. The corruption of language is the precursor of all things bad. We used to have depressions. The downward cycle in the market economy. A depression conjured up images that were cruel and therefore had to be remedied. Depression became recession, which invokes less destructive images even though, particularly for those made jobless, it's precisely the same thing. One million unemployed was considered an abomination when we had depressions. Now that we have recessions a permanent pool of two or three million unemployed is viewed as decently acceptable.

221

We used to have a Ministry of War. Now we have a Ministry of Defence. The Labour Exchange is now a Job Centre. We had poverty, now we have areas of multiple deprivation. But the word "poor" defeated all attempts at euphemism. Blessed are the poor. They were tipped to inherit the Earth, along with the meek. The very rich always wanted to call the poor something else like lazy bastards or neo-criminal inadequates. They failed. The poor had a good PR outfit working on their behalf. It was called the Labour movement.

Then came Peter Mandelson, who now re-defines "poor" as "socially excluded". But the poor help one another. If a tragedy befalls a particular family the poor help that family. They close ranks. The poor are more social in the best sense of the word than those who have plenty.

Some years ago Jonathan Dimbleby came to Scotland to do a television documentary with me. One Saturday after filming we took a carry-out back to my home in a tenement in Faifley, Clydebank, one of the most hard-up areas in the town. As we went up the stairs I knocked on every door. Within minutes we had a party involving all our neighbours. Plenty of chaff. In no way raucous. People sang, told jokes, listened to records, even danced a bit. It was comradely, joyous, and there was real warmth.

A few weeks later in the *New Statesman* there was an article by Jonathan about his experiences on Clydeside and the richness of the social life despite the poverty and areas of squalor. He described this particular evening, the genuine and wholesome camaraderie, and concluded that it couldn't happen in Hampstead. Since then I've been to a party in Hampstead. He was dead right. It couldn't happen there. At Hampstead parties people stand around eating wee sausages with sticks stuck in them, talking sombrely in small groups. In Govan they call that a funeral wake.

Poverty like everything is relative. You can't compare the poverty of Western Europe with the poverty of the Third World, although some would like to do so. Or compare the poverty of today with the poverty of yesterday. Poverty in Britain today is chronic by today's standards. Many millions live below our poverty line. The gap between rich and poor has grown enormously. There is no solution to this festering problem that doesn't involve some wealth redistribution.

The poor are short of money. If this weren't so they wouldn't be poor. They are financially excluded. Most of us are financially excluded from the Savoy Hotel when visiting London but the poor are financially excluded from basic essentials like decent housing and food. That's why they and their children tend to die before their time. Peter Mandelson is now hawking himself round Britain seeking votes that might secure him a place on Labour's NEC. This week he's in Scotland.

Donald Dewar deserves better than this. His leadership of the devolution debate over the past few difficult months has been outstanding. All who favour a Scottish parliament should close ranks behind Donald. I believe a Scottish parliament will tackle the poverty in our midst with a zeal that Westminster could never match.

THE QUEST FOR HEROES

3 SEPTEMBER 1997

SHE was young, beautiful, cared for life's victims, touched people, and was herself touched. Vulnerable as those she comforted. The Princess begowned by the world's best couturiers was perceived as a victim, too. Her marriage was made not in Heaven but Buckingham Palace. His carnal interests lay elsewhere. Diana was not ethereal but earthy. She had known men, was the mother of two boys. A Mother Earth who looked like Venus with arms that wanted to embrace the world. She made some other royals look drab, but then so does Nora Batty.

Her death was a tragedy. The outpouring of grief was to be expected. But its extent is revealing, in some respects disturbing. Our world has no heroes or heroines, just celebrities. Modern wars do not produce heroes. The Gulf war was like *Star Wars*. A push-button affair. Missiles and rockets galore.

Our most successful businessmen are technicians and accountants. A Bill Gates or an Arnold Wienstock. Our trade unions were massacred during the Thatcher years. The mass struggle of working people for their rights has been legally circumscribed. The emergence of working-class heroes has dried up. In politics, the technocrats have taken over. Every speech carefully planned to say nothing and make it sound good. Principle is no longer part of the political agenda. Careerists scurry around seeking personal or factional advantage.

Into this world stepped a young woman who had everything and yet identified with those who had nothing. In terms of imagery, Diana was a rebuke to the global status quo. In her death that status quo is organising the show. The palace that considered her a thorn in its side now wants to reclaim her. Politicians are muscling in. Newspapers that exploited her in life are now making millions from her death.

They all want to make of her a candyfloss princess. A heavenly collector of charity money. Nothing wrong with charities, but the problems of this world won't be solved by them alone. Every time I give money to a medical charity I'm conscious that every penny that gets through to the health service is noted by Government departments that then adjust their health service expenditures accordingly. Pub raffles to provide TVs for every ward and toys for children's hospitals are reasonable, but not for life-saving machinery. Has a child's life to depend on the success or otherwise of a pub raffle? Our collective charity can be expressed only through paying taxes sufficient to ensure that all of us are looked after, in good times or bad.

Diana was helping charities that looked after the victims of war. Men, women, but mostly children had lost limbs by treading on landmines produced in the West. Was she to be content tending their infirmities while more and more land mines were being produced and deployed? She joined the campaign for a world-wide ban on land mines and was accused of playing politics. To wipe away the blood of land mine victims is charity, to try to ban land mines to prevent further bloodshed is politics. Those who make land mines also make a lot of money. Some politicians also make a lot of money. Some politicians believe the making of money is sacrosanct and human life is not. Diana's activities were undoubtedly needling sections of the British Establishment.

I believe the press hounded Diana to death. That the driver of the vehicle which crashed had too much to drink has been established. This doesn't exonerate the paparazzi. According to the Ritz Hotel, the car that was to be used by Diana and Dodi was surrounded by photographers. It drove off without the couple as a possible diversion. Diana and Dodi went to some other exit where another car had been pressed into service. It was the driver of this car who was under the influence.

What is beyond dispute is that the paparazzi pursued them on motorcycles into that tunnel. Eye witnesses allege that they buzzed the car. If this is proven then surely the French privacy laws, that we are told are stricter than ours, which doesn't necessarily mean much for we don't seem to have any, will be invoked. I hope the papers get all that's coming to them. The circulation war among the tabloids has created a jungle where anything goes. Some time back I protested in this column at the harassment of the Duchess of York. I'm no monarchist. The reverse in fact. But the right of the individual must be for everyone or it will be for no-one.

Fergie had been sunbathing topless, in a private secluded garden. A press photographer climbed a tree and took snaps of Fergie, breasts an' a'. It was splashed on front pages. I pondered at the time about what might have happened when the photographer returned to the family hearth. Did his kids clamber on his knees and ask: "Daddy, what did you do at work today?" And did he reply, "I climbed up a tree and photographed the tits of an unsuspecting young lassie." What about the editor who published them? The proprietor who didn't sack him? Yet we are asked to leave the regulation of the press to these people. It's like leaving the protection of children to paedophiles.

In a democracy everyone should have the right to privacy, including public figures. No-one has the right to stop the media investigating crime, the abuse of power, the misuse of public or corporate funds, the critique of political programmes and parties, the arts, etc. What public figures do in bed with consenting adults is their own business, not ours. In the recent General Election, a Tory politician withdrew as a possible candidate because of a press report that alleged a homosexual affair. Homosexuality isn't a crime but allegations such as this pander to the homophobes in our midst. Homosexual allegations against Gordon McMaster, fear of their publication, is considered a factor in his suicide.

We have no right in the media to wield such power. I want a more investigative and irreverent press in areas of public interest. Diana's death is being dangerously over-hyped by an assortment of interests. On Saturday, I'll be watching Scotland play Belarus at football. I'll be a willing participant in any manifestation of respect for this young lady. In London, we're likely to see the orchestrated street grief and maybe near hysteria of people that yearn for heroes and instead get hucksters.

HYSTERIA PAVING THE WAY
FOR A BACKLASH

5 SEPTEMBER 1997

IF it's all right for shops to open in London after Diana's funeral, why is it all wrong for Scotland to play football, one hour later and 600 miles away in Aberdeen?

Is buying a pair of knickers in Marks and Sparks more respectful to Diana than watching a game of football? A game that was to be preceded by two minutes silence by all who were there. The players were to have worn black armbands as a token of respect. Is getting pissed in a pub more decorous than this?

Diana's mother has sanctioned a dance in Oban on Saturday night. Dances are jolly affairs. Let me tell you, from long experience, watching Scotland play football seldom comes into that category. Diana's mother was right. In death there is sorrow but there should also be celebration of the life that was lived and alas is no more.

Why hasn't the Prime Minister bludgeoned the owners of London's big stores into putting up the shutters on Saturday afternoon?

Well, you see, they're expecting an influx of up to two million people and that represents a lot of retail trade. In other words, a lot of lolly.

Our Prime Minister won't ever say boo to the guys with serious money. Has he called for all pubs and clubs to close? Shouldn't he be demanding that BBC and ITV stop transmitting after the funeral and play sombre music instead? If they are to transmit, will entertaining programmes be banned?

I'll bet that on Saturday afternoon at 3pm some of the folk who demanded the cancellation of this game will be sitting in pubs and clubs cracking jokes with their mates. Some will be avid readers of the tabloids that hounded Diana to her death.

Sooner rather than later these same tabloids will be after Diana again. Deification followed by character assassination. Any dirt they have on her will be dished out. The dead can't take out libel actions. You can't invade the privacy of those who have gone. There is another killing to be made by the tabloids. They will pick over her bones like the vultures they are.

The hype is now dangerously over the top. The people in the media who are whipping this up, making a princess into a goddess, will also be responsible for the backlash that will assuredly come. Any day now, we will hear the first Diana joke. The tabloids will get in on the act and then it's back to business as usual.

In this atmosphere, certain madnesses and absurdities abound. Three footballers in a public statement asked not to be picked for the team to play on Saturday. Donald Findlay, QC, vice-chairman of their club, leader of the No No referendum campaign, also attacked the SFA, who had actually consulted the Royal Family and received its approval for the game to be played as proposed.

But then who is the Queen compared to Findlay? He's more royal than the royals or so he seems to think.

Rangers Football Club issued a statement attacking the SFA. This was issued by an official at Ibrox who is a member of the

International Committee of the SFA that decided to hold the game on Saturday, a man I happen to like and respect.

Actually this game, whenever it's played, is no big thing in the scale of world events. But that a government should bludgeon football into doing something it believes isn't right or logical is a dangerous precedent. There have been many dangerous precedents set in the last few days. I was urged by friends not to write this article though they agree with all the sentiments. They say there is near hysteria about, fanned by sections of the media, among whom we must include the BBC.

I have already written in the *Herald* about my respect for Diana and understand the sorrow at her death and share it. But each of my children, with all due respect, means more to me than Princess Diana and if there are parents out there who think otherwise then they should go and see a doctor.

Such mass over-the-top emotions, on public display, are not healthy and will eventually tarnish the image of a young woman who deserves better.

HISTORY IN THE MAKING

10 SEPTEMBER 1997

I AM not exactly a kilt man. For tartan my affection is slight. Haggis? You can keep it. I view music hall songs with words like "it's a braw, moonlicht nicht, the nicht" as jokes against the silly Sassenach concept of Jocks. A concept stemming from Southern guilt about the slaughter at Culloden, the genocidal aftermath, and the romantic Celtic twilight industry spawned by Walter Scott.

As night follows day came shortbread tins and Harry Lauder. Porridge in your sporran, a caber up your kilt, hoots mon, stop yer ticklin' Jock, wi' a wig-wig-wiggle-waggle o' the kilt. Don't get me wrong, Granny's Hielan Hame has got haw maw from me many a time. I actually had a hielan granny. But in no way does this even begin to define my Scottishness. I believe Scotland is the finest country in the world because it's my country. Walter Scott did get it right sometimes. "Breathes there the man, with soul so dead, who never to himself hath said, this is my own, my native land!"

A Scot who doesn't love Scotland can't love the world. That's where I'm coming from. Scotland is on the map but isn't simply a geographical location. Scotland is a nation. On the other hand there is no such thing as a British nation. It doesn't and cannot exist. Britain is a state. A unitary state embracing the nations of England, Scotland, Wales, and the province of Northern Ireland.

All nations have a right of self-determination. For big nations that right was historically easier to exercise because of their bigness. For small nations it was a different matter. Big neighbouring nations wanted to swallow them up. It later became known as expansionism. England invaded and subjugated Ireland. England many times invaded but failed to subjugate Scotland.

This is a historical fact. Big nations sought to annex small nations and expand their domain. This happened all over the world. Geography played a right dirty trick on the Poles who were stuck between Germanic and Russian hordes. When one mob wasn't trying to overrun them the other was. A reality that applied till just a few years ago.

The 1707 Treaty of Union with England was opposed by the great majority of Scots. There were mass demonstrations of opposition in all the towns and cities. The Scottish Convention of Royal Burghs voted against it. But the electorate was less than 1% of the population. The people had no say. The Scottish nobility had already sold the jerseys. In 1603 on the death of Elizabeth, King James of Scotland ascended to the English throne and scarpered south as fast as his royal coach could carry him. The fleshpots for kings were bigger down there. His Scottish court went with him.

After 1707 the exodus was greater. At that time Scotland had arguably the finest schools and universities in the world. But the Scottish nobility sent their sons to English public schools where they would be taught to speak like English Gentlemen. Even to this day the sons of the Scottish landed gentry speak without trace of their ancestry. They expunged every trace of Scottishness. That's why they have to wear kilts, like badges, when up here.

The fear of union with England was based on a real danger that had nothing to do with England per se. In a unitary state within which a small nation lives cheek by jowl with a very much larger nation, the identity and interests of the smaller nation might be submerged by the sheer numbers of the larger nation. The British Parliament arising from the Treaty of Union was not to be in Edinburgh but in London, many hundreds of miles away. It would meet in the English Parliament with all its feudal paraphernalia.

The English Establishment became the British Establishment. To this day Scots are governed by an English Establishment. That some Scots are absorbed into this Establishment changes nothing.

When Henry VII of England offered his daughter Margaret in marriage to James of Scotland, Henry's privy councillors opposed it on the grounds that England might fall into the hands of Scotland through royal descent. Henry rejected this scornfully. "Supposing, which God forbid, that all my male progeny should become extinct and the Kingdom devolve by law to Margaret's heirs, will England be damaged thereby? For since it ever happens that the less becomes subservient to the greater, the accession will be that of Scotland to England . . . as a rivulet to a fountain." He was absolutely right.

The Treaty of Union gave no protection to the Scottish nation. With the advent of a wider suffrage and democratic representation the fight for a Scottish parliament became focused on changes that would restore our rights to govern ourselves within the framework of the Union. This has been a constant of Scottish political life ever since. It won't go away and has to be resolved.

It can be resolved by ourselves tomorrow. And let me tell you what I mean by ourselves. It means everyone who lives in Scotland. A nation isn't a racial entity. It is a historically evolved community of people. A social, political, and cultural phenomenon. Most Scots are Gaels emanating from Scotland and Ireland. Most of us are from both strands. In the North-east you only have to look at some of the place names and family names to recognise the Nordic influence.

The influx of Jews fleeing from the anti-Semitic pogroms in

Central and Eastern Europe has enhanced our culture and society. People from Asia have come to our shores and I welcome them and love to hear young Asian kids in the streets speak with a Glesca accent. The Chinese are now a settled part of our communities. Then there are our English brothers and sisters who have come to live among us. All of them are Scots by birth or adoption. Such diversity is enriching to the overall culture of the Scottish nation. We are all, in this context, Jock Tamson's bairns.

History in the making, and the No No campaigners have tried to reduce it to a tuppence-ha'penny affair. Or a thrupenny opera. They are basically telling us we're not fit to have more say in our own affairs. That London knows best. That's rich coming from Michael Ancram. Monsieur Poll Tax himself. A member of a Government that ruled Scotland without a shred of democratic legitimacy.

Look who's urging us to say No. Ancram, a Tory MP for an English constituency. And Lady Thatcher. Need I say more?

MASSACRE OF THE DISSIDENTS

1 OCTOBER 1997

PETER MANDELSON didn't win a seat on New Labour's National Executive. This was greeted as evidence that Labour dissidents still mattered. This response to the event reminded me of a playground joke from my schooldays. A wee man is going to work, discovers he has left his lunch pieces at home, returns and finds his wife in bed with a massive brute of a neighbour. The brute leaps from the bed, grabs the wee man, plonks him down in a corner, draws a circle round his feet with a piece of chalk and growls:

"If you move, even a teeny wee bit, outside that circle, I'll break your back in three places."

The brute resumes whatever he is doing then departs the scene without even an as you please. The wife turns furiously on the wee man. "How could you just stand there without doing something?" "But I did something," he protested. "When he wasn't looking I was jumping in and out that circle."

Mandelson's defeat was a triviality compared with another vote that took place at the party conference on Monday. The delegates voted overwhelmingly to massacre the Labour Party's internal democracy. The NEC is to be neutered. The party conference will become a glorified chat show. A National Policy Forum will initiate limited strands of discussion.

The whole package is Leninist. All power to the leader.

A few years ago the Labour Party could have laid claim to being the most democratic political party in Britain.

Now it is arguably the least democratic. All of this happened in the first day of conference. But we also heard a speech from the Chancellor. The speech, you might have expected, would deal with the specifics of economic policy; it didn't. Talk of guaranteeing everyone a job became, when you examined it, simply that everyone could be trained for a job. I know a lot of people who are trained for a job but have been jobless for years. Not a word was said about the actual creation of jobs.

Gordon Brown's speech did advocate the flexible market and the acceptance of market liberalism. But that, you might rightly say, is the essence of Thatcherism. New Labour talks of change, always on about change, and yet it's difficult to discern any real change from the Tory government in the management of the economy, apart from handing over the determination of interest rates to the Bank of England.

New Labour is keeping within Kenneth Clarke's public spending limits which will mean the closure of wards, hospital beds, and hospitals over this winter. New Labour's reform of the welfare state hardly differs from those advocated by Peter Lilley. If you read carefully what New Labour is saying about pensions the proposals are essentially similar to those proposed by the Tories, including privatised pensions.

I've been in Madeira for the past few weeks. I liked the place. The island is irrigated by a network of man-made water channels, cut through the landscape and mountains. They're called levadas. This network was publicly owned and subject to laws that ensured that water was distributed fairly. In the middle of the nineteenth century the network was privatised. This led to disputes, crop failures, and bankruptcies. The levadas were restored to public ownership at the end of the Second World War. The water system was modernised. The craggy hills and majestic mountains of this island cradle plains and uplands that are lush and teeming with fruits and flowers.

I was talking about this to a couple from Lowestoft. They explained how since water was privatised in England they had had a domestic meter and that some folk in their community, fearful of the costs, are only pulling the chain in their lavatories once a day. The point is that in other countries natural resources and assets are looked upon as natural publicly-owned assets. Only with the advent of Thatcherism did the political culture change in this country. The Madeirans were wise enough to initiate a change back to a more civilised way of living.

Is New Labour going to bring water back into public ownership in Britain? No. New Labour was vehemently opposed to rail privatisation by the Tories before the General Election. Is it going to take railways back into public ownership? No. In fact New Labour is considering further privatisations for London Underground and Channel 4.

What then has changed since the General Election? On all major economic issues—nothing at all. There is a rhetoric of change but no change. It's business as before. Tax, we are told, is to be reduced some time in the future for the low-paid, but the low-paid don't pay tax.

The only real change to be seen has been within the Labour Party itself, where democracy is being annihilated. The vote was carried in favour of the leadership by the block votes of the largest trade unions. The union leaders were subject to much arm twisting during the past eight weeks. They were bluntly told, vote for our reforms or we won't honour our manifesto commitments on workers' rights.

If that isn't sleaze the word has no meaning.

After Monday the conference work was effectively finished. Tony Blair's speech on Tuesday said nothing but said it well with touches that were Elmer Gantryish.

The only phrase that stuck in my mind was that after listing British inventions he claimed that change was in our British bone and blood. Most, if not all, the inventions he mentioned were by Scots, but we've never claimed this was a Scottish genetic phenomenon but due to our culture of education and the pursuit of knowledge. But there they were. The serried ranks of the idolatrous. A hall full of clappy happies. Flags and bunting. And a leader talking of blood and ethnic virtues. This is certainly a change at a British Labour Party conference. Mind you, the Tories have been at that for years.

FORMULA ONE
AND £1M OF FREE LUNCHES

12 NOVEMBER 1997

LET me see if I've got the facts right. Bernie Ecclestone gave lavish donations to the Tory party. From 1992-97 these amounted to something like £10m. With the advent of Blairism he changed sides. In January of this year he gave £1m to New Labour, 10% of the party's 1996-97 income. Other big personal donations that we know about came from Matthew Harding, £1m, and Paul Hamlyn, £600,000.

These men were massive beneficiaries of the Thatcherite revolution. A revolution that Mr Blair pledged to continue as her rightful and respectful heir and trusted custodian of her holy grail; that those who have plenty or have grabbed plenty for themselves shall have more, and those that are without, like single parents and working-class students, shall have less, for this is the way of the market. Bernie Ecclestone virtually runs Formula One grand prix racing. In the financial year 1993-94 his salary was £29.7m. The highest ever recorded in the United Kingdom.

Labour is committed to banning cigarette advertising. Smoking kills more than all other drugs put together. In the central belt of Scotland it is a massive killer. Many pals and workmates have died from a deadly combination of smoking and exposure, during their working lives, to asbestos. It's an insult to our intelligence to say that tobacco advertising doesn't influence people and lower their defences to the diabolical hazards of smoking. Why else spend billions each year on advertising and the promotion of these products?

Yet that is the argument of Max Mosley, president of the FIA. I heard him advance it on television. Give me proof, he argues, that the tobacco companies' sponsorship of Formula One racing has persuaded one person to start smoking. Of course it hasn't. The tobacco companies are God-made philanthropists. One day the tobacco bosses were sitting round a table doing what tobacco bosses do, chewing gum, when one of them said: "I've got a great idea. Let's give a hundred million quid to Formula One racing." "What's in it for us?" said one of the bosses. "Nothing, that's the beauty of it," said the proposer. And so they had a whip round.

The tobacco bosses sent one of their own to see Max and Bernie with a hat full of a hundred million smackers and emptied it on to their laps. (They must have big laps. A few kilometres or so.) "All this is yours," he said, "with no strings attached." "Is there nothing we can do for you?" said Max. "Well I suppose you could scatter our brand names about the place. Round the track. Over the cars, helmets, driving suits, drivers' bums, and any other surfaces you can find. Not, mind you, that it will do us any good. We simply want to do our little bit, add our little morsel, to the treasure house of mechanical creativity." Bernie, somewhat overcome, said: "We will drink to that." And in the ways of Formula One racing skooshed a bottle of champagne over the little group. It might not be good for the suit but it does make it unlikely you'll ever get done for drunk driving. Of course, officer, I smell like a distillery, but I'm in Formula One racing.

After the General Election, Labour Ministers in the Department of Health set about honouring the electoral promise to ban tobacco advertising. Frank Dobson told a conference of nurses that tobacco advertising would be banned in sport. A most justified step. To link smoking and athleticism of any kind must be the sickest of sick jokes.

On October 16 the Prime Minister had a meeting at Downing Street with Messrs Ecclestone and Mosley. After this meeting the Prime Minister personally ordered that Formula One racing should be exempt from the ban on tobacco advertising. Mr Ecclestone denies that there is any connection between this decision and his substantial donation, and who can say otherwise. The Prime Minister denies that there was any connection, though he knew the magnitude of Ecclestone's donation. Max Mosley was also a substantial donor to New Labour.

Cynics say there is no such thing as a free lunch, which is nonsense. I've had free lunches from people I have immediately or subsequently criticised without the slightest hesitation. If you're going to be corrupted it surely takes more than a free lunch. But £1m is a helluva lot of free lunches. How with the best will in the world can you excise from your mind such largesse? Does it not insinuate itself unconsciously, subconsciously, without being bidden, without a word spoken. These, after all, are good guys, on our side, on the same wavelength. Yes, that would be the way it was but alas that isn't good enough. There's the decision.

The worst thing about the whole business is the decision. Restore the ban on tobacco advertising in Formula One and some principle is served. But it won't happen. It is Blair's mistake but that won't be acknowledged. Someone else will have to take the rap and poor Frank Dobson looks the most likely candidate. New Labour claimed that it decided to raise the whole matter with Sir Patrick Neil, the new public standards watchdog, immediately following the reversal of policy. Sir Patrick says he never received a faxed letter from Tom Sawyer, General Secretary of the Labour

Party, until 7pm last Friday, a few hours after the media was clamouring for the party to confirm that Ecclestone was in fact a major donor.

Sir Patrick gave his reply on Monday. He told New Labour to return the one million quid. Labour announced shortly afterwards, at 5pm, that it would do so. Earlier that afternoon Mr Ecclestone's solicitor stated on behalf of his client: "A statement at the weekend denying my client gave money to the Labour Party still stands." Shortly afterwards Ecclestone had no option other than admit he was a financial supporter of New Labour but claimed he had "never sought any favour. . . ." Maybe so, but why the evasions?

Simply to list the circumstantial facts is damning. More damning than the allegations made against some Labour councillors and at least one MP. Yet they have been suspended, without actual proof of culpability, pending an investigation by the party's NEC. Is Tony Blair to be suspended pending investigation by the party NEC? Of course not. In New Labour the leader is above reproach and beyond restraints. He makes policy on the hoof. Changes policies in private discussions with the wealthy to whom he forever panders and then lets departmental Ministers carry the can. This is corruption, the corruption of power. In politics the corruption of principles means that everything else is up for grabs. If you sell your principles, nothing is safe. I personally know no-one who has been killed or maimed by a landmine but know that landmines should be banned. I know thousands who have died from inhaling cigarettes. To condone the promotion of tobacco is an outrage. To do so for economic or financial reasons is an obscenity.

A CLEAR CASE OF
CALIGULITIS

3 DECEMBER 1997

SINCE being duly elected MP for Govan on May 1, 1997, neither head nor remaining hair of Mohammed Sarwar has been seen in the Chamber of the House of Commons, until last Friday. Sarwar attended the debate on a motion to ban hunting wildlife with hounds. He voted for the ban. This delights me not primarily because such hunting kills foxes and stags, but for another more compelling reason, that some humans actually derive pleasure from killing them.

So cheers for Sarwar. But where was he on other occasions when matters vital to the electorate in general and his constituency in particular were up for debate and decision? He was absent under instruction from New Labour's leadership—permanently "paired" by the whips' office as a technical justification of his non-appearance. He can't ask a question in the House and is barred from sharing a platform with other Labour MPs. All we need is Bernie Ecclestone, appointed by Blair, to walk in front of Sarwar ringing a bell and intoning "make way for the unclean".

Sarwar, you might well assume, must have been found guilty of the most heinous crimes. Your assumption would be entirely wrong. He has as yet been found guilty of nothing. New Labour has devised a bizarre new system of internal justice that makes Hangin' Judge Jeffreys look like a bleedin' heart liberal. Stalin needed show trials before sending his erstwhile comrades into outer darkness. Blair sends his with the suggestion that he might get round sometime to proving them guilty.

This high-and-mighty disregard for the presumption of innocence until guilt is proven was always bound to fall foul of the law. I wrote of this some months ago in the *Herald* and reported that Labour lawyers in London were alarmed at the cavalier attitude displayed in the suspension of MPs and councillors. They were of the opinion that such actions might not be sustainable in law. I read last weekend that Labour lawyers in London were warning Blair he might be in serious trouble if he proceeded against some of the Glasgow councillors and Scottish MPs on the grounds already defined.

The trouble is that Blair sees himself as a man of destiny. And men of destiny tend to consider themselves above the constraints of office that apply to mere mortals. It's called Caligulitis. Blair appeared at a time when Labour hacks were malleable. Excluded for so long from power and the tantalising fleshpots of office they were willing to sell their souls to get a little turn themselves. When a few like myself suggested that power was not an end in itself, but a means to a better life for the many, that power should be used to correct the injustices of the Thatcher years, I was told, haud yer wheesht, we'll come to that when we have power.

As soon as Blair was in Downing Street he started campaigning for the next election. Appearance was everything. The grind of photo opportunities and media management continued, unabated.

Trotsky believed in permanent revolution. Blair believes in permanent electioneering.

He aims to kill off the Conservative Party by making it redundant. The Tory opposition can only protest forlornly that New
Labour is carrying out Tory policies. But Tories in the English
Shires and Home Counties are rejoicing. Why worry about the
possible demise of the Tory party when there is a brand-new Tory
party at hand? You know something, I wouldn't have William
Hague's job for all the money in Geoffrey Robinson's tax-avoiding
offshore trust fund. Liberal Democrats are being sucked into an
alliance that could spell the end of Liberal traditions: traditions too
left-wing for New Labour to accommodate. You get the impression that Paddy Ashdown will sacrifice anything for an electoral
system based on proportional representation. He might get PR on
the ruins of his own party. The only effective opposition will come
from within Labour ranks. This was already true at the General
Election.

I spoke at the start of the hustings for Labour, and it was, as you
would expect, in Govan. I made it clear that I would voice my
criticisms of New Labour, which in Scotland was no electoral
disadvantage. This was agreed. I said that after the formation of a
New Labour government, the political fight for the future of Britain would take place within the Labour Party itself. Then the
excrement hit the fan. From on high New Labour barred me from
speaking at any other meetings.

I didn't care. What I said was true and would become reality
before the year's end. And it has. The back-bench revolt of Labour
MPs against benefit cuts for single parents is the only real opposition that Blair's Government has faced. The hundred plus who
have signed the letter of protest to Gordon Brown will be under
unremitting pressure. They will be told in words of few syllables
to withdraw their names or to say goodbye to promotion. Some
will succumb. Some will abstain, which in this context is a coward's castle. If this battle is lost there will be other battles to come,

and who knows, by that time the trade unions might be off their knees.

Blair always understood where the main opposition would come from. That is why he sought to remake the Labour Party in his own image. To neuter the party conference and turn it into a leadership rally. To neuter the NEC and make it sing from his hymn sheet. Branches too had to be marginalised. Dissent stamped out. Members recruited on a form emblazoned with his photograph as if their membership were a pact between him and them. They receive a glossy magazine each month in which the leader is liberally featured. They pay their dues by banker's orders. Policy statements from the centre will come direct to the home and voting will be by postal ballot. There will be no opportunity to debate or vote on amendments. They will only be able to tick a little box, yea or nay. Most won't vote. New Labour will be a fan club.

Scotland was always a problem. Blair's blandishments didn't really work up here. Men of destiny don't take kindly to that. The Scottish parliament could be another danger to the monolithic party through which he wants to exercise power. The Scottish party had to be tamed. Accusations of sleaze are accepted without investigation of substance. The accused are condemned out of hand. The party leadership in London uses this to take a grip of things in Scotland. It's also intended to demonstrate New Labour's masculinity. It doesn't seem to matter that the accused have not yet been found guilty of anything.

This has left Govan without an MP. I believe Mohammed Sarwar is more sinned against than sinner. But he cannot escape his responsibility to the people of Govan. He is their elected MP. Nothing anyone says can alter that fact. He must take his place in Parliament now. The only other honourable alternative is to resign his seat.

HALLELUJAH FOR GOOD GOD
I DON'T BELIEVE IN

24 DECEMBER 1997

LET me tell you something. I don't believe in God but the God I don't believe in is a good God. It beats me that some people can actually believe in bad, vengeful, fire-and-brimstone gods who are forever putting the frighteners on people. Compared to them Auld Nick's a charmer.

Take Jesus. Now He's a God after my own heart. A punter, woodworker, revolutionary Rabbi, thorn in the side of the cosy conformists. He preferred wine to water. Befriended prostitutes. Told those without sin to cast the first stone, certain in the knowledge that no-one is without sin and therefore if they obey his dictum no-one would ever be stoned except those who drank his wine. Hallelujah!

Jesus went into the Temple and banjoed the money changers. Kicked over their tables. Told the greedy that they had only a snowball in hell's chance of ever getting through the portals of Heaven. His Heaven was obviously a Tory-free zone which effectively puts the bar up on Blairites as well. Jesus says: what you did to the least of men you did unto me. And that includes single parents, the lame and the halt, the poor who are forever blessed, even if you call them an underclass. You cast them into the gutter and when your time comes I will cast you into outer darkness where you can gnash your gums with others of your ilk, like Jeffrey Archer and Noel Edmonds. That I maintain is a fair precis of what Christ was about.

As gods go you can't get any better than Jesus. That's why tomorrow I will be celebrating his birthday with what used to be called gusto. Quibblers tell us that it isn't his actual date of birth, which we do not and cannot know. What in the name of Christ is wrong with inventing one? See quibblers, see me, I could see them far enough. They tell us he wasn't born in Bethlehem. So he was born in Coatbridge or Stowe in the Wold! What does it matter? Three wise men didn't come to see the infant Jesus, say the wise guys. So what? There aren't three wise men in the whole of Westminster. Quibble about that for a change.

So the early Christians purloined a pagan midwinter festival and made it their own. Good thinking. Those pagans must have known a thing or two. In the middle of winter we need a good knees up and now we've got two, Christmas and new year, and they have merged into one massive binge. In this miserable godforsaken world what's wrong with that? Yet the moaners are at work. It's true that jingle bells get clattered with the clamour of cash registers. Do what I do, ignore the tinsel. Clock on to people. Family and friends. Suffuse in the warmth of their company and have kind thoughts for those who will miss loved ones this festive season. As my old maw used to say: "See and enjoy your bloody self."

That's what I try to do. Not stridently but in a quiet and composed way that befits my age. At least that's the theory; in practice the years slip away and I'm a youth again, in mind if not in body. I will drink too much and afterwards pay my dues. People used to talk of getting in a Ne'erday bottle. Now you need a crate. Jesus was lucky, he made his own.

On Christmas morning our home is pandemonium. My youngest grown-up daughter's the most pandemonious, aided and abetted by her mother and grandmother, who, at their age, should know better. Their first task of the day is to get me out of bed. They used to play music loud, music I don't like. Country and Western and Barry Manilow. But with my growing deafness this became a diminishingly effective ploy. They now gather in my bedroom and try to pull the duvet off. Where did we get that word, duvet. It's still a quilt to me. Even the dog and cat get in on the act. Stirred into near frenzy by all the activity, they jump on the bed and pummel me around. The most insidious tactic of all is to get my granddaughter to plead with me to get up. I succumb. There is no other day of the year when I'm up at four in the morning unless I'm just coming home from a party.

My agonies are still not over. When I'm having my bath my betrothed, obviously under the influence of mulled wine, comes breenging in and sinks all my boats. Childish I know, but what can I do but grin and bear it? Thereafter things get better. Presents piled under the tree are opened. There's much ooh-ing and ah-ing. Kisses of thanks are exchanged. I will have enough socks to clad Ranulph Fiennes' next expedition to the Arctic wastes. He could go to Edinburgh for half the price.

We eat a proper Scots breakfast. According to the experts a thoroughly unhealthy concoction. But it's Christmas Day and a little backsliding is surely in order. Jesus, I'm sure, would have understood. Might even have agreed. I then slip away to my bedroom ostensibly to peruse some books I've been given. In fact I'm trying to sneak a little more sleep. Turn on my side away from the door. Prop the book on the pillow held up with my hand, and snooze. Sometime later I awake with pins and needles in my left hand. It's a bugger.

By this time, though, I'm wide awake and rarin' to go. A visit to a local is in order. Everyone seems to be dressed in their brand-new pressies. Some of the men stiffly, so as if only the starch of their new shirt is holding them upright. I'm in that category. A few malts and all is well. Women look prettier and men not so ugly. Small drinks and tall tales are swopped. We're glorious, o'er all the ills of life victorious. There isn't a problem we cannot solve.

Some are a bit less than jolly. Probably rent by the guilt of sly embraces or a let-me-tell-you-frankly expression of opinion at an office party or works night out. Be jolly when celebrating at this time of year. Eschew matters of gravity. See not the mote on the eyes of others over the festive season and while you are in your cups, for assuredly as night follows day you will point them out in the most brutal detail and end up with an enemy for life.

I love Christmas dinner with all the trimmings and loved ones. It's a time to meet old friends and new ones. I tend to greet strangers as long-lost friends, especially if they're cute. I prefer humour to jokes for jokes are often cruel. I wallow in a sense of fellowship. That's my Christmas. Sometimes fleetingly I might look sombre, for even in the midst of joy we cannot completely exclude thoughts of those in pain, in misery, victims of injustice, or the cruelty of men, both here and elsewhere in the world. These are sentiments I associate with Christ the man you might call God. But while we might not agree about that and about Heaven we must surely agree not to make Earth a hell. Merry Christmas. And may your god be with you.

BEWARE BLOODSUCKERS, BOTH LARGE AND SMALL

14 JANUARY 1998

JUST because you're a hypochondriac doesn't mean that you're not ill. Take me. I'm not a hypochondriac until someone tells me about symptoms for any illness known or unknown to man, then— wham, bam, alakazam, quick as a flash—I've got them, with knobs on. This first happened to me in my tender years. A battered, rather shabby old book appeared from nowhere; probably a neighbour gave it to mum. It was a kind of encyclopaedia of ailments. I started thumbing through the pages, then got engrossed, then terrified. My youthful demeanour was devastated. I was done for with a deadly combination of beri beri, fallen arches, asthma, bronchitis, and flu.

I somehow survived and vowed never again to read a medical book. In these matters ignorance can indeed be bliss. My resolve held until last week. I was in my daughter's home. Sitting sipping a beverage. Talking about Aristotle, Hegel, the virtues of free-range eggs, the survival prospects of Partick Thistle, and other

251

such urgent matters, when it happened. I innocently picked up a book that was lying on the table and, as is my wont, perused it. The title was: *The Doctor's Book of Home Remedies* subtitled *Thousands of Tips and Techniques Anyone Can Use to Heal Everyday Health Problems.*

Everyday Health Problems! The book fell open at a section on the tick. Now I know next to nothing about the tick except for the aforementioned Partick which, of course, is a suburb of Govan. Here's what I read: "Ticks are not fussy about what type of animal provides their meals. Humans are fair game for them . . . Ticks pose a special problem because they dig their little jaws into your skin . . . forcefully plucking it out may leave its mouthparts embedded, setting the stage for infection."

It advises easing the tick out with tweezers. "Don't pull too fast." You might also apply "a little heat on the tick's backside". Then there's the fact that "a drop of petrol, paraffin, benzene or surgical spirit placed on the general region of the tick's head will make it loosen its grip". Then a warning. "Note that these substances are flammable and should not be used with a hot match." By this time I was pondering the use of a stun grenade exploded close to the tick's ears. The book advises a gentler method. Suffocating the tick by covering it with "a drop of wax or nail polish. Either will close off the tiny breathing openings on its side . . ."

But the pièce de résistance was the Benforado Method, called after Joseph Benforado, professor emeritus at the University of Wisconsin-Madison who had been a Scout camp physician in earlier years. Here it is. "Take a large nail and warm the tip in a match flame. Slide the flat side of a pocket knife blade under the tick's abdomen. Place the heated nail tip on the tick's back so it is sandwiched between knife and the nail. When the tick's legs begin to wiggle in response to the heat, turn the knife blade 90° so the tick is standing on its head. Keeping it sandwiched, gently pull the tick up and away from its grip. If the legs do not wiggle the nail is not warm enough. Try again." Dr Benforado explains: "The object is to annoy the tick rather than roast it." I think the tick is bound to be annoyed by the good doctor's method—but if that fails what's left? The SAS? Alistair Campbell?

By this time my mind was made up. Prevention was better than the cure. What we needed was a home guard against a tick invasion of our bodies. Maybe mosquito nets over the beds. The wearing of wellies all the time including to weddings and black tie dinner dances. People may mock my dress style but better that than a backful of ticks and the Benforado Method.

Later that day I cooled down. My betrothed persuaded me that ticks didn't fly and didn't live in concrete jungles, but in the countryside. That made sense. People who lived in the countryside always did look a bit wabbit to me. It must be all these ticks sucking away at their blood like rural Draculas or bookies.

Mind you, we've got enough real things to worry about without inventing others. Let me give you a for example. If you're a pensioner or a potential pensioner start worrying now. The Government's plan to reform the welfare state has the strategic aim of ending the welfare state which was and is based on a system of universal benefits. Everyone while working or earning paid into the fund. Everyone was paid the same benefits when retired, sick, disabled, or unemployed, with supplementary payments for those in special need.

Benefits were being paid to those who had money but this was clawed back through a progressive system of taxation. The principle of universality was thereby maintained. The idea that the founders of the welfare state hadn't foreseen the funding difficulties of the future is an insult to men who were profoundly more intellectual than today's chancer politicians. Their system of universal contributions, universal payments, and progressive taxation isn't working because progressive taxation has been eroded in the past 18 years. Today Britain has the lowest taxation for the rich in the European Union and North America.

The present Government has committed itself to further reductions. Without a proper progressive taxation regime the welfare state would always have been unsustainable. That's the position we are getting into today. Workers who have paid for a private pension were urged to do so to supplement the state pension. Their private pension will be used to take away part or all of their state pension. In other words their private pension will become a substitute for the state pension to which they subscribed during their working lives. That's highway robbery.

But it won't help the poorest; quite the reverse. Pensions will be means-tested and we know what this means because it applied during the depression of the 1930s and indignity piled on indignity. The basic pension is already falling because Thatcher ended the link between pensions and average earnings. Labour was pledged to re-establish that principle but refuses to do so. The aim is to pay a pension only to the "very poorest". And the poorest's pension will be driven down and down.

What applies to the pensioners will apply in different ways to all others in receipt of benefits. The underclass will become further isolated. The poor, but not so poor as the very poor, will complain at the monies going to the very poor, at their expense. All the others will do the same and the very poor will become scapegoats and their benefits will be further reduced and nobody will protest except them and no-one will be listening. The welfare state that brought social stability, social justice, and dignity to the streets of Britain will wither away. See New Labour. I'd rather have the ticks.

THE MORALITY BENDERS

21 JANUARY 1998

IN THE CONTEXT of a Richter scale which could objectively measure the impact of great twentieth-century discoveries, such as Fleming's penicillin, and Einstein's E=mc², I suppose it really doesn't matter whether President Clinton's penis is bent or not. On that scale of things, such small fry wouldn't even register.

That it is bent is alleged by a woman who claims to have given it a right good shufti when he dropped his pants in front of her when he was Governor of Arkansas.

For all I care, his penis could be triangular, microscopically minuscule, or painted in psychedelic hues. Though I do admit to a wee prurient ponder; if the allegation is true that it's laterally bent, how does he pee without wetting the guy at an adjoining urinal? In this much ado about nothing, what is completely and conveniently forgotten is that politically the man is as bent as hell, and nobody seems to care.

His abundant political infidelities go unmentioned while his alleged domestic infidelities get laldy. Principles in politics have become less important than penises, on both sides of the Atlantic.

The stramash about the recent biography of Gordon Brown deals with conflicting ambitions, and not about conflicting political principles. In the aftermath of John Smith's death, there were certainly all kinds of queries raised with me by people in the media, here and in England, about Gordon's sexuality.

I assumed they originated from anti-Labour sources in the press with close links to the Conservative Party. I now realise they were probably attempts to discredit Brown to the advantage of Blair in the run-up to the election of the new party leader.

When asked if Gordon was homosexual, I said no. On reflection this reply wasn't good enough. It pandered to homophobics. I should have said: "I don't think Gordon Brown is homosexual but if he is—so what!"

During the General Election a Tory candidate in Scotland was publicly assailed for alcohol problems. He sought a cure in a treatment centre, where he met a lady with whom he formed a relationship.

The publicity drove him to resign, and brought him close to a major breakdown. A possible successor Tory candidate in the same constituency was then publicly accused of having a homosexual affair many years ago. He fled the country.

Being a homosexual isn't a crime in this country, as long as sexual relations are conducted in private with a consenting adult. Similar restraints apply to heterosexuals.

This is as it should be. Don't tell me that we have a choice as to our sex and sexuality. In my class at school was a lad who was manifestly different from the rest of us. He was religious. We were apprentice atheists. When we played football he was knitting. We considered him a bit of a cissy, but in a friendly way.

Many years later, during the work-in on the Upper Clyde he phoned me late one night. I hadn't heard of him since we left school. He lived in London. He wanted to give a donation to the UCS fighting fund. I was not in the least surprised to find that he was homosexual. He couldn't be otherwise. It was in his genes. To blame a homosexual for being homosexual is to indict him for being born.

To the homosexual his or her sexuality is as legitimate as hetero-sexuality is to the rest of us. People are responsible for what they believe and what they do, but not for their race or sexuality. We have no choice on these matters. This is more widely understood when it comes to race, but we are more ambiguous when it comes to sexuality. The homophobic, in a sense, is a sexual racist.

Over the years I've come to the conclusion that the homophobic man who wants to beat up poofs has serious suppressed doubts about his own sexuality. He doth protest too much. I believe there is a phoney morality knocking around just now. It was promul-gated by Reagan and Thatcher. A harping back to the non-existent idyllic family life of nineteenth-century Victorian times. In reality these were the times of the poorhouse, the workhouse, the cruel exploitation of child labour that we now rightly condemn in the Third World. The times of Charles Dickens, and *Oliver Twist*, and of dark, satanic mills.

Victorian morality was a myth. The bewhiskered bourgeois father was a 22-carat hypocrite. Chastity and fidelity were for his womenfolk. He frequented brothels staffed by daughters of the desperate poor. J B Priestley attacked this hypocrisy in his play, *An Inspector Calls*. It was a time of violence and lawlessness, at home and abroad. Jack The Ripper was a Victorian. So was Cecil Rhodes, who murdered many more than Jack ever did. Victorian Britain pioneered the concentration camp that Hitler adapted for his own bestial purposes.

Blairism is the application of Victorian ethics to the Britain of the 21st century. He brandishes the two-parent family like a truncheon.

The cuts in single-parent benefits made no sense fiscally, for they stemmed from moral disapproval. All talk nowadays is of self-reliance, no bad thing within limits, but not a word about a great simple truth.

Human beings are first and foremost social animals. We were social animals before the family emerged. Today we are more interdependent than ever before. The division of labour is now global rather than national.

Look around your house, everything in it is a product of social labour and commerce.

The solution to all major problems of our time, from the environment, to lighting in our streets, has to be a social solution. This is the nature of our species, and of modern times.

I'm a family man. It's nothing to boast about. It came naturally to me. I glory in my daughters and granddaughters. For others it may be different. What's good for me may not be your cup of tea. If we don't understand and respect such differences, then we've learned nothing. I also recognise that the offspring of higher animals are more vulnerable and dependent for survival on their parents than the offspring of less-developed forms of life. The human child is among the most vulnerable and dependent.

The integrated family, the product of certain historical circumstances, has been an effective unit for the nurturing of babies and children, both physically and psychologically.

It may survive changing circumstances because of the sustenance it provides. But this at all times has to be underpinned by social support. In Victorian times children died like flies in slums because of forces outwith the control of the family unit.

Self-reliance didn't work and couldn't work. No single family could control these forces. The only way was to control them socially. This became the principled battleground of twentieth-century politics. Social need versus private greed. Now there are no principles at stake. The parties and politicians are divided only by ambition. And what is left? The penis and the spin doctor, and the spin doctor is bent as well.

ARMS AND A MAN

18 FEBRUARY 1998

IN THE LONDON of the so-called swinging Sixties I got to know a young Iraqi. He was a postgraduate student and political refugee. His young wife was a lovely girl. They were a delightful couple: idealistic, sympathetic, empathetic supporters of good causes worldwide. They dreamed of a democratic Iraq instead of the cruel and corrupt despots who had ruled their country for many decades with the co-operation of foreign oil companies.

Then there was a coup. The rhetoric of the leaders, all army officers, was about democracy and how, given time, they would bring it about. But that is often the rhetoric of despots seeking to replace another group of despots. My young Arab friends, on hearing of the coup, decided to return to their homeland to try to help in the building of a democratic Iraq. I urged delay until the true nature of the new regime was clearer. Our young friends argued that of course the forces of dictatorship would be active but that was a reason for democrats to go to rally to the democratic banner, not to stay away.

259

The argument was persuasive but it was with a heavy heart I met them the evening before their return to Iraq, in a little Italian cafe in Bedford Street, just off the Strand. The Caff was owned and run by the boxer Henry Cooper's in-laws. I remember the girl telling me that once Iraq was free and democratic they would start a family. Within weeks the true nature of the new regime was shown to the world. Democratic dissent was crushed. The regime came to terms with the oil companies. It was business as usual.

Months later I heard what had happened to my young friend from Iraqis who had managed to escape back to Britain. He had been arrested along with his colleagues. As the most charismatic and influential, he was bound arm and foot. Laid on the street outside the prison. Others were forced to watch, including his wife, as a steamroller ran over his body, time and time again. Nobody knew what then happened to the girl. The regime that did this became a firm, if erratic, friend of the West.

I hate the Saddam regime. It is in lineal descent from those who murdered this young lad. I hate Middle Eastern despots, including the Saudi royal family and the other tawdry sheikdoms. If I may again paraphrase Lord Acton's famous and brilliantly accurate axiom—absolute power and absolute wealth have absolutely corrupted them in every conceivable way. They are intellectually and culturally stagnant. Morally, the pits. While exuding Islamic piety in public places back home, the sheiks and princelings are to be found whoring, drinking, and gambling in the crudest playpens of the Western world. Yet they are our allies and deemed honorary members of the free world. "Free world"—they couldn't spell the words.

Saddam's power derives from America and Britain. Without their support he wouldn't have lasted. They built him up both economically and militarily. They armed him to fight the ayatollahs in Iran, including giving him the means to make chemical and biological weapons. He used them against the Iranians and the Kurdish population of Iraq. Can you recall America and Britain

demanding that the Security Council of the United Nations au-
thorise the strongest military action against Iraq for this crime
against humanity? Neither can I.

America and Britain, we are now told, have supplied Saddam,
since the Gulf war, with the ingredients of chemical and biological
weapons, which brings us to another strand of the Middle East
equation. The region has been a source of fabulous wealth this
century through the modern world's over-dependence on oil. We
are talking here of wealth beyond the wildest dreams of men in
times previous. This wealth, its ownership and exploitation, creates tension, as men and nations manoeuvre for a piece of the
action. This tension leads to further tensions between competing
blocs. They need arms and armies to defend their wealth against
those who want some of it for themselves.

The whole of the Middle East has therefore become an absolute
bonanza for the arms trade. A trade that has become an added
source of enormous profits. Arms have been sold to anyone with
money to buy.

The *Daily Telegraph* this week published a unique letter from
General Sir Hugh Beach, Admiral Sir James Eberle, and General
Sir Michael Rose. I quote: "Apart from ethical considerations there
are compelling military reasons for tightly regulating arms sales to
regions of tension and instability." And: "During the Gulf War,
the Allied forces faced a heavily armed Iraqi military, supplied
through the export of arms and equipment from the European
Union in the 1980s." These three top military gentlemen concluded by calling for support for "a code of conduct that provides
effective controls over both arms manufacturers and governments".

Please note the "and governments". The 1980s was when the
credo "markets cannot be bucked" was brazenly proclaimed by
leaders of the western world. For close on 20 years now, in the
pages of the *Herald* and elsewhere, I've argued against this proposition. In effect it means that there is no moral dimension to
economic decision-making. No general good that could possibly

transcend market considerations. It's a formula that justifies the pimp, brothel-keeper, drug baron, arms salesman, unscrupulous tabloid owner and editor, in any and every circumstance. I accept the necessity of market forces, but to enthrone them as the gods of human relations is obscene.

This is what the West has done in the past 20 years. Mrs Thatcher, when Prime Minister, considered herself a glorified arms salesman. Remember her tour of the Middle East with son Mark in tow. She boasted she had secured arms sales worth billions for the United Kingdom. She now calls Saddam a monster. She helped create the monster. The acolytes of the arms trade tell us that it creates jobs. Such an attitude would justify Hitler's concentration camps on the grounds that they created job opportunities for gas fitters. As someone identified with the right to work, let me add that such a right has to be qualified by what you want to work at. As a pimp or drug dealer, you're not on.

Saddam, we are told, is ready to destroy the world with half a glass of anthrax. How is a rocket going to find and take out a half glass of anthrax without spilling some, and maybe killing only half the world's population. You don't need a presidential palace to conceal a glass. You could plank it under the floorboards of a room and kitchen in downtown Baghdad. Is Unscom, the United Nations commission for monitoring the destruction of Iraqi weapons of mass destruction, going to search them as well? The United Nations doesn't know whether it has already destroyed his stockpiles or not. How are rockets going to destroy biological weapons it isn't sure exist? What we do know is that Clinton is in trouble back home. And a war or a threat of war against a "monster" could come in handy. Though why a British Labour Government should tag along beats me.

AN OPEN LETTER TO
SEAN CONNERY

25 FEBRUARY 1998

DEAR Sean, you may not be, in theatrical terms, the greatest thespian ever, nor was Spencer Tracy, Cary Grant, or Humphrey Bogart. You are a film star, and a great one. You wouldn't be stereotyped, and broke free from the bonds of Bond. Your career has blossomed with a diversity of roles that brought you critical acclaim and an Oscar. Your Scottish accent shines through in every part—Russian submariner, Papal envoy, American marine corps hero. So what? John Gielgud speaks like a Surrey family solicitor whether playing Herod or a butler.

So that's no hassle. The movie is the great and most singular art form of the twentieth century and you, Sean, are one of its luminaries.

It does look as if New Labour doesn't fancy you. I'll let you into a secret, I don't fancy New Labour. They're just about the biggest conglomeration of male prostitutes since the collapse of the Roman Empire. I'm talking here of intellectual prostitution not the more

263

wholesome kind. They've sold the principles of the Labour movement for the gladhand of the men of money. You might have a few
bob Sean but compared to Rupert Murdoch the backside is hingin'
oot yer trousers, metaphorically speaking, of course. New Labour
is not primarily interested in getting cash from them, though they're
getting plenty. They want the support of their newspapers, the
clout that comes from such wealth, used on behalf of New Labour.
They've got it, but at a terrible price.

Like Faust, New Labour sold its soul to the devil. We even
know the when and the where of the transaction. It took place on
an Australian offshore island about a year before the General
Election. Tony Blair met Rupert Murdoch's executives. A deal was
done. The *Sun* became a fervent supporter of New Labour in the
run-up to the General Election. What did New Labour promise
in return? Put it this way. New Labour now favours predatory
pricing as practised by the Murdoch empire. The aim of such an
exercise is to put rival newspapers out of business and consolidate
Murdoch's near-monopoly in the market. New Labour favours
altering the law to allow greater cross-ownership of newspapers
and television. As things stand Murdoch owns 40% of the British
press in terms of readers, and Sky satellite television. Further
growth in organic terms is stymied by law. New Labour promised
Murdoch it would amend the law to his advantage. Labour was
founded to end the gross concentration of wealth and power in a
few hands. Instead New Labour has become the handmaiden of
the Murdochs.

New Labour is now the most right-wing Government in West-
ern Europe. Kohl's Germany is a bastion of social democracy
compared to Blair's Britain. British Ministers roam the European
Union preaching that all other governments should follow Brit-
ain's example and deregulate markets; putting the peoples of
Europe at the mercy of blind market forces. This is Thatcherism.
The victims of this philosophy are to be seen in your beloved
Edinburgh. In the vast housing schemes there are youngsters with

no jobs, no future, no hope, looking for substances that might blur the cruel reality of their existence. The society that threw them on the scrap-heap blames them for being on the scrap-heap. New Labour tinkers about with a bit of window-dressing, palliatives, soundbites, but leaves untouched the source of the problem.

The leader of the Tories at the Palace of Westminster, Hague the younger, is pushed to find a reason to vote against the Government. He niggles and then says, as this policy is essentially our policy, we'll vote with the Government. The real opposition in the lobbies comes from a group of disenchanted Labour back-benchers, Alex Salmond and his group, and sometimes the Lib-Dems.

Sean, to be blackballed by New Labour is no badge of honour. I know some of the scoundrels they've 'honoured' in the past. You wouldn't be seen dead in their company. Anyway, the gongs on offer resonate with the mores of feudal times. Being Sir Sean would add nothing to your lustre.

As Tennyson wrote: "A simple maiden in her flower, Is worth a hundred coats-of-arms." Our own Robert Burns put it this way: "A prince can mak a belted knight, A marquis, duke an' a' that; But an honest man's aboon his might, Guid faith he maunna fa' that! For a' that an' a' that, Their dignities, an' a' that, The pith o' sense and pride o' worth, Are higher rank that a' that."

Some years ago a group of Scots got together to organise Scottish honours in the form of a medal made of Scottish gold and silver. I was the recipient of the first and last gold medal. They couldn't afford to continue the tradition. I cherish that medal more than any bauble of the British Establishment. My fond dream is that a Scottish parliament will have its own honours bereft of feudal trappings. Who knows, Sean, you might get one of those. Something to be really proud of.

The bad-mouthing you're getting is also par for the course. New Labour is a nasty lot. Its spin doctors are feeding all sort of malignant stories to the press to blacken the names of dissidents and rivals within the party. The Lord Provost of Glasgow is being hounded from office, accused of cronyism by a Prime Minister who appointed a crony of his, the man with the penchant for interior decoration at our expense, as Lord Chancellor. As you know, Hollywood is a cesspit of backstabbing. New Labour makes it look like a kindergarten.

Come back to Scotland, Sean. These are exciting times. The fate of Scotland is in the balance. New Labour is trying to take over the Scottish Labour Party, in fact it more or less has, hell-bent on stacking Scotland's parliament with Blairites. They won't succeed. The true voice of Scottish Labour will be heard, whatever it takes. Re-alignment in Scottish politics is long overdue. Your own party is programmatically social democratic. This places it substantially to the left of New Labour. It will do well in the elections but will not be able to form a government on its own. The Lib-Dems will suffer unless they break from the apron strings of New Labour. Things are in a state of flux and there's everything to play for.

Sean, we had two mutual friends. Alec Kitson drove the Co-operative milk cart through the streets of Corstorphine. You were his delivery boy. Alec became one of Scotland's most outstanding trade union leaders. He died last year. I gave the oration at his funeral. You were filming on location but sent a warm message that was read to the congregation by the Lord Provost of Edinburgh. The other friend was Iain Stewart. A Tory grandee in the Harold Macmillan-Rab Butler tradition. A supporter of the welfare state. He helped me with contacts during the fight to save ship-building on the Upper Clyde. On other things we agreed to disagree, which is part of the give and take of life. Iain helped you set up a Scottish Educational Trust to help talented Scottish youngsters in need. This was funded by your salary from one of the Bond movies.

We can have a Scotland, Sean, where no youngster is in need because our nation will cater for the needs of all our people. We have the brains, the talents, the creative imagination, the technology, to do so. All we need is the political will. All the best, Jimmy.

RETURN OF THE
URBAN SPACEMAN

4 MARCH 1998

LAST week a Minister of the Crown outlined a change of government policy concerning village schools. The gist was that any
proposal by a local authority to close such a school had to be
referred to central government, which would rule against unless
exceptional arguments were adduced to justify closure. "Fair
enough", and other sounds of agreement came from my recum-
bent form. Village schools, I presume, are a very important part of
village community life. I presume this because local schools are a
very important part of community life in Govan, Easterhouse,
Craigmillar, and every urban, working-class area of Scotland.

Glasgow and all our cities and towns are actually an accumulation of large and small villages. Disparate village communities are
the vital cultural segments that constitute the overall city/town
persona. Yet community schools are being closed in towns and
cities. Closures driven by insufficient government funding. The
Minister said nothing about these closures. Had it something to do

with the Countryside March on London? Yes. The Government is in retreat from the green wellies and their tumbrils.

. It's doing U-turns and somersaults ten to the dozen. So the wee foxes will continue to be thrown to the hounds and torn to pieces. Any day now we'll be told to eat mad cows, on the bone, or on the hoof if the animal could stand up long enough to get it home. As for roaming in the gloaming, cut that out. Instead we'll be told to roam in the Dome. The landed gentry must be placated. They don't have many votes but they do have political clout, money, patronage, newspapers, and Channel 4 racing at their disposal. A thousand hardly visible threads inextricably link the landed gentry with the English Establishment.

I'm a product of an asphalt jungle who loves the countryside and I ain't alone. The green belt is more important for us than for rural dwellers. Green belts are the lungs of our towns. Take them away and we'll suffocate, more or less. That's why I'm against any further encroachment. It isn't, in other words, a country versus town issue.

I'm for helping the working farmer. They might in the past have reaped it in and showed scant concern for other sections of Scottish society who were fighting for their livelihoods, but today working farmers are suffering. A lot might go out of business. A balanced economy needs a thriving agriculture. I would like to see it based on organic methods of farming and believe there is a growing market for such produce.

What is certainly the concern of all Scots is the fate of our magnificent wilderness, overwhelmingly located in the Highlands and Islands. My grandfather was a Highlander. The Highlands and Islands belong to me and to every Scot. The problems of these areas cannot be solved until we tackle the festering sore of land ownership. The vast estates are a feudal anachronism. Large parcels of Highland glens and hills are sold off to anyone with money, like selling margarine in a supermarket.

Did you see any placards on the Countryside March calling for action against absentee landlords in the Highlands? I didn't. Yet the ownership of land in the Scottish Highlands is certainly a countryside issue. Were there crofters on the march? Maybe, but they were swamped to extinction by the fox-hunting brigade. The countryside is not inhabited by a homogenous populace of progressive-thinking people, nor are the towns. But there are neanderthal reactionaries entombed in the shires that beggar description. They were pulling the strings on Sunday.

More than anything else I'm concerned at the Government's capitulation to these rural reactionaries even before a horn was blown, just as they capitulated to urban high finance before the count was finished at the General Election. Electoral opportunism overrides everything else in the calculations of New Labour's leadership. The Government seems incapable of taking a moral stand on anything. An ethical foreign policy! One of Britain's giant companies that benefits from government contracts has appointed the discredited former Tory Minister Jonathan Aitken as an arms salesman in Arabia.

Is this New Britain's ethical contribution to peace-making in the Middle East? We've heard no criticism of this from government circles, but we have heard of an increase on prescription charges. We've heard of Chris Patten's book vetoed by Rupert Murdoch because it was critical of gross violations of civil rights in China. Murdoch didn't want to upset China's leaders, lest they damage his business interests in that country. New Labour has said nothing. Murdoch is an ally of Blair. Hence his silence.

The legitimate concession about proposed closures of village schools should be applied to proposed closures of urban schools. Have the decisions to close been taken on fiscal grounds irrespective of social and community consequences? That would be a disgrace. Stable communities are the bases of stable societies. The breakdown of urban communities, I'm sure, is a root cause of many of the social problems that bedevil the life of Western societies.

269

The Government displays scant respect for urban people because it reckons their votes are safe. The working class is perceived as voting fodder. The punter has become the victim of his or her loyalty to Labour. But we are not dealing now with Labour but New Labour, which is a creation orientated to Middle England. Loyalty is double-edged. You only owe loyalty to those who are loyal to you.

Why not an urban march on London? There's a thought. Instead of small scattered protests, bring them all together in cohesive unity embodied in a charter of demands on jobs, welfare, schools, pensions, urban squalor, public transport, recreation, and leisure, etc. Don't ask but demand that they listen to us. There is no virtue in an overdose of patience when confronted with mounting injustices. Now, who would lead or organise the urban march is a problem. Labour Party branches, who would be up in arms against a Tory Government doing the same things as this lot, are muted. Trade unions have been told not to rock the boat or promised legislation that would help them a little will not be enacted. In other words, the Labour movement has been severely constrained or even emasculated. It lies dormant and supine. A sleeping giant.

For how long? That depends. This weekend in Perth the Scottish Labour Party conference will take place. If there is no fight back, no challenge to increased prescription charges, no questioning of neo-Thatcherite economic policies, a bland acceptance of a proposal that takes away the basic democratic right of branches to select their candidates for the Scottish parliament, then I suggest the game's up. The Blairites will be in control, change from within will be impossible because the democracy of the party, from the bottom up, will have been replaced by centrist power from the top down. The Labour movement exists independently of the Labour Party, it founded the Labour Party. New Labour cannot and does not serve the cause of labour. The parting of the ways increasingly seems inevitable.

THE DILETTANTE
AND PARTY DEMOCRACY

11 MARCH 1998

ABOUT three months before the General Election I had decided to leave Blair's Labour Party, having become convinced that the man and those around him were essentially Thatcherites. His ideological commitment to her concept of economics became clearer as he tried to explain his position.

She was for a deregulated market, which is simply another name for the brand of nineteenth-century laissez faire capitalism that more or less dominated the world until the start of the Second World War. It created vast wealth and mass poverty. The poor lived in wretched ghettos, often demoralised, sometimes desperate. Some sought escape from the hopelessness of their lives in cheap booze. Laissez faire capitalism created cyclical booms, catastrophic slumps, and two horrific world wars. It was an unmitigated disaster.

The human toll was ghastly. My parents lost three daughters. The oldest was 18 months. We lived in the disease-ridden tenements of the Gorbals when Britain was the richest country on earth. The very young died like flies. Those who survived were often physically marked for life in the form of rickets, stunted growth, etc. These cruel conditions were compounded by the massive slump of the 1930s. Life was hell. Relief came through another horror—the Second World War. My father could find no work in the Thirties until war was declared, and then the men of the slums were needed to fight for Britain and work for the war effort.

I have my sisters' death certificates. They died, so it says, from various diseases of the lungs and chest. I don't believe it. In the space reserved for "cause of death" should be written "Laissez faire capitalism". It was and is a cruel and evil system. It is no way for human beings to live. It contaminates even the very wealthy it spawns. Marx said it left "no other nexus between man and man than callous cash payment". He was at least right about that. The Scottish Labour movement was foremost in the fight against this evil system.

My family moved to a council house in Govan. It had two bedrooms, a living room, kitchen, and inside toilet. I remember the bare floors, furnishings that were minimal, but, compared with where we had lived, it was a paradise. The slum clearance plan had been put in place by John Wheatley, Minister of Housing in the 1924 Labour Government. Our abode was called a Wheatley House. Is it any wonder that I love the Labour movement?

In the Labour movement we had socialists, left-wing social democrats, social democrats, right-wing social democrats, all legitimate elements that could rightfully encamp under Labour's banner. We argued like hell, but within certain parameters. We were all against laissez faire capitalism. We hated the beast. We never in our wildest dreams envisaged a Labour Party leader that would one day actually embrace the bloody beast. A beast that given the chance, will devour us again.

The 1945 General Election was a turning point in British history.

I was a schoolboy at the time and remember the joy and tears of happiness in our home and among all the neighbours as the election results came through and Labour had won. The two words I heard most were: "Never again." And I don't think they were talking specifically of the war, but of unemployment, bad housing, under-nourishment, depressions, impoverishment, the means test, the indignities that all this entailed.

The 1945-51 Labour Government delivered a welfare state that brought a bottom-line security to everyone, from the cradle to the grave. Those who haven't experienced it can't imagine the utter destructiveness of lifelong insecurity on the human psyche. Men and women lived their entire lives one pay packet from penury. All that changed in 1945. To be fair, it has to be said that Tories like Harold Macmillan, Rab Butler, and Ian Macleod subscribed to that post-war consensus.

This consensus governed Britain from 1945 till 1979. Things were by no means perfect, but for the ordinary people these were the glory years in the recorded history of the UK. Killer diseases rampaging through communities were wiped out, and not just by new medicines but from vastly improved social conditions. Then in 1979 a zealous dogmatist of the hard right became Prime Minister. Her idea of progress was to mount a white charger and gallop back to the last century. The welfare state was referred to contemptuously as the nanny state.

She claimed it was no responsibility of government to create jobs. Markets were deregulated. Public assets sold off at giveaway prices. Taxes on the rich were reduced to the lowest in Europe. Public spending became a dirty word. The health service began to fall apart. The welfare state was under attack. There was mass unemployment. A new chronic poor emerged that was to become known as the underclass. They lived in ghettos. They are dying much younger than the rest of us. The infant mortality rate is higher in the ghettos. Many are demoralised, some seek escape in drugs. Déjà vu.

Blair accepted Thatcherite economics. That means accepting Thatcherite social policies. Economic priorities determine social priorities. Blair did his deal with Rupert Murdoch. As his agenda emerged it was seen to be indistinguishable from Thatcherism in its fundamental handling of the economy. And that tells you everything you need to know about a potential government. I've known Harold Wilson, James Callaghan, Michael Foot, Neil Kinnock, and John Smith. That means every Labour leader over the past 35 years. All loved the Labour movement. Blair doesn't. He has no feel for it. No background in it. To me he's like a political dilettante. His obvious locus in politics was with the Tories. Cherie probably guided him towards Labour. I wish she hadn't.

These were my feelings months before the election as any reading of this column will testify. I didn't want to be associated in any way with a government I was convinced would betray the cause of labour and in the process do great damage to the wider Labour movement. I had urged others who shared my fears to speak out. They wouldn't. And gave me the usual crap about not wanting to rock the boat. I was convinced that the Tories couldn't win. People all over Britain were at last rejecting the cruelties and crudities of Thatcherism. The election was lost by the Tories, not won by New Labour, as any objective analysis of the result will show. And, anyway, the pursuit of power unrelated with what you want to do with it is completely unacceptable in a democracy. I was going to pack it in but was persuaded by colleagues to wait until after the election when a fight to curtail Blair might start.

I've waited and my worst fears have been confirmed. The Blairites have destroyed Labour Party democracy. North of the Border comrades scurrying for seats in a Scottish parliament have kept their noses clean. It is totally squalid, and has nothing to do with modernisation. It is an unholy mixture of reactionary and Tammany Hall politics. The last straw for me was New Labour's Scottish Conference in Perth. New Labour, it seems to me, is no place for a socialist or social democrat.

DEALING WITH DISSENT

25 MARCH 1998

"STALIN needed show trials before sending his erstwhile comrades into outer darkness. Blair sends his with the suggestion that he might get round sometime to proving them guilty. This high-and-mighty disregard for the presumption of innocence until guilt is proven was always bound to fall foul of the law."

The above words appeared in my column on Wednesday, December 3, 1997. Months earlier I had written in the *Herald* that Labour lawyers in London had told me that New Labour would be in serious legal trouble if it proceeded against Glasgow councillors on the grounds already defined. The charges simply wouldn't stand up in a court of law. I knew it. You knew it. And New Labour didn't?

It did. The party was told months ago. Why didn't it act then? It meant admitting it was wrong and New Labour's arrogance makes that hard to thole. Things came to a head, as they were bound to do, when Glasgow's Lord Provost and Deputy Lord Provost took legal action against moves to expel them. The court did as it was bound to do and found for Pat Lally and James Mosson. Instead of accepting this with a little grace, New Labour intends to try to "get" Lally and Mosson by other means.

This will be compounding stupidity with venom. That our/my diktat must prevail whatever the merits of the argument, is the twisted logic of autocracy, not social democracy. Those in the Glasgow City Council Labour Group who thought that, as Lally was almost down and out, now was the time to put the boot in and pay back old scores, are themselves being damned. There are no profound discernible matters of political principle between them and Lally that I've heard of so it's safe to conclude that it's all about personalities and the scramble for office.

Meanwhile, the citizens of Glasgow under a Labour Government will pay higher council taxes for fewer services, just as we did under the Tories. Why aren't they arguing with the same fervour about that? Instead they accuse Lally of cronyism. Scottish local government is full of cronyism but it's tuppence ha'penny stuff compared to what's going on in Westminster. Lord Irvine, he of wallpapering fame, is Lord Chancellor not because he's the legal brain of Britain or has great political experience. Oh no, he's the Prime Minister's pal and ex-workmate. If that isn't cronyism the word is meaningless.

When I complained about this I was told: "Of course the Prime Minister surrounds himself with like-minded people. All Prime Ministers have done this." That doesn't make it right. He could be surrounding himself with yes-men but the healthy exercise of power requires people around who will not hesitate to tell you when they think you're wrong or communicate truths to you that are unpalatable. It's called collective leadership and responsibility. The truth is that the present Prime Minister acts like a president in a non-presidential system that therefore has no checks on his presidential powers. In this, as in so many other things, he follows the example of Thatcher, though she attended Parliament more often than Blair does.

Such a circumstance is a grave constitutional threat to the fundamental principles of British parliamentary democracy. In our system a de facto president can become a dictator for there's nothing to stop him. There is no separation of executive and legislative assemblies as in America. Only MPs can stop a Prime Minister who would be president, and this one has 400 in his hip pocket. About half of them are in government, from parliamentary private secretaries up to the Lord Chancellor. Most of those remaining would like to be in government and all the patronage is in the hands of the Prime Minister. We are in danger, as we were under Thatcher, of living under an elective dictatorship.

In the past such a matter might have been discussed at a meeting of Labour's National Executive, but now the NEC is an appendage of the Prime Minister's private office. It could have come up at Labour's UK conference but its powers, too, have been truncated and now it is to be a rally where the leadership tells delegates what's what. Next year's Scottish Labour Conference will be a policy forum; its terms of reference so ambiguous as to render it powerless. Who, then, will determine Labour's policy for the Scottish parliament? The leadership in London, i.e. the Prime Minister and his advisers.

The stramash in Scottish local government since the election stems from London. Scotland was always likely to be a thorn in the side of Blairism that had to be excised. New Labour had made great play of Tory sleaze, even when it was media sleaze, as in the case of David Mellor. Given allegations of Labour sleaze, Blair's conditioned reflex was to condemn without finding out if there was any substance in the allegations. He was more concerned by appearances than substance. Innocent people were thus put through hell for New Labour's obsession with soundbites and all the malarky of murky spin doctors.

Labour's opponents in Scotland grabbed the wrong end of the stick. The real sleaze was in London. There we were seeing the corruption of power and political principle. With almost every day that passes there is more proof of this. According to the Italian newspaper *La Stampa*, Tony Blair, in a telephone conversation last Wednesday, asked Romano Prodi, the Italian Prime Minister, to support Rupert Murdoch's bid for the Berlusconi media empire. A spokesman from 10 Downing Street said: ". . . he [Blair] would have no difficulty at all speaking Prime Minister to Prime Minister in seeking to defend and promote the interests of British companies."

To call Rupert Murdoch's empire British is stretching the English language to breaking-point. An Australian who took American citizenship to enable him to add American television and film companies to his media empire owes fealty to no country. He is czar of his own empire. His global power is an affront to democracy. Any self-respecting Labour Prime Minister would want to curb rather than enhance Murdoch's power. But Blair is Murdoch's man. He sold his soul not for a mess of potage but for the support of the *Sun*. Bad deal, but then maybe his soul wasn't worth much.

DO AS I SAY, NOT AS I DO

8 APRIL 1998

IN OCTOBER 1997 Professor Steve Bruce of Aberdeen University was automatically expelled from the Labour Party because he voted Liberal Democrat in the General Election to help ensure the defeat of the Tory candidate in his home constituency of Gordon, which Labour couldn't possibly have won. I thought it a bit heavy-handed and was told he had to be expelled under explicit party rules; that if party members didn't vote Labour why should non-party members? Once a decision was taken to adopt a Labour candidate all members in the constituency, irrespective of previous opinions, had to support his or her candidature. Put like that, you had to agree, but where does that leave us now?

In last Friday's *Herald*, under the heading, "Labour campaign director voted SNP" Catherine MacLeod wrote: "Tony Blair has agreed to appoint a man who voted SNP at the last General Election to a key campaign role in the forthcoming elections for a Scottish Parliament." No elected constitutional body of the Scottish Labour Party was informed, let alone consulted, about this appointment. It would seem the principle of devolution doesn't apply within New Labour. Blair's new man in Scotland is Paul McKinney. He was a member of the Labour Party in Govan at the General Election. He acknowledges that he voted SNP in that election.

Under the same party rules that led to Professor Bruce's automatic expulsion, McKinney should no longer be a member of the Labour Party. Yet here he is elevated to arguably the highest post in the party north of the Border. A Labour Party spokesman told the *Herald* that part of McKinney's job will be to demonstrate "the opportunist, economic illiteracy of the SNP", and he will do so as someone who voted for this "opportunist, economic illiteracy" at an election less than 12 months ago. Given the job description the man has absolutely no credibility for the job. It's a hoot.

It gets worse. Tony Blair knew of Mr McKinney's voting record before he was offered the job. Does this mean that Blair can break the rules of the party to save a man who should have been expelled under membership conditions, rule 2A.4(b)? Yes. Blair is New Labour incarnate. The rules, and constitution, and everything else, are what he decrees. His high priests such as Mandelson act as upholders of his holy grail. McKinney is twice blessed. He is a pal of Mandy's and sometimes kips at his place when in London. So, in fact, the rules don't apply to him as long as he keeps on-message and doesn't cross the high priests.

But then things start to get really dirty. A Downing Street spokesman, which usually means Alistair Campbell, told the *Herald*: "Paul is now a firm supporter of the Labour Party. That he voted SNP as a protest against Sarwar will not be an obstacle." What exactly does that mean? That it's all right for Labour Party members to vote against Sarwar when he stands as a Labour candidate? Why? Up to the General Election the only fact indisputably known was that the first ballot to select Labour's candidate in Govan was comprehensively and grotesquely rigged to ensure that Sarwar lost.

The second ballot was conducted by the NEC of the Labour Party and was transparently not rigged. Sarwar won handsomely. Why then should any Labour Party member have voted against him at the polls? Members of the Labour Party in Govan are entitled to know. The electors in Govan are entitled to know. The people of Scotland have a right to know.

This man has been handed a very important job in Scottish politics. We are entitled to scrutinise his credentials for the job. We have a secret ballot in this country. But Mr McKinney's vote at the last election is now a public issue because he made it so. Blair's private office has made it so. Where does this leave Sarwar?

The leader of his party has endorsed for a key party post a man who in contravention of the party rules voted against him at the General Election, and proudly proclaims the deed. The punters in Govan and in other constituencies in Scotland are entitled to ask if he and Blair know things about Sarwar that we don't know.

The serious allegations against Sarwar came only days after the election. He was accused of corruption, electoral fraud, and goodness knows what. Having investigated previous allegations against him that were proven to be false—that's what brought me into the case in the first instance—I presumed his innocence until or unless his guilt was proven. Blair took the opposite view. He presumed his guilt until his innocence was proven. That was nearly a year ago and neither a civil nor criminal case has been brought to court.

If Sarwar is guilty of fraud and corruption then let him be driven from public life. If he is innocent, then some people have their sins to answer for. The only alternative to his guilt is that he was stitched up, and if this is the case the culprits will be found in the ranks of New Labour. I'm convinced New Labour has a vested interest in postponing a conclusion, or want to find Sarwar guilty of something, anything. The prestige of the leader is all that matters. Yet again this resonance of Stalinism.

Jack McConnell is resigning as Blair's man in Scotland to become chief executive of a new lobbying organisation for the Scottish

Parliament. One day leader of New Labour in Scotland, next day a boss of political lobbyists in Scotland. McConnell has already told us that he wants to stand for the new Scottish Parliament. All his contacts in setting up this lobbying organisation for the Parliament of which he hopes to be a member will of course, be completely erased from his mind if he becomes an MSP. Is this not a mental or psychological impossibility? I believe that this career structure he envisages is in violation of the spirit, if not the letter, of the Nolan Report.

In the meantime, is the Scottish Labour Party or the Govan Labour Party going to initiate disciplinary procedures to expel Comrade McKinney?

THE LEADERS WHO HAVE
LOST THE WILL TO FIGHT

13 MAY 1998

SINCE the General Election New Labour has treated trade unions with contempt. Honeyed words for the Confederation of British Industry, the Institute of Directors, and the poisoned chalice for the TUC. The Bernie Ecclestones and Lord Symons of this world were ushered in the front door of 10 Downing Street while union representatives were smuggled in the back door and told "no favours", shorthand for "the jackboot pressing on your throat will not be lifted". Or, "the laws passed by the previous administration which made British unions the least free in the Western world will remain in place". Who says New Labour doesn't keep its promises?

The real power of trade unionism rests on workplace organisation. Without that, nothing else matters. Without that, trade unions are hollow bureaucratic superstructures that will slowly sink into the sands. The unions needed Labour to deliver (God forgive me for this cliché) a level playing field, which means the legal right to organise in the workplace. To organise the unorganised is always a process, often a very slow process. It never happens overnight. To impose a 40% threshold of support as a starter is to erect a barrier for trade unions that is virtually insurmountable. It is a formula for continued non-unionism.

This is what the Government is offering the unions. There was no threshold mentioned in the General Election manifesto, but months ago it was known that Blair wanted 40%. The strategy was to get the TUC to suggest 30%. Meanwhile, Millbank Tower was encouraging the CBI to press for 50%. Blair would then split the difference. This he has done. The trade unions are knackered yet again. Why did the TUC approach these negotiations volunteering concessions? It was stupid.

Even the rawest shop steward knows that. And one presumes the General Council of the TUC isn't stupid.

I think too many trade union leaders have lost the will to fight. Some never had it and assumed positions of power through union in-fighting rather than fighting for the members.

In the beginning trade unions were illegal. Leaders fought to organise workers and were hounded for doing so. They were hanged, jailed, deported to places like Botany Bay. They didn't beg for rights but demanded them. Their struggles and sacrifices helped the cause of political reform that gave workers a legal right to organise. This was an important part of the democratic revolution in this country. The right of workers to organise is a fundamental democratic principle. The right of organised workers to withdraw their labour is a fundamental democratic principle. There were no strikes in Nazi Germany, Fascist Spain, Stalin's Russia, or Zalazar's Portugal. Total industrial tranquillity is possible only in a totalitarian state. As is total political tranquillity. Such tranquillity is really servility. Put in context, the occasional nuisances of a free society can be most alluring.

There were great difficulties for trade unions during the Thatcher years. They were un-free. What was not forgivable was the way they threw in the towel. They had mass memberships, money, and organisation. They could have campaigned above and beyond party politics, putting the rights of workers in a civil libertarian context. Instead, they put all their eggs in the Labour basket.

Everything will be okay when there is a Labour Government. Even when there was a Labour Party that might undo the damage of the Tories this was always a feeble response. The unions had to re-assert their rights irrespective of governments. This they failed to do. Then when Blair was elected leader of the Labour Party the whole thing fell apart. He made it clear that his strategy was to continue with the main tenets of Thatcherism and all that meant for trade unionism.

Even then the TUC pandered to, instead of pressurising, the Blairite leadership.

They were told not to rock the boat before the election and therefore didn't punch their weight at Labour conferences. After the election they were told to stay on message or else certain manifesto promises deemed to benefit the unions would not be honoured. Instead of fighting back they once again kowtowed. Now they've been humiliated. Whatever else is in the package, the 40% precondition is intolerable and has to be fought. Trade unionists are not social workers. Trade unions exist to maximise the wages and salaries of their members, to obtain the best possible working conditions, and safety at work. They also want to negotiate what were once called fringe benefits.

The function of company boards and managements is to maximise profits and dividends for shareholders. This function is considered legitimate and even commendable by this Government and the last one. On the other hand, any wage increase for workers beyond something like 3% is considered regrettable and condemned as inflationary.

THE ROAD TO HELL

20 MAY 1998

AS EVENTS unfold in Indonesia, the Western World tut-tuts and suggests it's time for Suharto to go. Where he should go isn't clear. Somewhere. Anywhere. Out the road. It's all his fault. Their global system that put him in power is blameless. The American CIA organised the military coup that brought him to power. Britain took over and gave him the arms he needed to crush all opposition. The rotted bodies of the victims polluted the rivers. The tanks and water-cannon used in recent days on the streets of Jakarta were British-made. The aircraft he used to strafe the native people of Timor were British-made. In a very real sense Suharto was American and British-made. He's a man they could do business with, and did. Foreign corporations took over and dominated the economy. Before doing so they would ask, what about the trade unions? Don't worry, Suharto will take care of them. What about laws and regulations that might hinder us making a billion bucks or so? Suharto will sort them out as well. It was all a kind of Locate in Indonesia project.

Now the Indonesian economy has gone down the plug-hole. There is a political as well as an economic crisis. Suharto is an embarrassment, not because he's a bloodthirsty swine, he always has been. He's an embarrassment because he can no longer contain his people. A dictator who can't dictate is a dead loss. He has to go to make way for someone who can. Though the Indonesian people might have something to say about that. The clincher came when the poor took to the streets. Parading students throwing stones is one thing, but the poor from the lower depths had a different agenda. They marched on the shopping malls and plundered them. They smashed any symbol of a regime that put plenty on display and then told them: hands off. These goodies are not for you. As they and their families starved in the ghettos, the city teemed with food and riches. Theirs was not the hunger of drought and natural disaster. It was man-made. They starved in the midst of plenty.

Indonesia today embodies the failure of the global economy in the Third World. In Asia, Africa, and Latin America there is social and ecological disintegration. Economic output has soared since the 1950s. Far outstripping population growth. Yet millions more are starving. Still the cry goes out, economic growth is the way forward. I heard this when I was a teenager. Don't fight for a redistribution of the cake. Let's work together to make a bigger cake and all our shares will be bigger. It was to be easy. A piece of cake. We've got a bigger cake. A much bigger cake. The poor are just as poor, and there are more of them. There are more billionaires, too.

We've had almost 50 years of economic growth in Western Europe and North America, and we have more poverty, higher unemployment, greater inequality, crime has escalated, and our living environment has been degraded. Many people are stressed out. Depression is widespread. Fear of the future is greater today than I've ever known it. Drugs are widely taken. Our prisons are full. More prisons are being built. A holiday camp for an earlier generation of British workers is being turned into a prison for the current generation. Kids are subject to curfew. Some vigilante groups are on the prowl. We can't swim in our offshore polluted waters. It might not even be safe to sit on the beaches. Our beef is suspect. Blood from British donors is not sent abroad because it may be contaminated. Methinks the concept of continuous economic growth as the solution to all the manifest problems of society has been overstated.

But, the argument goes, we have no say in the matter. The global market is unstoppable so we will just have to lie down and take what's coming to us. What an inspiring message. A real confidence booster. Surrender as the best line of defence. To some extent there's been a global market for at least 100 years. In recent years technology, as in all things, has speeded up the process. I have no quarrel with the global market, but what they're really saying is that the global market will be controlled by global corporations. These corporations will be controlled by a small unaccountable elite whose sole aim will be short-term financial gain. Communities will die by their say so. They will exploit natural resources for short-term gains. Democracy will die through disuse as real power on this planet will be in the hands of this unelected elite.

The plight of human beings will not feature in the criteria of their decision-making. They will colonise the world's resources. They have more or less done this already. They are robber barons on the grand scale. That such power over the lives of billions should be ceded to this tiny handful is nightmarish and an affront to humanity.

People should be at the centre of all mega-economic decisions or people will be diminished and miniaturised. Nations working together must regulate the global markets or the global corporations will take over the world. It's that stark. In this context the European Union is a godsend.

Europe acting as one is financially and politically strong. Its collective population exceeds that of the US. Europe can define the terms under which global corporations will be allowed to operate within Europe's boundaries. They must not be allowed to play off one European nation against another. Their adherence to a firm ecological policy should be a precondition of their involvement with Europe along with their committed respect for the labour and commercial laws of the Union. In other words, we have to regulate the global market as it affects us.

Here we have a problem. Tony Blair has embraced the global market without constraint or qualification. He is going round Europe urging nations to follow Britain's, i.e. Thatcher's, example, and deregulate markets in preparation for the global market. This would be good for Rupert Murdoch but a disaster for all the nations within the United Kingdom. It will be a surrender to the global market, and all that entails. People will have no say. Our democratic rights will erode. Inequalities will grow, alongside a deepening poverty. Frustrations will turn to anger. The dispossessed will forsake their ghettos and march. In a society racked with consumerism they will be demanding a piece of the action. Their political impotence will further enrage them.

Where will it all end? Who knows? People already feel that political parties have let them down. That governments have let them down. That God has let them down. Nobody will let them up. Fewer will go to the polling stations. Fewer to churches. Where are those pills? That fix? That bottle of cheap wine? And in the absence of leadership there is a blind rage. In East Germany alienated youth are turning to the Nazis. In America to screwball religions. It's the anguish of people who despair of the future. Money-centred social structures have no place for those at the bottom of the heap. They have no time for anyone except those at the top. You know where I stand. Markets not tempered by humanity are abominations. The global market untouched by human compassion will simply be a bigger abomination. Let me quote you something from a book called *When Corporations Rule the*

World by an American called David G Korten: "Even in the world's most affluent countries, high levels of unemployment, corporate downsizing, falling real wages, greater dependence on part-time and temporary jobs without benefits, and the weakening of unions are creating a growing sense of economic insecurity. The employed find themselves working longer hours and having less real income. Many among the young—especially of minority races— have little hope of ever finding jobs adequate to provide them with basic necessities, let alone financial security. The advanced degrees and technical skills of many of those who have seen their jobs disappear and their income and job security plummet mock the idea that unemployment can be eliminated simply by improving education and job training."

This is a precise pen picture of Blair's Britain. The prelude to the global corporations' takeover of the world. I'll support any political party that will challenge this strategy, for it is indeed the road to hell.

REALITY IN OUR LAND
OF CRIME AND PREJUDICE

27 MAY 1998

JONATHAN AITKEN, former Tory Cabinet Minister and upper-class flyman, claims he lied for his country. A claim that was emblazoned across the front page of the *Daily Telegraph*. I suppose Mata Hari could have claimed to have got "laid for my country". A "sacrifice" arguably more honourable than his. At the same time the BBC's *Panorama* about the two British nurses jailed in a Saudi prison was totally lacking in objectivity. Scenes were acted out by members of Equity who obviously learned their trade in the melo-dramatic school of silent movies. All the Saudis looked like a combination of Sir Jasper the bad squire and a Mafia hit man. This programme was for starters, the main meal was to be the seriali-sation of the nurses' stories by the Mirror Group and the *Daily Express*.

The usually wog-bashing *Sun*, New Labour's favoured and favourite tabloid, took the moral high ground, and espoused the fairness of the Saudi courts. After, it has to be recorded, offering a large sum of cash for Lucille McLauchlan's diaries. The offer came too late. The spoils had gone to the Mirror Group. The diaries, it should also be noted, were deliberately written for publication, at a price, on her release from prison. This presumption of release was interesting. The story from the very start was enmeshed in big money.

The two British nurses were charged and convicted of murdering an Australian nurse. All were white. Parry was sentenced to death which meant being beheaded in a public place. McLauchlan was sentenced to eight years and 500 lashes. The prospect of Parry having her head chopped off on television must have sent some businessmen and Government Ministers scurrying for a change of trousers. It could lead to mass protests against a Saudi regime that truly is neanderthal. Things could get out of hand. Relations could be severed. The oil-rich Saudis are our biggest market in the Middle East, particularly for arms and warplanes.

Under Saudi law the family of the victim can waive the right of execution on receipt of blood money. The brother of Yvonne Gilford accepted a sum well in excess of £500,000 to do precisely that. It was paid by British Aerospace, the biggest British arms company. The Saudis wanted no estrangement with a Britain that could always be relied upon to join with America in defending the Saudi regime whenever it was threatened. This was the purpose of the Prime Minister's visit of a few weeks ago that presaged the release of the two nurses. It was to tell King Fahd that it was business as before, as it was with Mrs Thatcher and John Major. Nothing had really changed.

I'm glad that Yvonne wasn't beheaded and Lucille wasn't lashed. Such punishments are barbaric. But the way their release was engineered was both shabby and mercenary, and the media aftermath has been similarly tainted. It is hypocrisy of a very high order indeed to condemn Islamic law for allowing the payment of blood money, if the condemnation comes from newspapers that pay blood money to those convicted of murder. In response to this criticism the papers involved tell us that the women are innocent. That may be so. But I don't know that, and neither do they. Why would the Saudis frame two British women whose conviction would be such an embarrassment to them? What was in it for the Saudis?

If judicial systems are to be condemned for the regularity of false convictions then the British judicial system stands condemned. For years now I've wondered if any guilty men were in British prisons. Year after year convictions have been quashed because of false confessions, fabricated evidence, dicey forensics, police violence, the planting of false evidence. I could fill this column with the names of those falsely convicted in British courts. Some died before they could be reprieved. There is evidence that in a few parts of Britain the CID harboured the biggest villains in town.

By no means is this the full picture. Most coppers in Britain are good guys, but that doesn't make the police force perfect. The judiciary in this country is, to a considerable extent, independent. But no-one can be totally abstracted from their upbringing and social circumstances even when they sit in impartial judgment. A thousand little unconscious threads from one's own direct social experiences are woven into one's persona. Our judges, with very few exceptions, come from a very narrow social base. Has there ever been, will there ever be, a High Court judge from Easterhouse? Judges have had a tendency to accept what the police say as opposed to what the accused says. I've never kicked anyone in the head. To do so requires the victim to be on the ground. I was taught in Govan that you don't kick a man when he's down. The lumpen thugs did and we rejoiced when they were sent to prison for years. Recently in Scotland young middle-class students in a public school kicked another young man to death and got four years each. I think they would have got much longer if they had come from Drumchapel.

In the Sixties I worked in London, near to Covent Garden, and about 50 yards from the prestigious Garrick Club. One early evening I saw this toff coming out the Garrick absolutely steam-boats. Two beat coppers grabbed him by the arms. Come on, sir, you've had one too many. Shall we get you a taxi home? This they duly did. Helped him into his seat. Wished him goodnight. I thought, aren't our coppers nice. The very next day, at almost the same place, I saw a market porter who had obviously been sampling the bevvy. He was blootered, though not as blootered as the toff the night before. The same two coppers came on the scene, but the benevolent tolerance of the night before was no longer there. The market porters of those times were very well-paid. He could easily have afforded a taxi. But he wasn't offered one. Instead he was huckled off to the police station. Maybe I'm only imagining things, but the thought persists—if the porter had only worn pinstriped trousers and a bowler, had spoken with a different accent, he might have gone home that night in a taxi. The point I'm getting at is this. To presume the innate superiority of our institutions over those of all other people's is presumptuous nonsense. Our law has many fine features, including democratic reforms brought about through mass struggles. Our very right to vote had to be fought for. Our institutions are tainted with residues of feudalism. Our tabloid press in particular is consumed with the awfulness of xenophobia. In England they are manically xenophobic. They invent stories. They make news rather than reporting what is really happening. They are in the business of manipulating minds to further a political agenda that benefits their owners. Press bosses are now the Tammany political bosses. To them deference is paid by prime ministers and presidents.

If what the Mirror and Express groups have generally said in the past week about the Saudi regime is true, and I think it is, then these two newspaper groups should be campaigning for sanctions against Saudi Arabia. That will be the day. There's too much dosh involved. And dosh is more important to them than democratic principles and civil rights.

CARRY ON CARPING

3 JUNE 1998

KENNETH WILLIAMS was a nasty little man. I've never felt it necessary to record this opinion, for his capacity to do real harm was limited by a personality that evoked only transient belly laughs. In recent weeks, however, there have been television appreciations of Williams as if his was a major thespian talent sadly unfulfilled. Last Monday on BBC2 someone said that Williams was always receiving scripts that were an insult to his intelligence. That's hard to visualise.

The *Carry On* films were his forte. I appreciate the bawdy but the best requires subtlety. The *Carry On* capers have none. No nuances. All balls, tits, and single entendres. They are naughty seaside postcards transposed for the silver screen. Williams contributed a braying laugh, flaring nostrils, a set of hyperbolic facial expressions, and a grotesque campness that must have reinforced the prejudices of all viewing homophobic nuts. Yet some people are talking as if he was some kind of unfulfilled English Walter Matthau!

I once met Kenneth Williams, in rather unusual circumstances. Michael Parkinson made mention of this meeting in the BBC programme mentioned above. It happened like this. Early one week, I got a phone call from Michael at the shipyard in Clydebank. He asked if I had seen his show on Saturday evening. I hadn't. He explained that Williams had been one of his guests and towards the end of the programme had made a scathing attack on trade unions. Michael described his comments as crap. This caused a bit of a stooshie.

Over the weekend Williams was demanding that he be given an entire *Parkinson* show to debate and defend his "crap". The BBC conceded but insisted that someone should defend trade unionism. Mike wanted me to do it. I was due to speak at a public meeting in Fairfield Hall, Croydon, on the Friday evening, with meetings all day Saturday and Sunday in London. Add a major network, the biggest viewing UK television programme that was being hyped up as a kind of shoot-out at the OK Corral, and it was becoming a very heavy weekend for me. I had sworn to doctors in Glasgow that I would take things easier. They were bound to hear of, if not see, the Parkie show, and I would get pelters on my return.

But Michael Parkinson was getting stick for his outburst, and by then I was a pal. He's one of the good guys. One of the finest professionals to grace British television. His dad was a Yorkshire miner who got the black dust and left his native roots to work in Morris Cowley, Oxford. Once at a BBC reception he told me that Michael had been a disappointment. When I asked why, he replied; if he had stuck to cricket he might have been No 3 for Yorkshire and England. Compared to that prospect, any other kind of success was failure. In the glitter and false glitz of the occasion the old man's down-to-earth values were like a breath of fresh air.

After the meetings on Saturday I was taken by car to the studios and allocated a dressing room where sandwiches and coffee were provided. Sleep was out the question. I've never mastered the art of sleeping in small doses. But was happy to settle for lying back, relaxing with eyes closed, trying to think without anxiety. I was refreshed and shaving when Michael knocked on the door. He was very anxious. The flak had obviously been more severe that I had thought. I started getting anxious for Michael.

I didn't know Kenneth Williams, he hadn't really impinged on my consciousness. He was right-wing in politics and hostile to trade unionism, that was clear. But I've liked people who disagreed with me and have disliked others who have agreed with me. Unanimity in itself has no virtue. There is, after all, something unanimous about death. On the other hand life and dissent are indivisible. Kenneth had first of all to explain his position. He had demanded the programme. I hadn't been involved in the previous shebang. Michael's role was to haud the jaikets. As Williams spoke I was shocked not at his views but at the intellectual superficiality of his arguments.

There was something else: his ignorance was compounded by arrogance. There were asides that were mean and carping. I decided to let him go on and on. Not to interrupt. Not to respond to his questions except in a few terse words. Let him rant on. Give him enough rope etc. My failure to respond was construed as weakness. His supporters in the studio audience clapped and mocked my refusal to elaborate in replies. I was listening to his case and would respond in due course, was my attitude. His rantings got wilder, his arguments weirder. He didn't like sick people or the mentally handicapped, he told us. He was exposed as a nasty little man, an intellectual pigmy, floundering in a hole he had dug for himself.

The studio audience, which the BBC ensured was 75% on his side because it believed that he was incapable of sustaining an intellectual argument for an hour, turned against him. One young mother of a mentally handicapped child gave him a roasting from the floor. At the end the audience were booing him. As the credits went up on the screen someone from his agency came on to the stage to get him off, muttering loudly, "this is the last chat show for you". Kenneth Williams was a bully. Cruel. Insensitive. And a 22-carat bampot. There are many such monsters in showbusiness.

I did a chat show series for Grampian. One of my guests was Roy Castle who had been a feed for Jimmy James whom I rated a comic genius. The act was a comic trio, with Roy and another feed. James played a drunk with an Anthony Eden hat and a cigarette that went from one end of his mouth to the other. As the three of them surrealistically conversed their heads would go in and out in imminent danger of a collision that never happened but added a frisson to the proceedings. After the programme Roy told me of his experience at Bernard Manning's club when he topped the bill. At the finale Manning came on stage, grabbed Roy by the arm and told the audience what his fee was. He then proceeded to count it out note by note into Roy's hand. Castle was a multi-talented, nice, vulnerable, gentle man. Why didn't you kick him in that man's tender spot, I asked, though it was actually phrased more indelicately.

He couldn't. It was not in his nature.

Hollywood director and anti-Semite Howard Hawks mercilessly bullied Lauren Bacall when she was a teenage newcomer to the big time. When I asked her why no-one had objected in a Jewish-owned studio, the reply implied that his movies made money, and that was all that mattered. The monsters are seldom exposed by showbusiness itself. In fact they're often honoured. Is this because they're too numerous, too powerful, or both?

There's no business like showbusiness, except modern politics. Politicians read speeches written by someone else. So do actors at the Royal Shakespeare. Spin doctors produce shows called party conferences, photo opportunities, press conferences. There are many people in showbusiness that are genuinely talented and dedicated. But the business encourages narcissists. Our political leaders are becoming increasingly Caesarean. Politics is beginning to look like a branch of showbiz—but without a leavening of talent.

HOW THE PEOPLE'S GAME
IS BEING HIJACKED

10 JUNE 1998

ONE of my earliest recollections is of being taken to a football match by my mother. There was no admission fee. No fences to keep you out. No dressing rooms or clubhouse. Just a marked-off pitch ringed by spectators, including many women like my mum, supporting their local team. One of the players for our team was a family friend called Martin. I think he fancied one of my sisters or she fancied him. Something like that. Martin was a good looking guy, built like a tank, and when he tackled his opponents, they seemed to fall over.

Why this should be was a matter of dispute between the women and the referee. At the start they were on first-name terms with the ref. As the game progressed this was dropped. "Hey, Thomson," they would roar, "that wis never a foul," as another opponent fell to a perfectly good tackle from Martin. Thomson would reply in kind. He gave as his considered opinion that the women might be better deployed washing the clatty stairs and closes up which he presumed they lived.

Dialogue was an ongoing phenomenon. When our boys clattered into an opponent it was clearly "a ferr shoulder charge". If the other side did the same it was a diabolical act of aggression. Despite everything, real skills were on display. Players who could take on men, jouk past them like sprites, and create scoring chances for their mates. I remember one called Sparra Hope (sparrow if you're from Edinburgh). Sparra went on to play for Clyde.

Later Dad took me to see the Juniors. Many of the players looked ancient, and still do, though I'm getting a bit ancient myself, but then I don't call myself a junior. I remember going to a game at Tinto Park, Benburb's home ground, with my pal. Standing beside us was a lady built like Hyacinth Bucket from the television sitcom. She proudly told us her son had just signed for the visitors. Despite her imposing physique she seemed a gentle, motherly sort. Halfway through the second half her son was tackled from behind. In fact he was kicked up the behind. I swear his feet left the ground before gravity got a grip of things and brought him down to earth with a resounding thud. The matronly lady was off like a cheetah in pursuit of prey. She surmounted the perimeter fence like a gazelle, ran to the culprit who could have been the model for the original drawing of Desperate Dan, swung her large handbag that must have been full of bricks, and smashed him in the moosh. He dropped as if poleaxed. The ref tried to intervene and she hit him a glancing blow that sent him birlin' like a peerie, before he crumpled in slow motion. Her son by this time had made a remarkable recovery and beseeched her to leave the field of play before she pruned the ranks any further. Apart from that he added: "Hiv ye no' gied me a big enough riddy?" The lady left the stadium with dignity.

Nobody stopped her. She still had the handbag. When the game resumed nobody tackled her son.

We lived near Ibrox Park. My mother let me go to the reserve games, but not to the big games. In Rangers' 2nd XI at that time was Willie Woodburn. The best centre-half I've ever seen. He was unique at the time. A ball-playing central defender. He had a problem. He thought it was against God's express wishes that Rangers should ever be beaten. When they were in any danger Willie became the Almighty's avenging sword. He handed out chastisement with such zeal the refs took a dim view. He was suspended *sine die*, a punishment that now seems unbelievable in its severity. In the last 20 minutes of any game the gates were opened to let people out and we could get in for nothing. Afterwards, when the crowd had dispersed, my pal and I would collect empty beer bottles and humph them down to a garage in Copeland Road that paid a penny for each bottle. During those 20 minutes I saw glimpses of great players. Tommy Walker. Billy Steel. Torry Gillick. When I started work at 14 I could pay my way in. I remember players such as Bobby Mitchell and Jimmy Mason of Third Lanark. Charlie Tully of Celtic. Jimmy Watson of Motherwell, whom nobody but me seems to remember.

I remember starting my engineering apprenticeship for it coincided with my first glimpse of the great Hibs forward line of Smith, Johnston, Reilly, Turnbull, and Ormond. At each stage of my life there is a footballing corollary.

The day I went to do my National Service was the day Hungary trounced England at Wembley. I watched it in a pub in Bedford. When I moved to London the Spurs team of Blanchflower, McKay, Greaves, etc, was coming to fruition. I saw the young George Best. The Brazilian and Dutch masters. The artistry of Pele, Maradona, Puskas, Cruyf, Di Stefano, and a host of others. I was back in Scotland to see Jock Stein's great Celtic team; for two years the best club team in Europe, and arguably the world.

My dad took me to Hampden to see the Victory International against the Auld Enemy shortly after the last war. I was just a kid. Scotland won 1-0. The sheer unalloyed joy as the final whistle blew was untainted by the sectarian divisions that so marred club games in Scotland. Henceforth my team was Scotland United. I went to Wembley. In so far as my budget allowed, I've supported Scotland on forays abroad. Yet this year I won't be in France with the Tartan Army.

The game is now so commercially hyped that the real fans are being squeezed out.

Incredible sums will be made. Fans are officially getting 8% of the tickets. Corporate entertainment 20%. God knows were the other 72% have gone. Clearly many have gone to ticket-tout organisations. Fans are thus forced to pay way over the top. The number of tickets involved in this scam is so large that it could only happen with the connivance of the organisers.

Professional football had to become more businesslike. Stadiums had to be developed, and not just for safety. The facilities had to be brought into line with people's modern expectations. The refinement of skills in a relatively short career, and the dedication this requires, had to be rewarded with salaries that could set a young man up for life.

But what has happened is a disgrace. The people's game is being taken from the people. Football is historically a social and cultural phenomenon. You can't apply the mores, appropriate to the production of margarine for profit, to the running of a football club. Punters who don't like a brand of marge will switch to another. Try telling Hibs fans that they could do the same. If that link is ever severed, football is in serious trouble.

The Scottish Premier League next season will play 30-odd games on a Sunday night at 6.05pm, at the behest of Sky Television. Saturday afternoon football is an integral part of our culture. Sunday nights are for winding down for the sobering reality of Monday. If football in the US takes off in a big way, TV might want a 2am kick-off. If attendances drop, so what? They could dispense with spectators and replace them with cardboard cut-outs and canned soundtracks.

The deregulated football market is now a jungle. Some players' salaries are incredible. Punters are being unscrupulously squeezed for more money to fund these salaries. Each year more good players will be thrown on the scrap heap to help pay the salaries of a few. With such expenditure continuous success becomes a necessity. Indigenous talent is left undeveloped as our big clubs get out the cheque book and sign another transnational mercenary. Next year the need for success will be even greater. Some day the punters, increasingly marginalised, will pack it in. I'm already getting pissed off with the massive media overkill surrounding this World Cup. Much of it is cringe-inducing. Football might still be the beautiful game, but the trappings are increasingly tatty and ugly.

DOING THE HONOURABLE THING

24 JUNE 1998

THE BRITISH honours system stinks. It must be about the best honours system that money can buy. Knighthoods and life peerages are doled out to time-serving chancers, place-seeking chanty wrasslers, party hacks being put out to grass, and deep-pocketed donors to party funds. New Labour's honours list keeps up this tradition. Substantial donors to New Labour funds were suddenly found to be such estimable citizens that knighthoods and peerages were the least a grateful government could bestow.

School janitors, lollypop men, office bearers in the Women's Rural Institute, are regularly given some of the minor gongs to bring a tinge of democratic inclusiveness to the proceedings. And anyway, awards for legitimate public service, for academic and professional excellence, are justified in any society.

But it's a bit of a liberty to burden them with gongs that relate to the long since defunct British Empire.

In some parts of the world people might take umbrage at anyone introduced to them as a Commander of the British Empire.

After all empires, by definition, suppressively occupied the territories of other peoples. The British Empire was no exception. I think empire gongs should be more honourably retitled.

Knighthoods are pre-empire. Feudal. The knight was no romantic. No honourable Ivanhoe. He was a member of a repressive class. They were to the fore in the Crusades that are among the filthiest abominations in the annals of human history. Yet as we approach the millennium our Government uses this title, so steeped in blood, as an honour. The peerage is worse. The peer is part of the nobility. The Scottish nobility made the lands of the clans their private property. Robbed the people of the common lands. Not just in the Highlands but all over Scotland. They were robbers, brigands, and monotonously treacherous. If members of the Scottish nobility had any sense of decency, they would be so shamed by their forebears and all they stood for, and how the family fortune was amassed, that they would pack in their titles, give their loot to charity, and seek to purge the family infamy by voluntary social work in places like Drumchapel. Instead they go to America in kilt or tartan trews and beg money for the old homestead from the children of the children of the men and women their families drove from Scotland. I'm not inclined to visit the sins of the fathers on their children. But this is different. Today the nobility in Scotland have wealth and privileges based on the cruel and plundering activities of their forebears. They wave title deeds to land that was stolen from our forebears. To add insult to injury their nomenclature is used as an honour for those who want to wallow in a feudal title.

Lordluvaduck it's pathetic. I've known very good men succumb. Ted Hill was the best leader the Boilermakers' Society ever had. He accepted a peerage. I met Ted at a reception in London. We had a pint afterwards. He told me he wanted nothing to do with the title but his wife would have made his life hell had he refused. His wife was a member of the Communist Party. Some weeks later Ted was inducted or whatever the hell you call it, into the House of Lords. There was a press photo of him, big, lovely, lumpy, working-class lived-in face sticking from the top of an ermine robe. It was so sad. Ted was never the same again.

Many good Labour men have gone that way. Time and again I've heard the same refrain. "I can do a job in there. Legislate the place out of existence. I won't use the title. Just keep calling me Erchie". Ten years later they're still there and so is the "place". Soon they will have to call Norman Lamont, My Noble Lord. May the Big Lord upstairs have mercy on their souls. Mind you the expenses are a bit tasty. The truth is that the House of Lords is a feudal monstrosity that has no place in a modern democratic society.

The argument about a second chamber is a different matter. To have a House of Lords where only life peers appointed by Prime Ministers shall vote, is no real improvement. We are simply replacing the diktat of ancient privilege with the diktat of latter-day Prime Ministerial privilege.

Blair's list, made public last week, shows what this means. Big donors to New Labour were made peers. Those who rendered services to him were similarly elevated. Such patronage in the hands of one man damages democracy. Even an elected second chamber along party lines would simply replicate the political alignments of the House of Commons and therefore wouldn't make much difference. Why not a new approach? A second revising chamber elected from candidates with no extant party political connection, nominated by social and community groups and professional organisations, also not affiliated to any party?

We could then get shot of the House of Lords, lock, stock and barrel, and all the attendant snobberies. It could be turned into a museum with stuffed images of M'Luds, that will hardly be less animated than the originals, and be a reminder to future generations of times when Britain had no democracy and class privilege was everything. Any such proposal is unacceptable to the Blairites because they are control freaks.

The name on the honours list that hurt me was that of Melvyn Bragg. We've been friends for years, not intimates, but with mutual respect from afar. He was on the left. A democratic socialist. His family was steeped in the Labour movement.

Some years ago I opened a Labour Club in Wigton, a lovely little town in the North of England. The people were lovelier in the only sense that really matters, in character. All Melvyn's family were there. Aunts, uncles, the lot. I pulled the first pint and the festivities commenced. It was a good, clean, wholesome Labour gathering, with a bit of devilment as well. Not a career politician in sight. I was one of the original signatories to Charter 88 and was pleased to see his name was also appended. You can argue about his merits as a novelist but his work in bringing art, in the widest sense of the word, to a mass audience on TV, was meritorious. He pandered neither to the philistines nor the elitists.

He never concealed his beliefs. He made a lot of money from Thatcher's deregulation of television, as did Greg Dykes, and others. It was nice to see some good guys making a few bob for a change.

Then they funded Blair's campaign for the Labour Party leadership. I criticised this at the time in the pages of the *Herald*. Labour's internal elections hadn't been conducted on the basis of heavily funded campaigns. This was an American phenomenon where it led to a situation where only millionaires, or candidates backed by millionaires, could win office. We surely want none of that here.

Melvyn told us he would only enter the House of Lords if the idea was to end it within two years. He is now a member with a remit from Blair to tart it up for the millennium. "Still call me Melvyn," he insists. Why?

SOMETHING ROTTEN
IN THE STATE OF ENGLAND

1 JULY 1998

IN FRANCE Scotland played three games, drew one, lost two, scored two goals, conceded six, secured one point from a possible nine, and ended bottom of the group. Now I don't want to quibble, but if this wasn't a fairly comprehensive defeat, then, bejabbers and bejasus, what the hell was it? I pose this question because the players were greeted as conquering heroes on their return to Scottish soil.

Our penchant for being self-congratulatory at being beaten is coming unhealthily close to masochism. The team didn't deserve uncharitable criticism. It gave of it's best. It's best was not yet good enough. But nor does it merit hyperbolic acclamation, which gets things out of perspective. To pose a consequential question; after this, what are we left to do when we win the World Cup in four years' time?

Sabbath mornings usually find me at ease. I wallow in the Sunday papers, over the only mixed grill breakfast of the week that I'm allowed, but not last Sunday. My repose was shattered by a screaming headline: "It's payback time for 'hand of God', says Hoddle". This wasn't a promise by England's manager to win the World Cup for God, Who, he might have thought, had given England a helping hand along with Hoddle's resident faith healer. God, after all, is an Anglican, and is rumoured to be absolutely tickled pink to be of the same faith as Tony Blair. But alas, the story behind the headline was much more mundane. It was a threat of revenge for a goal scored by Diego Maradona in the quarter-finals of the 1986 World Cup, when Argentina slaughtered England 2-1.

Our freens south of the Border claim that Maradona deliberately fisted the ball into the net for one of the goals. As a neutral who has watched replays of this goal, a thousand times or more, on British television (a number only exceeded by replays of Sir Geoffrey Hurst's third goal for England in the 1966 World Cup final where a Russian linesman gave England a goal that manifestly wasn't, presumably as an act of revenge for the siege of Leningrad during the last war), I believe it was Maradona's head that propelled that ball over the line. And no-one will convince me otherwise. The same goes for the entire population of Govan, as sophisticated a bunch of impartial aficionados of the beautiful game as you could ever find in a month of Sundays. Let's be fair, the mix-up in the minds of our sassenach cousins could stem from the fact that wee Maradona's head actually looks like a hairy fist.

I'll tell you how I know. He was drinking one night in a pub near Govan Cross, rolling his own weird kind of fags, when a punter leaned over and said: "Haw wee Marra [that's what they call him in Govan], you've goat a coupon like a hairy fist." Need I say more! Well, yes. Maradona's second goal was so good it deserved to count for two.

In other press reports I read of references to the Falkland war. It was too much. I sought refuge from these jingoistic rantings in the more sedate columns of a Scottish Sunday paper, only to read the result of a poll carried out by the *Sunday Times* that claimed something like 60% of Scots were now supporting England in the World Cup. Izzatafact? If so it's the best kept secret in the history of the human species.

But my Sunday routine was in tatters. I discarded the papers to watch Channel 4 racing from Doncaster. John McCririck was brandishing a newspaper with the story that since England's recent defeat of Colombia the yeomen of England have recovered their sexual potency and no longer needed the stimulation of viagra pills. McCririck rejoiced in this new-found Anglo-Saxon fecundity and said something like English males would give their wives and girl friends some "GOTCHA". This was the dreadful headline in the *Sun* that marked the sinking of the *Belgrano* in the South Atlantic, during the Falklands war, which killed hundreds of young Argentinians.

When German hooligans rioted in France, the president of the German Football Federation wept with remorse and volunteered to withdraw the German team from the competition. When English fans have rioted the spokesman for English football shrugs his shoulders and says "it has nothing to do with us". The manager talks of revenge. English newspapers invoke the Falklands spirit. An English television commentator makes gloating remark about "Gotcha". Television adverts that occupy slots surrounding the World Cup are aimed at morons. The people who produce these adverts aren't morons but among the most intelligent people ever to work in the British media. They've been told that the core audience are morons. Treat people like morons and they're more likely to behave like morons.

These hooligans are ugly. And I don't mean physically. There is an ugly brutishness about them. They didn't come from outer space. They are products of English society. The fans sing 'Rule Britannia'. Is there any other group of fans who sing of imperial supremacy. This doesn't seem to bother the English FA or scribes. The hooligans are not seen as part of a wider social malaise, a chauvinist culture that is the root of all the troubles. England suffers from post-imperial tensions. During the Falklands war the atmosphere in London was obscene. Thatcher was doing her Warrior Queen Boadicea stuff. In pubs you risked chastisement from patriots if voicing a mild criticism of the war. Union Jacks were everywhere. Like Last Night at the Proms, every night. When ships returned from the Falklands to English Channel ports they were greeted with young women waving knickers in the air, holding posters aloft proclaiming "Knickers to the Argies". In Scotland there was a complete absence of jingoism, of gloating triumphalism. Similarly when Thatcher preached that there was no such thing as society, only individuals looking after No 1, she was rebuffed by the Scots through the ballot box. We faced a double whammy. The glorification of war and greed. Selfishness became overtly respectable in England. The Scots rejected this philosophy. The English masses didn't. They were conned into a process that coarsened people and society.

The English thugs in France are essentially Thatcher's children. There is a political and cultural dimension to the problem. I have more in common with a Liverpool docker than with the Scottish nobility, taken as a whole. But the men who marched in support of Enoch Powell's racism were London dockers and porters from the Smithfield Market. We have a host of problems up here but there is something rotten in the state of England. I thought a Labour government would tackle the problem head on. Instead it panders to the reincarnated prejudices of the Thatcher years.

I want Argentina to beat England. (I write before the game is played.) I say this without rancour. An English triumph would simply be unbearable. If they won the World Cup, which is highly unlikely, we may have to seal the Border, and declare a Scottish breakaway. We don't want to cry for you Argentina, all we are saying is give us a goal. PLEASE!

AN ANGLOPHILE'S HATRED
OF ENGLISH CHAUVINISM

8 JULY 1998

IF YOU had ventured into the Reid abode last Monday afternoon, contrived an entry through the exterior security door, then the interior security door, into a lobby where two raw-meat-eating rottweilers prowl, and eventually opened the door to the inner sanctum you would have seen the titular head of the household watching television, while teetering on the brink of a nervous breakdown. He can hardly bear to watch the screen. Two tail-end batsmen are giving their all for Queen and country. They have to survive a good few overs to save the nation from the disaster of an innings defeat. They are faced with a bowler thought by many to be the best in the world, and at the other end by a toaty wee man who releases the ball when bent over like a half-shut penknife while seemingly scrutinising the ground immediately underfoot. He too, despite his bowling action, is very good.

They survive. I whoop with joy. Sing a few choruses of 'Swing Low Sweet Chariot'. England have won. Not quite. It's a draw. But

313

in context this is a victory. I cuddle my wife. She was born in England, so was a daughter, but don't tell anyone. Well there you have it. I had to come out the closet sooner or later. I'm a fervent supporter of the English cricket team. Seeing as it's confession time let me further avow that the small group of poets, including Shelley, Keats, and Byron, who gathered under the aegis of Leigh Hunt, in a cottage on Hampstead Heath, during the early part of the 19th century, have had a great influence on me. They were all English, though Byron was part Scot, and wrote 'Dark Lochnagar'. An Englishman, Daniel Defoe wrote the first ever novel, *Robinson Crusoe*. He also wrote a poem 'The True Born Englishman' with the inescapable conclusion that the English gentleman was descended from a shower of jumped-up mongrels and chancers. Much the same as our gentlemen.

For as long as I can remember I've rejoiced in the robustness of Chaucer, the magic of Milton, the glory of Shakespeare. Francis Bacon was among those who first sought to explain the world through the world itself. Darwin was a genius.

Tom Paine, a staymaker from Dorset, was the pamphleteer of the American revolution and democracy. The English Chartists contributed enormously to the creation of democracy in these isles, and to the early formative years of the Labour movement. I am deeply in debt to an Englishman, Christopher Hill, for showing me that history is not a series of accidents but a process of underlying social and economic contradictions, of causes and effects. He did this in his classic work on the English Civil War. A war that also produced the Levellers, the first coherent political movement based on socialist principles. I am an unashamed aficionado of the English novel. England also gave the world cricket. Is it any wonder I'm an anglophile?

It's because I'm an anglophile that I hate English chauvinism. It's a betrayal of all that's good in the English tradition. Chauvinism isn't nationalism. Nationalism is a consciousness of national identity. At its best it exudes a pride in all that is good in your own heritage. This also implies shame for those things that are bad in the same heritage. Such an attitude engenders respect for all that is best in the heritage of others. A healthy nationalism is the cornerstone of internationalism. The word literally means solidarity between peoples of different nations. The 'Flower of Scotland' is not my cup of tea. But the words are of a battle to repel an invading army. 'Pomp and Circumstance' is not a bad piece of music but the words put to it are crass jingoism. "God who made thee mighty make thee mightier yet". There is no plea to God to make "thee" better or more decent, just "mightier".

Mightier over other nations. In the anthem God is asked to make the Queen "victorious" over other nations, including rebellious Scots.

This is the language of imperialism. It's been taken up with fresh vigour in England today. This is not English nationalism but English chauvinism. John Lloyd writing in *Scotland on Sunday* quotes one of the English rioters in Marseille: " 'This country ruled three quarters of the f****** world.' " John concludes: "The loss of imperial themes to English working-class culture has been larger than was at first thought; the larger, since the socialist themes, which to a degree took their place, are now going as well." A writer described his feelings about the England-Argentina game in the *Daily Mail*. "It was like the Battle of Agincourt, the Battle of Britain." Matthew Engel in the *Guardian* writes about England's defeat by Argentina. The jingoism was becoming unbearable. "I can't recall previously seeing a match at any sport which I wanted England to lose." Engel adds: "The tabloids have actually been rather restrained. They have not needed to feed Jingo. Jingo is already a bloated monster." Jingoism and Thatcherism have taken root in England. Unless they are uprooted the English nation will be in serious trouble.

The economy is heading for a slump. There is abundant historical proof to show that the interplay of economic slump and rampant chauvinism creates the ideal breeding ground for right-wing extremism. New Labour adopted Thatcherism to win in England. The English Labour movement has thus been ideologically disarmed. The latest report of the Organisation for Economic Co-operation and Development (OECD) says that Blair's Government is pursuing "largely the market-oriented policies of the previous government."

Social priorities are determined by economic strategies. Socio-economic priorities reflect the morals of a government. The men in suits, and on the make, are everywhere, indistinguishable from their predecessors, even unto sleaze.

The Government is planning to spend £8bn on two new aircraft carriers. The equivalent of 20% of the NHS annual budget. The Foreign Office argues that they are necessary for flying the flag. That's gung-ho gunboat diplomacy. All of this goes down badly in Scotland where Thatcherism never even got a toehold. New Labour is now in danger of becoming equally alien in Scotland. That's what the *Herald* polls reflect. A year ago I predicted that any attempt to impose Blairism in Scotland would result in a major realignment of politics in our nation. The debacle surrounding the selection of candidates was anticipated. I also argued that New Labour would fare badly in both next year's local government and Scottish Parliamentary elections.

Weeks ago I warned that our Scottish Parliament must be protected against the sleaze of political lobbying that is so rampant at Westminster. That chicken, too, has come home to roost. No great prescience was needed to make these predictions. They were, as they say, on the cards. Scotland wants to govern itself through its own Parliament. It wants to play its part in peacekeeping, and humanitarian actions throughout the world, but wants nothing to do with imperial flag-waving or global power politics. It wants a market economy that is regulated to serve the people as a whole. Scotland wants to be part of Europe. It will do so, if possible, as partners with England. If not it will do so anyway. That I believe is the growing mood of the Scottish people. A mood that will grow

into the settled will of the people as disenchantment with Westminster continues to grow.

THE PLEASURE OF MULTI-DIMENSIONAL PEOPLE

15 JULY 1998

I WAS sixteen and going to London as a delegate to a conference. It was the first time I'd been out of Scotland. The journey, in an old-style four-berth sleeper compartment, was, to say the least, memorable. One of the guys snored harshly. If people have to snore, why don't they snore like me? Softly. I was much too considerate in those days. It never even crossed my mind to gently wallop him above the right ear with a screw tap. That was the kind of young gentleman I was. An idiot.

Sleep was out the question. About five in the morning the train stopped. I pulled back the blind. We were in a place called Leighton Buzzard. It sounded like a town in the American Wild West. Who were those shifty-looking guys on the platform? The James gang? There was Jesse. I knew it was him. He looked like a Jesse. And there was Frank. A Henry Fonda lookalike. I looked at my dormant travelling companions, strangers in the night. They looked as if they hadn't a tosser between them. The gang got on the train, didn't come into our compartment. Maybe they didn't want to wake up the snorer. The swine.

On the Saturday night there was a conference dance in a hall called Baths. I asked one of the attendants where the baths were. He looked at me as if I was daft. "What makes you thing there are baths here?" he asked. "Because it's called Baths," I replied. "Look mate, me mother-in-law is called a human being, but she bleeding well ain't." Cockneys have no regard for literal accuracy. They sing of Hackney marshes. I've been there. There ain't no marshes in Hackney. The place probably gave birth to Hackney carriages and "hacks", those who write in hackneyed prose. In Govan a hack was a split lip caused by a cold, not a belt on the mouth. But, to get back to the dance in the non-existent baths. The band was billed "Ralph Sharon nearing Shearing". George Shearing was a blind Cockney jazz pianist who had a hit in the charts entitled 'Lullaby of Birdland'. Ralph Sharon was an outstanding musician in his own right.

Now let me take you a big leap forward in time. A couple of weeks ago I was in my den watching the World Cup when daughter number three poked her head round the door and bellowed "there's jazz on the telly". I didn't believe her. I pore over TV listings in search of music programmes. Any kind of music except pop. I find it musically unintelligible. Daughter number three returns. "It's Tony Bennett. He's singing at the Glastonbury Festival." I switched over. Thousands of youngsters, begrimed bejasus, in a sea of mud. They were lapping up the magic of Tony as he strode the stage in his immaculate tuxedo. The voice has gone a bit. The top notes are strained, but, what the hell, like Sinatra he has elevated saloon bar singing to a musical art form.

He is also a good guy. When Martin Luther King started his long march from the Deep South to Washington, demanding an end to racial discrimination, Tony was one of the first whites to join in. And it was dangerous. White civil rights activists had already been brutally murdered by the Ku Klux Klan.

Sinatra also took a stand against racism. Towards the end of the war Sinatra was visiting high schools to talk about the dangers of racial and religious intolerance. In Gary, Indiana, in 1945, 1000 white students from the Froebel High School went on strike against the "pro-negro" policies of the new principal, who allowed the school's 270 black students to share classrooms with whites, to join the school orchestra, and to swim in the school pool one day a week. Sinatra went down to speak to the students and their parents. To a hostile audience he said: "I implore you to return to school. This is a bad deal, kids. I know something about the business of racial intolerance. At 11 I was called a 'dirty guinea' back home in New Jersey. We've all used the words nigger or kike or mick or polack or dago. Cut it out, kids. Go back to school. You've got to go back because you don't want to be ashamed of your student body, your city, your country." He was withering about the witch-hunting House Un-American Activities Committee. He opined: "The minute anyone tries to help the little guy he's called a communist." He tried to help the victims of McCarthyism and incurred the wrath of John Wayne who was Attila the Hun in cowboy boots.

All these thoughts were flitting through my head as I listened to Tony Bennett, and also his pianist, Ralph Sharon. The same guy who played at that dance all those years ago. There he was, looking for all the world like an elderly, benign, Anglican vicar, who had come out without his dog collar to make a little music. He was making a lot of music.

Benny Green, who died some weeks ago, was in Ralph's band all those years ago. He played the tenor sax. Benny was a self-taught polymath. Some years ago I was doing a programme for BBC radio in London. I was working on the script with the producer at Bush House and wanted to use a quotation from George Bernard Shaw. Shaw's first job was as a music critic. His knowledge of music was extensive but he deplored the way most critics paraded their knowledge in print and penned a devastating critique of their pedantry. We couldn't find the quote. Then the producer had a brainwave. "I'll phone Benny, he's sure to know." Benny Green, a Shavian, too. He dictated the piece over the phone.

Benny was a pal of Ronnie Scott. I first heard Ronnie live in the Paramount Cinema, Renfield Street, Glasgow. Ella Fitzgerald was topping the bill. The supporting act was a group called the Jazz Couriers fronted by two tenor players, Ronnie Scott and Tubby Hayes. It was arguably the best British jazz I've heard. Some years later, in 1959, I was involved in the organisation of a festival in Vienna. There was a budget that enabled us to take and pay for top musicians from Britain. I argued that the Jazz Couriers should be included. They were a great hit. Tubby went to stay in the US. He played with many of the top names in American jazz. He died through drug addiction. Last year Ronnie committed suicide while in a black depressive state. I don't think he was ever into drugs or at least not heavily.

He had that marvellous London, Jewish, wit. A laid-back laconic style. He might tell an audience of his experiences while doing a gig in a place like Mablethorpe. In his wee hotel room he plugged in his electric razor and the street lights dimmed. It was all kind of zany.

But back once again to my radio broadcast on prose and poetry. The BBC had a specially invited audience, mainly of friends and people that I liked. These included James Cameron, that doyen of British journalism from Dundee, and his delightful Indian wife, Moni, Jonathan Dimbleby and his highly talented wife, Bel Mooney. Afterwards we had a party. Someone asked when we were returning to Glasgow. I said in the morning unless someone could find us some tickets to hear Dizzy Gillespie play in Ronnie Scott's club. Jonathan explained that he had a table booked for Ronnie's club that very night and Joan and I would be his guests. The place was mobbed and loud as people ate and talked and had to talk louder to be heard above the hubbub. In the midst of this clamour Ronnie was playing chess with someone who looked like a bouncer. He

321

was mean, d'ya know what I mean? I would have bet his feet were prehensile. Then Dizzy started playing and the hubbub ceased.

Ronnie Scott was involved in the early days of the peace movement in this country. He was a self-debunking cultured man. One of life's great pleasures is to know and enjoy multi-dimensional people. I've been most fortunate in this respect, for which the Lord be thankit.

WHAT NEW LABOUR NEEDS

5 AUGUST 1998

AS A CONCEPT, God is very tricky to replace. Believers believe that providing they pay their dues they have a spiritual insurance policy that guarantees infinite life after death. They are loath to give all that up for the relatively short, sharp stab at mortal life represented by the only other game in town; atheism. That's why I never argue about God or no God. The beliefs of the believer are based on a faith that goes beyond reason. There can be no argument or debate that lays no claim to reason. So what the hell. Let sleeping gods lie.

I can live with a God who creates matter, especially that particular assortment of matter that is planet Earth, and then left us to it. Through trial and error, hypotheses, amendment, further investigation and by the exercise of our God-given or evolutionarily acquired reason we can gradually build up knowledge about the forces and laws of nature, so that we may use such laws and forces to our advantage. Over many millennia that has been the basis of all human progress. But if God is an interventionist and keeps moving the goal posts, then the game's a bogey. Why should scientists bother to unravel the secrets of the universe and the laws of physics if some omnipotent power can suspend or change these laws, almost by whim? Such a God would be a celestial magician. When a scientist goes into his laboratory and puts on his dustcoat he has to believe that he can search and discover truths about the world through scientific methodology and the deployment of reason. If he doesn't he isn't a scientist but a mystic.

Religion doesn't worry me, for I know too many good and enlightened people who are religious. It's the bloody fundamentalists who get on my wick. Two of my daughters were recently in Canada and went to see something called "The Toronto Blessing" at the city's airport. There had been a "vision" in a hangar. Regular healing rallies now take place there. My daughters, who respect the religious beliefs of others, an attitude that their parents encouraged, were utterly shocked. One poor fellow who apparently suffered from hepatitis was brought onto the stage. The ministers laid hands on him. The congregation had their right hands held aloft towards the victim. He collapsed on to the floor and lay there, presumably in a trance, for the rest of the evening. Then the head minister asked all who suffered from asthma to come forward and be healed. Many did. The ministers and the congregation, hands again aloft, did some chanting and moaning. The supposed asthmatics started trembling. Members of the congregations were going into spasms. Some became hysterical. My daughters left thoroughly dismayed.

All claims about divine cures and miracles are destructive to the pursuit of cures through the work of medical science. Why spend billions on the NHS when we can all be saved through prayer and divine intervention? In the World Cup the English team had it's own faith healer. I will believe in these "miracles" when someone is carried into sacred waters with one leg and walks out with two. I mean no offence to anyone but such tricks demean the concept of God. What kind of faith depends for sustenance on the Almighty pulling rabbits from His cosmic hat with His voice booming from the heavens "and now for My next trick"?

It is arguable that the greatest threat to world peace now comes from religious fundamentalism in the Middle East, the Indian sub-continent and Eastern Europe. The North American Christian fundamentalists are a frightening lot. They hate everybody bar fellow fundamentalists and given half a chance they'll hate them too. I believe that they have a malign influence on American life. Think of it. All the forensic skills of the FBI are trying to identify a semen stain on a young lady's dress. This has nothing to do with murder or rape. No crime has been committed. At the very worst it will prove sexual activity between two consenting adults. On real moral grounds President Clinton can be indicted, as the most powerful man in the world, for not taking action to stop the ethnic murder in Kosovo or the starvation in Ethiopia. Instead he is being hunted down for some sexual hanky pankies. That speaks volumes of a sex-obsessed society, born of the sexual repression of white Anglo-Saxon Calvinism. Here in Britain too there are ominous signs. I have serious misgivings about politicians who wave their religion like a banner. Mark them well and if you ever sup with them bring a long spoon. New Labour last year went formally religious. Ex-Marxist student leaders turned Government Ministers started queueing up to join the Church of England. The same people are hounding dissidents in the Labour Party. Don't they know that Christ was a dissident? They are now vilifying Frank Field, a man whose views I deplore. But he has a right to hold and express these views. Over the weekend he was portrayed as a pariah by Government Ministers and spin doctors in off-the-record briefings. It was a campaign of character assassination and constituted a gross abuse of governmental power. He was deemed to have been disloyal to the leader. All criticism is considered disloyal, treacherous and even blasphemous.

We've had purges in the selection of candidates. We will have attempts to purge all opposition from the National Executive at the next Labour Party conference. The Prime Minister gave his annual report in government not to the House of Commons but to a gathering of acolytes in the back garden of 10 Downing Street. It was compared in style to the American President's address to the nation. It was more like Stalin addressing the Central Committee of the old Soviet Communist Party. The only thing missing is the Show Trial, but give him time. We were promised a Freedom of Information Act. Instead we have attempts to extradite from France an ex-MI5 officer who wants to expose on the internet things such as how the agency plotted assassinations in our name. New Labour at the election was against student tuition fees, now it is for them. Systematically and comprehensively New Labour has abandoned all the values and principles of the Labour movement.

Why an old friend like Gus Macdonald would want to throw in his lot with this mob beats me. Minister of Trade and Industry at the Scottish Office for 10 months until a Scottish Parliament is elected, and then what? Scottish manufacturing industry is already in recession. The indications of a general recession are manifest. New Labour promised to end Tory booms and busts, but as I warned a few weeks ago on this page, the cycles of boom and bust are endemic to the free-market economy. You will only have a chance of ending these cycles if you regulate the system. It isn't the Tory Party that causes booms and slumps but the Tory system that New Labour upholds with undiminished vigour.

Gus cannot change the course of the British economy as it impacts on Scotland in the next 10 months and, if he doesn't change the system, he couldn't do it in the next 10 years. If New Labour contests the Scottish elections next year in the throes of a recession then it could well get slaughtered at the polls. Blair will then blame the leaders in Scotland for the debacle. Gus as the Minister for Trade and Industry will get caught in the flak. But on a matter of principle an elected government should be composed of elected representatives. Blair has blithely drafted into his Government unelected men of big business, further undermining the already

flawed democracy of our governmental institutions. It's disgrace-
ful. Of course the Tories did it, but Labour is supposed to be
different. And that is the nub of the matter. New Labour ain't. It
isn't more spin doctors it needs in Scotland, but new policies.

OVER THE POINTS WITH
TRANSPORTS OF JOY

12 AUGUST 1998

WHEN I was at primary school a teacher would occasionally read us bits of poetry. They were mostly about daffodils and other exotic flowers. Her readings didn't exactly go down a bomb in Govan. The only flower we were familiar with was the "pee the bed", and she never mentioned that. What I liked were not so much the words as the sounds and rhythms of her undulating voice. Maybe this explains why I still believe that good poetry has a melodic line and a beat. I do, however, remember some phrases, like "transports of joy". She was dead keen on them.

In the transport line we had direct experience only of buses and trams and even the trams weren't exactly joyous. But the phrase stuck in my mind. Years later when I did a lot of travelling some train journeys were transports of joy. For example, if time and circumstances permitted I always preferred to travel by train, rather than air, to London. You could have a good meal on the train. A very good glass of wine. At one period the best-value-for-money plonk to be had anywhere in Britain was on British Rail. You could read, write, have a drink, look at the passing, changing countryside, walk around, have a wash. You could even have a shave. And at journey's end walk off relaxed and ready for the fray.

The size and contours of Britain are tailor-made for trains. If the journey from Glasgow or Edinburgh to London could be done in something like four hours there would be no logistical logic in going by air. Good, cheap, clean, safe, sufficiently frequent rail services, including connecting lines from the main termini to surrounding population areas, would render long-distance travel by car a form of madness. The same would apply to the long-haul transportation of freight. A much improved environment would be a consequence of such sensible travel provisions for the public, but they do not currently exist. I could tell horror stories about rail travel in recent years that drove me back, time and again, to the car.

Let me cite a most recent and more local example. Last Friday my daughter and her partner arranged a night out for her mum and dad in Edinburgh, to hear a great guitarist, Martin Taylor, in concert. She found there was a train from Glasgow Central to Edinburgh. The train left 18 minutes late. By the time we got to Edinburgh it was too late to get anything to eat before the concert. We had to leave early to ensure we got a taxi to the station so as to get the 11.30 last train to Glasgow. It was packed.

At Queen St Station there was a queue for taxis, the rain was heavy, the taxis few. We decided to brave the elements and walk to the Central Station where taxis were more frequent. We still had to wait about half an hour to get a cab. It would have been so much easier to have gone by car. I would normally be in Edinburgh a few times over the following weeks for Festival events that interest me. Now I'm not so sure.

I detail this experience not to have a moan but to make a point. John Prescott recently announced the Government's Transport

Strategy. It sounded great in aspirational terms but, before you can get people out of cars and on to public transport, you need a public transport system that is preferable to cars. The alternative is coercion through fiscal and legal means. You can't, in a democracy, compel people to use public transport with inadequacies and costs that curtail their social, cultural, and business activities.

The last trains between Edinburgh and Glasgow are too early. They should be timed to allow people to go to concerts or the theatre and have a meal afterwards. Why do trains stop so early from the city centres to outer parts of the conurbations? The same applies to buses. Taxis are an integral part of public transport and yet are seldom mentioned in this context. I seldom use my car except for longer distances. Try going from Glasgow to Grantown-on-Spey by public transport, or a multitude of other places. We have a forced car-dependency culture, and for social and environmental reasons this has to be changed.

The first priority is a public transport service that is viewed as something of a social service. But is this compatible with a free-market philosophy?

Contemplating that young school teacher reciting poetry got me thinking of how poets can say things that often encapsulate great truths in relatively few words. Berthold Brecht was a poet as well as a playwright. In the early Fifties East German workers left their workplaces to protest at living and working conditions. These protests were crushed by grim threats of legal action. The writers' union, an adjunct of the Communist Party, produced a leaflet condemning the workers. Brecht's reply was this short poem:

> After the Uprising on June 17th
> The Secretary of the Authors' Union
> Had leaflets distributed in the
> Stalinallee which said that the people
> Had forfeited the government's confidence
> And could only win it back
> By redoubled labour. Wouldn't it

> Be simpler in that case if the government
> Dissolved the people and
> Elected another?

There is something of this relationship creeping into the Government's attitude to the Scottish people. A few weeks ago when he was in Scotland the Prime Minister was being interviewed on television by a gracious young lady from the BBC. She asked him if he wasn't fed up coming to ungrateful Scotland and being vilified when elsewhere he was lionised. He demurred as if to suggest that He forgave us, for we know not what we say. You got the feeling, though, that if we persisted in our foolish ways he might just replace us with people in his own image.

This attitude was also discernible in the attitude of the leader of the Glasgow Labour Group towards the strike of the city's social workers. He invoked Thatcher's laws against the workers. He may live to regret that. The issues of the dispute are too technically internal for judgments to be made by those not involved. What we do know of is the mounting frustration among all public-sector workers. Over the past 20 years they've borne the brunt of public expenditure cuts. Their wages lag seriously behind those in the private sector. The workload has intensified. People leave or take retirement and are not replaced. The burden grows on those remaining. They've seen some services privatised and workmates, working beside them as employees of private employers, doing the same work as before, for lower wages. Put these together and more that can't be listed, and you have an explosive situation.

Workers might go on strike over an apparently trivial issue whereas their actions are born of bitter frustrations over a wide range of issues. If public-sector unions, at the top, don't address these problems, then rank-and-file leaders will emerge who will try to do so. If the Government and Labour-controlled councils don't take heed, we could be heading for another winter of discontent. And don't blame the workers.

WHY ECONOMIC LEVITATION IS A DANGEROUS THING

19 AUGUST 1998

THE SOVIET system was a monument to the folly of men who think they can command an economy, like a well-trained dog, and it will do their bidding. This might have worked during the dawn of man's dominance on this planet, when the "economy" might have consisted of gathering herbs and killing small mammals for the prehistoric pot, but in the twentieth century, an economy was part of a system that was both national and international. It was based not only on production but on trade and commerce. Things were exchanged in markets—not for other things, but for money. We had the emergence of corn exchanges, indeed, of all kinds of exchanges, including stock exchanges, and banks to underpin this trade. Economic laws were identified. They sprang from the actual process of production and exchange. Laws of value and exchange, the determination of value, and related prices, were of fundamental importance. The mechanisms of the market became the arbiters of price. No more efficient system has yet been devised for this function and it is likely that none ever will. Two men in particular discovered these economic laws: Adam Smith, and the man he influenced, Karl Marx. But the Soviet Union totally ignored them. Now, you can ignore objective laws—but the consequences can be drastic. You can ignore the law of gravity and fall with a great thud that knocks the life from you. To ignore economic laws can have a similar effect.

In 1986 and '87, I was in the Soviet Union researching and filming for a television series. Everywhere we went, the signs were unmistakable. The economy was crumbling. Nothing seemed to work. The country was fabulously rich in mineral resources; it could have been the richest oil producer in the world. But oil was seeping out of pipeline joints that stretched all over that vast countryside. The remedy was a simple, if large-scale, maintenance job. Yet it wasn't done. I sampled the best apples I've ever tasted on a collective farm in Georgia and found that half the harvest never reached the towns but rotted on trains shunted into sidings or in forgotten warehouses. The farmers didn't care—they were paid for producing apples, not for their sale.

From the beginning, the Soviets were obsessed with production. This is true of all developing countries. Indeed, it's possible—though I'm not sure of this—that strict central control of the economy in such countries might even be necessary. What I am sure of is that, in an economy that has developed beyond that stage, rigid central control from the top becomes a shackle on economic development. The Soviet Union had reached that point, maybe in the late Thirties and certainly by the early Fifties. Industries, if they are to survive, have to be efficiently productive, and that can't be measured solely at the point of production. The Soviet Union had virtually no internal market except a small but thriving black market. All economic plans were for production. Nobody in government seemed to give a toss about how these products would fare in a genuine market. There was no market. Soviet consumers had to take what they could get, not what they wanted. There might be plenty of shoes in the shops, but no real choice. You could buy a television—but the main cause of domestic fires was exploding television sets; they were seriously defective.

In the Soviet Union, workers had rights as producers that didn't exist in the West. They had a right to work. Redundancy was unknown. But they had no rights as consumers. I remember during the Seventies going to the Soviet Union and being asked by the wife of a friend there if I could bring her some sanitary towels. These were impossible to get in Moscow. Members of the Nomenklatura, the party and state apparatchiks, had no such problems. They had access to special shops that sold consumer goods from the West at 1929 prices. The system that promised so much in 1917 had degenerated into something profoundly different. Soviet society was moribund. The economy was stagnant.

In 1987, I met Professor Aganbegyan, then chief economic adviser to Mikhail Gorbachev, who was trying to unravel the economic chaos that prevailed. I asked him how the Soviet economic system, which was allegedly based on the teachings of Marx, had totally ignored every law of economics known to man, including those enunciated by Marx. "That," he told me, "is a question I keep asking myself."

Without market mechanisms, prices had to be arbitrarily decided by a committee. Their decisions could make an efficient industry seem inefficient, and an inefficient one look efficient. Nobody really cared. Everyone waited for orders from above. Personal initiative dried up. This was the command economy. It sprang not from economic theories, but from Lenin's concept of a centrally controlled party that centrally controlled everything, including the economy. This reached absurdity under Stalin. The story is told of the commissar in charge of the production of nails in the Thirties. The target for his industry was expressed in weight and couldn't be achieved with the existing machinery. One of his aides said jocularly: "It's the different sizes of nails that's the problem. If we only produced six-inch nails we could smash the target." The commissar made his decision. For some time afterwards you couldn't get your shoes mended, since the only nails available were six inches long. The commissar for nails was made a Hero of Socialist Labour.

In an *Observer* article in the very early Nineties, I warned of the dangers if the Russian economy collapsed. Clapped-out Soviet industry couldn't possibly survive in an unregulated market. The economy might completely disintegrate, and society could then slither into anarchy and gangsterism. I argued that such fundamental change had to be carefully managed. The pace of change was important. The West should be urging restraint. Instead, Thatcher and Reagan wanted to dance on communism's grave. Aid from the West was made conditional on an immediate change to a free market. Young Russians were given the impression that with a free market, they could all live like West Germans or the Southern English, with stacks of consumer goods and natty clothes. I kept telling them that Bangladesh, Mexico City, the Third World as a whole—not forgetting skid row in New York, the cardboard city in London, the vast underclass of the deprived and unemployed in the West—were also part of the free market system; that Russians, given the parlous state of the economy, might find themselves part of the Third World. And that, more or less, is where they are now. Post-communist free market Russia has created multi-millionaire gangsters side by side with a poverty worse than it was under the old regime. Miners haven't been paid for more than six months. They're only now going on strike. Yeltsin is a joke and always was. Gorbachev has passed from the stage and a comeback seems impossible. Dangerous men are lurking in the background. So are thousands of nuclear devices. If the rouble is devalued, can the Hong Kong dollar be far behind? What knock-on effect will this have in Japan and the rest of Asia? And where would this leave us? Let me put it this way: the Soviets never had a monopoly on political dogma.

We have it in the West. It's the cult of the deregulated market.

It has many names—Reaganism, Thatcherism, Blairism—and has all the makings of a new evil empire with a global command economy run by the faceless executives of transnational companies. Some might even be members of the Russian Mafia.

WHY MIGHT IS RIGHT,
SO LONG AS YOU'RE WHITE

26 AUGUST 1998

MY CHILDHOOD was spent in the dark shadows of world war. After '45 there was the briefest of respites before wars resumed in Greece, Korea, Indo China, the Middle East, Latin America, the Caribbean, Laos, Cambodia, the Falklands, Afghanistan, the lands of what was Yugoslavia, and others I can't recall at the moment. At no time has the world been at peace during these years. Millions of landmines litter the Earth's soil. They blow off the legs of Third World children. Princess Diana's one real claim to fame was that she highlighted this obscenity. The landmines were made in developed countries. More high explosives were dropped on Vietnam than in the 1939-45 war. The United States was mostly unconcerned when the casualties were almost exclusively Vietnamese. Yet when the pine boxes containing dead young Americans started arriving regularly on American soil, the peace movement became a mass movement.

All wars since 1945 have taken place in the lands of the Third

World. These were the new killing fields. The superpowers used them as jousting grounds, test beds for their new weapons of destruction. Also at stake were rich mineral resources to be exploited, spheres of influence, and geopolitical power. This was the era of the Cold War, but it was killingly hot for the Vietnamese, Cambodians, and Palestinians. Implicit was an exchange rate for lives. One white North American or West European equals 100 Mexicans, 200 Arabs (400 if the Arabs are Muslims), 1000 Bangladeshis, 2000 Ethiopians, etc.

The same applies to natural disasters, only more so. With modern technology we can sit at home munching pizzas, watching, via satellite television, famines kill millions on the other side of the globe. Or we can switch to another channel, without leaving the chair, and watch the Teletubbies. Decisions, decisions. Of course it's history and culture. We Wasps have to stick together, including Catholic and Jewish Wasps. And equally, of course, we are anti-racist.

We espouse liberal democratic values, the Enlightenment and all that jazz. We could cry for the people of the Third World but we've run out of tears for the black bastards.

I think the West, in the midst of the biggest accumulation of material wealth in the history of humankind, is a moral desert. It's hung up on sex, which should be of no interest to anyone except those doing it. Its leaders are obsessed with Mammon; they are the people Willie McIlvanney calls the non-dialectical materialists. They are developing a war technology that kills people and peoples without any possibility of retaliation, at least that's the theory. The President of the US only has to give his generals the nod and rockets rain down while he gets back on his helicopter to resume his holidays in Martha's Vineyard. Listen, I don't care what he does with his semen, it's what he does with his rockets that worries me.

During the Cold War we had MAD, or mutually assured destruction. The two superpowers more or less nullified each other.

Since the USSR imploded we have only one superpower. It has no such restraints on its actions or behaviour. President Clinton ordered the destruction by rockets of a pharmaceutical factory in Khartoum, the capital of Sudan. He claimed it was producing war gases. Citizens of Britain who were involved in the design and construction of the factory say its structure precludes such activity. British businessmen who were in the factory in recent weeks say it was producing only pharmaceutical goods. Structural experts have told us the factory was too open to have permitted the production of such gases. The *Observer* had a front-page lead last Sunday, which claimed that American Intelligence had told the President that there was no hard evidence to prove that the factory was producing nerve gases. He nonetheless destroyed it.

Now it could be that this raid had more to do with what the President did or did not do, or where he did or did not do it, with Monica Lewinsky, than the pursuit of terrorism.

It would be funny if it wasn't so serious. The territorial integrity of a sovereign state, no matter what we think of the current regime in that country, has been seriously violated. If this is acceptable then the nations of this world will be riven by wars, holy or unholy. The United Nations can pack it in, for it will have no role to play. We will have a New World Order where only might is right. That is why the United Nations must assert its authority or it will have none. The burden of proof as to whether this factory was producing war gases rests with the United States. If it fails to produce such proof, the United Nations has to carry out its own scientific investigation. If this factory was only producing medicines then the American government has to be condemned by the world community. The alternative is to go back to the Thirties with the rockets instead of panzers and, lurking constantly in the background, the use of nuclear weapons by the desperate who feel they have nothing else to lose.

The language of US Secretary of State Madeleine Albright has been particularly frightening. She talks of the next war, "the war

339

against Muslim terrorism". Her talk and Clinton's actions are the best recruiting sergeants Islamic fundamentalism has ever had. The great majority of the one billion Muslims in the world today are not fundamentalists or terrorists but poor, hard-working men and women, and their families. They are aggrieved at what they see as the West's double standards in the Middle East. The UN resolution that recognises the State of Israel within its prescribed borders, as well as the territorial rights to a homeland for the Palestinians, has been ignored for decades.

They have seen the oil riches of Arabia squandered by feudal kings maintained in power by the West for being "reliable" allies. Young Palestinians born and bred as stateless persons in refugee camps are understandably attracted to extremist groups. The United States hasn't lifted a finger to help them, but is quick to crush them if they get out of order. There will be no peace in the Middle East until the problem of Palestinian nationhood is resolved. The real interests of Israel will be best served by such a solution. Netanyahu wants no deal. He speaks for Israeli chauvinism.

It should be remembered that William Wallace was called a terrorist by the English. Nelson Mandela was called a terrorist by the white supremacists in South Africa. The founders of the State of Israel were called terrorists by the British Government, as were the founders of the United States. One man's terrorist is another man's freedom fighter. Terrorism can best be tackled by seeking a political settlement that is fair; force, if used at all, should be to that end. That is what is now happening in Northern Ireland. The Middle East is no different.

Finally, I don't know about you, dear reader, but I'm mightily pissed off with British governments that rush to support any and every military action by the United States. Some day it might cost us dearly. That apart, it's undignified.

THE BOTTOM LINE

2 SEPTEMBER 1998

THE JAPANESE economy that for decades had been the wonder of the Western world suddenly manifested "serious structural weaknesses", just like that. These fraught times in the global economy are being blamed on a series of unrelated crises that by sheer coincidence have had an impact on the world trading system at approximately the same time. I'm not partial to coincidence as an explanation of momentous happenings. It is usually an excuse offered by self-seekers to avoid admitting unpalatable truths. The tiger economies of the Pacific rim that had been the wonder of the Eastern world collapsed, just like that. The Singaporean economy, hitherto a minor wonder of the capitalist way of doing business, started convulsing, just like that. The Russian economy collapsed, just like that. In my opinion it was collapsed from the start.

But things don't happen, just like that. There are invariably underlying causes. I was born in the slump and depression of the Thirties. In previous centuries people had died from pestilence, droughts, the lack of sustenance in the world around. In this

341

century they hungered in a world full of food. Fish was brought into ports and taken out and dumped back in the sea. People had no money with which to buy fish. In the US they burnt corn to fuel locomotives while the jobless pleaded Buddy can you spare a dime?

Then there were jobs for everyone. Like a miracle all the men on our street got employment, including my dad. We got rations of food. For us it wasn't austerity but paradise. The miracle that brought this about was called war. The free-market economies of that time couldn't handle peace but by God they could handle war, and make a killing too. But what an indictment of society that people only escaped penury through war; that children walked taller and straighter in conditions of war, whereas they were stunted in the years of peace. We actually prospered, in relative terms, during the war years. Pity about the poor sods at the front or the victims of air raids. And don't think this disgusting absurdity wasn't noticed by people at the time. It was this factor that won Labour a landslide victory at the 1945 General Election.

People wanted a planned economy, full employment, and an end to the mentally crippling insecurity of the pre-war years. The Labour Government delivered. The market functioned but wasn't allowed to dominate or destroy the lives of people. Enlightened Conservatives, against the horrific background of the Thirties, accepted this new consensus. Slumps were no longer viewed as acts of God but as flaws in a system that had to be rectified. Keynesianism was all the rage. It wasn't perfect, far from it, but what a step forward. The American right had always fought Roosevelt's New Deal and in the post-war years regrouped under the banner of monetarism and unrestricted market forces. The intellectual centre was the Chicago School of economists. I remember in the Seventies on a David Frost show sitting between Keith Joseph and the then secretary of the CBI who was a Scot. Milton Friedman, head of the Chicago School, was beamed on to a screen in the studio. Keith Joseph was looking up at him, starry-eyed, as if Friedman was some mystic and splendid guru. I nudged the CBI guy to take a shufti at Joseph. He looked, shook his head and muttered: "He's away with it."

Little did I think that these nineteenth-century laissez-faire capitalist theories that prevailed till the start of the Second World War, and created social havoc through cycles of boom and slump, would re-emerge to define the political agenda as mankind edges towards the millennium. It seemed all too absurd. But it's happened. A new consensus prevails based on the dominance of blind or, at any rate, unrestricted market forces. The highly volatile eruptions in world markets today are resonant of features that were evident during the Twenties and Thirties.

A few years back an esteemed friend had toured the Pacific tiger economies and came back enthused. His was the "I've seen the future and it works" kind of response. I didn't see it that way. A free-market economy has its ups and downs.

It might surge and burn brightly, like a prairie fire, but sooner or later it burns itself out in some kind of slump. That's not praise or condemnation, simply a fact. It's the nature of the beast.

Russia was a disaster waiting to happen. It was huckled into a deregulated free market when anyone who knew anything about the state of the Soviet economy knew with certainty that its industries couldn't possibly survive in such a market. They were utterly clapped out.

Gorbachev was for a mixed economy with certain industries privatised in joint deals with Western capital, all operating within a kind of social democratic political culture. The triumphalist duo of Reagan and Thatcher would have none of this. As dogmatists of the right, they hated social democracy as much as they ever hated communism. They wanted capitalism red in tooth and claw in the land of Lenin, and that's what we've got. Since Yeltsin became president the Russian economy has stagnated with virtually no improvement in the gross national product. Yet billionaires abound not through entrepreneurial skills and the creation of new wealth but by privatising and appropriating for themselves state-owned assets. Something we are familiar with in this country. As I wrote in this column some weeks ago, the Russian economy was bound to collapse; it now has.

And from the West come the siren voices. Carry on as before. It's like a patient going to a doctor with an ailment and being prescribed medicine that he takes and gets worse, goes back to the doctor, and is prescribed more of the same medicine, and gets worse and gets more of the medicine, until he's at death's door and told by the doctor to take even more of the same medicine. If the Russians take this advice then all hell will be let loose. People are not being paid. Some are starving. There's runaway inflation. Life becomes unbearable. Civic life breaks down. There could be another revolution of the extreme right or the extreme left. This is what happened in Weimar Germany, and we got Hitler.

I think the current economic instability is directly linked with the new world order fashioned by Friedman, Reagan, Thatcher and their converts, Clinton and Blair. Up until 20 years ago the creation of full employment was considered a function of good government. Now it is a function of the market alone. If the market cannot do this, then hard cheese for the jobless. A few weeks ago a New Labour Minister came up with this brammer: "We are for full employability, not full employment." In any previous Labour Government he would have been sacked, now he'll probably get promoted.

Governments acting in concert have to start regulating national and global markets for agreed social objectives. The creation of jobs being one. The overheating in the global economy would be alleviated if consumption in the Third World, where many millions are destitute, was substantially improved. That which we should have done out of compassion, we should now do out of economic self-interest. But the bottom line has to be that economics should always be the servant of mankind, and not its master.

SEX,
SELLING FOOTBALL SHORT,
AND A SEMINAR IN SURREY

17 SEPTEMBER 1998

I'M an innocent abroad, and in Scotland too. Until recently I might have assumed Fellatio was an Italian opera singer or a Hollywood movie director. Now I know different, though what a cigar has to do with it still beats me. I thought oral sex was talking dirty, now I know it makes talk impossible. See the things people get up to, or down to, in the name of sex, it's a wonder there's any weans born at all. Biology tells us that sex was the means by which a species reproduced its own kind. Go forth and multiply, saith the Lord. Today people are going forth, doing their stuff, and not multiplying, if we are to believe all we read in the papers, and that's plenty. To me it all sounds anti-woman. Her need is getting left out the equation, and that must be hard to swallow. Is this sex? As a non-expert I don't know, but it certainly isn't cricket. The truth is I can't take seriously all this guff about Bill and Monica.

Sex between consenting adults is a private matter. That way we don't get to know the hilarious details and high jinks of what people get up to in the bedroom, broom cupboard, or wherever. Now we know what this couple were up to, and to know isn't edifying. But then sexual hanky panky, and the sexual act, which they never seemed to get round to, is side-splittingly comic. A form of slapstick comedy. Funny, absurd, risible, except for those involved, then it's a bit of all right. Whatever happens, Bill and Monica will forever be remembered for that cigar. Was it lit? Did he inhale this time? Were they blowing circles of smoke? Me? I think it's a diabolical waste of a good cigar. But in the midst of all the saloon bar guffawing it's also very sad.

Judged against the harrowing problems facing humanity, as we edge towards the millennium, how bloody irrelevant it all is. The details of the relationship between Clinton and Lewinsky should never have been made public. That it was, brings shame to the United States. No crime was involved. What he did was in bad taste, we are told. But who is to judge what is good or bad taste? If bad taste was a crime the penal institutions in America and Britain would be crammed with Senators, MPs, pop singers and professional footballers. England wouldn't be able to field a team in the European Nations Cup. Scotland could. Our lot are too old to indulge in such serial "bad taste". If bad taste was really a crime, Kenneth Starr would be doing life.

Roosevelt, arguably the best president since Lincoln, had a mistress. Eisenhower, the most underestimated president of recent times, had a mistress. John F Kennedy had more women than the average citizen of the Third World has had hot dinners. Richard Nixon, so far as we know, had no mistress. Lenin had a mistress. Stalin, as far as we know, had no mistress. That would suggest that adulterers make better presidents and party leaders than non-adulterers. I don't think that's true, but, on the basis of available information it would seem more likely to be true than any contrary suggestion.

In Britain and America political power and influence can be bought and sold like any other commodity. Politicians are, more often than not, front men for vested interests. Politics is about getting elected and re-elected. About getting office or failing to get office. The conflict is between two groups of self-seeking, office-seeking, money-grabbing, back-stabbing, career politicians with not a principle between them. They would do anything to win. Nothing is barred. In such a climate people get destroyed. In American elections that is commonplace; and we're going that way too. Why don't the Americans go the whole hog? Lower the Stars and Stripes. Raise aloft Monica's semen-stained dress as the new flag of the Republic, which reminds me of some things I wanted to ask. Is there no washing-machine in the Lewinsky household? If Clinton gets any more desperate will he nuke Saddam? Get Starr-struck? Weld up his fly? Or will he say as he should have said right from the start: "My private life is my business. Go to hell."?

People seem to think that principles are abstract phenomena until a principle or the lack of principle hits them directly in some shape or form. I've been regularly raging in this column about the dehumanising and destructive impact of unrestrained market forces on the lives of ordinary people. I believe its worst manifestations can be profoundly evil. Many fans thought this had little to do with their passion for football. With Murdoch grasping at Manchester United, they know now. Everything in our society is locked into what might be called the culture of cash. Everything, including our passions, is transmuted into a commodity to be bought and sold for profit.

If the very water of life isn't an exception why should football be? It isn't, of course. Most of our big clubs are PLCs listed on the stock exchange. Such companies exist to make profits for their shareholders. This is the first prescribed function of the directors and those who run PLCs. It's also a legal requirement that they should strive to do so. The fans you might think are necessary to reach that objective. Today it ain't that simple. The money taken at the turnstiles or through season tickets is becoming a relatively declining factor in overall earnings.

Television will be the massive earner. Sponsorship deals and executive entertainment will generate millions. Prices for the watching fans will go up and up. They are treated like animated profit fodder, who will buy all the dross from the club shops, including an ever-increasing number of high-priced club jerseys, usually produced by the sweated labour of disgustingly low-paid children in the Third World. The teams these fans are allowed to watch are often stuffed, not staffed, with foreign mercenaries who come and go like ships in the night. The clubs will eventually have no commitment to any community or nation but be part of a vast media global empire. Then anything can happen. Some bigger PLC will swallow up Manchester United, for it is by a long way the biggest earner in European football. Other clubs will go the same way, and that will eventually include Rangers and Celtic. Those that live by the market can die by the market. That's the real name of today's game.

In Sunday's *Observer* I read of a meeting (it's called a seminar down there) in Surrey, in a hall owned by Rentokil, of trendy lefties from the Seventies and Eighties who had helped propel Blair to the leadership of the Labour Party. They had all been involved with the now defunct magazine *Marxism Today*. The purpose of the gathering was to consider whether there was any future for the left in the age of New Labour. Eric Hobsbawm, an eminent, octogenarian historian, opened the proceedings with a lecture that was rapturously received. He told them, "It is a good moment for the Labour Government to do some rethinking of the assumptions on which the policies of too many governments, including this one, have been based since about 1980. These are basically the assumptions of laissez-faire. . . ." This was greeted as an intellectually brilliant insight into the socio-economic essence of British society today.

I've been saying this for five years now, and so have other punters in Scotland. Why are they so intellectually backward in places like Surrey?

WHEN THE POOR
COME KNOCKING ON THE DOOR

25 NOVEMBER 1998

THE GOVERNMENT proposes to monitor the quality of life in Britain by measuring 13 designated key indicators. In principle this is a sound idea to expand the criteria beyond the purely economic; for indeed we do not live by bread alone. In the long run the environment of the planet will determine whether we, as a species, will live at all. The health of our bird population is a good indicator as to the health of our environment. As is the wellbeing of the fish in our rivers and coastal waters and other facets of our flora and fauna.

What makes this whole exercise somewhat bizarre is the absence of human poverty from the list of indicators aimed at quantifying the quality of human life in these isles. I need no convincing that the wellbeing of our feathered friends is important to us. I need plenty of convincing that the poverty of human beings is less important; but we're not required to choose. The wellbeing of both is interrelated. This is why the omission of poverty from the list of indicators is beyond comprehension.

Those today who subsist on social security in urban ghettoes must be worried sick about the wellbeing of their families. The wellbeing of birds in remote glens might not, understandably for them, be a matter of major concern, as it is for those more comfortably placed.

The alleviation and eventual eradication of poverty is impossible without some redistribution of wealth. This is the jaggy nettle that the Government will not grasp, yet unresolved it threatens the quality of life for everyone. Just as the starving, desperate poor of the Third World will one day come kicking at our doors (they are already beginning to do so as illegal economic migrants), our indigenous poor will do the same in a smaller geographical framework. That too is already happening in trickles.

We live in a consumerist society. We are urged in every conceivable, insidious, way to consume more and more. The poor are not unaffected by this clamour; but they are excluded. Some may decide not to be excluded. Think of the urban riots we've seen in the United States of America and in Asia, Africa, Latin America, when political crises loom. Students and the middle class might initiate the movement for political change but then the urban poor join in and for them the targets are the shopping malls that they can't afford to shop in. How many times on television have you seen them grabbing everything they can get their hands on? It's the poor taking their share.

The permanent division of the world between those who can eat as much as they like, and some do to the point of obesity, and those who will go without and eventually die of starvation and undernourishment, is morally and I hope tactically unsustainable. The poor in Britain will also some day come kicking down doors, demanding of a consumerist, obsessed society their share. Law and order isn't upheld by courts, prisons, or law enforcement agencies. Law and order is sustained by the consent of people who must believe at the very least that society will give them the right to hope that things might get better. For millions in Britain that hope is no longer there.

A substantial section of the working class has been pushed down into a degree of impoverishment from which there is currently no escape. Something like 30% of our people are in this predicament. They have no real hope. The children of our new ghettoes are born to fail. The barriers are much higher for them than for my generation. They are tucked away in vast schemes bypassed by motorways and just about everything else. For those of us who are not poor they could be living in darkest Africa. Out of sight; out of mind.

Why should a young man or woman, denied the right even to hope, respect the rules of a society that condemns him or her to such a hopeless life? Listening to Jack Straw visiting further punishments on the heads of demoralised youngsters fills me with despair. He couldn't find time for a Freedom of Information Act in the Queen's Speech but made time for a Bill bringing swifter punishment to the delinquent children of the ghettoes. His priorities are grotesquely perverse.

Poverty in Britain is compounded by the indignities of the welfare system. These will get worse in the next few years. The Government is moving from universal to means-tested benefits. This is being justified as targeting those most in need. It's a lie. Universal benefits are a cornerstone of the welfare state. Benefits were viewed as legal entitlements, as of right, to everyone. Those who want to end the universal principle ask: why pay benefit to a millionaire? The answer is that benefits are based on universal payments from which, as a matter of principle, no-one should be excluded. Anyway, a progressive taxation system would ensure that most of the benefits paid to the wealthy would be clawed back through income tax.

The welfare state, for example, envisaged retirement pensions sufficient to a dignified status for all in the twilight of life. Eventually it was intended that they would become self-sufficient and would not need the top-up of supplementary benefits. Now all these concepts are being abandoned. When the poor are more or less on their own, as recipients of state benefits, those excluded from benefits because of their income will become a powerful force for further constraining state pensions and benefits. The horrors of the 1930s and the detested means tests could once again stalk the streets wherein the poor reside. This was and will once again be terribly dehumanising. A coherent society has to be inclusive. You can't exclude a third of the population, pass them out into some kind of outer darkness, and still be a civilised society. The reality is that the excluded will come knocking on our doors and demand a place in the sun—and only heartless bastards would deny them.

An inclusive society would benefit the quality of life for everyone in all sorts of ways. "Culture, stripped of snobbish accretions, is like the sum of special knowledge that accumulates in any large united family, and is the common property of all its members," wrote the essayist Emmanuel Bearl. That rings very true to me. The divisions in the cultural life of Britain are not inherent in culture itself but reflective of the social divisions in society at large. To end that would enrich the entire cultural life of the nation.

To illustrate the magnitude of the problems we face let me quote from the United Nations Development Report. "The three richest people in the world own assets worth more than the combined yearly incomes of the 48 least developed countries." The United Kingdom ranks fifteenth out of the top 17 industrialised countries in the new United Nations poverty index. Sweden, just behind Britain in its level of gross domestic product, has half Britain's level of poverty. If we are genuinely interested in the quality of life for the people of Britain then let's declare war on this poverty and let our leaders exude the passion that was so manifest a week ago when they wanted to go to war in the Middle East.

MORALITY IS ABOUT
MUCH MORE THAN SEX

16 DECEMBER 1998

IN MARCH 1930, long before most of us were born and when Al Capone was the best-known living American, the Senate of the United States debated censorship and obscene literature. Here are but a few fragrant fragments of the seamless oratory that fluttered across the Chamber. Senator Smoot of Utah had brought with him as exhibits the naughty poems of Robert Burns, Balzac's *Contes Drolatiques*, Casanova's *Memoirs*, George Moore's *The Story Teller's Holidays*, D.H. Lawrence's *Lady Chatterley's Lover* and the *Kama Sutra*. He described the authors as lower than beasts. "... If I were a customs inspector this obscene literature would only be admitted over my dead body. . . . I'd rather have a child of mine use opium then read these books." He would have been in deep manure if the child had fancied both.

Senator Blease of South Carolina told his senatorial colleagues that he was quite prepared to see "the democratic and republican forms of government for ever destroyed, if necessary, to protect the virtue of the womanhood of America. . . . The virtue of one little sixteen-year-old girl is worth more to America than every book that ever came into it from any other country. . . . I love womanhood. Take from a government the purity of its womanhood and that government will be destroyed." You will observe the absence of any reference whatsoever to the purity of American manhood, who were somehow expected to sow wild oats in their youth without the assistance of American womanhood. Something I still can't figure out.

I only quote these two blusterers to remind you that sexual humbug is nothing new in the U.S. of A. I blame England. It sent as pioneers to that far flung place, a bunch of strong willed but mealy mouthed puritans, who took the fun out of everything, including sex. Puritanism, in a sense, has gone. The humbug remains. President Clinton is the latest fall guy. He might be impeached next week for something that is not in any shape or form a crime. He undoubtedly indulged in some kind of sexual hanky panky, with a young lady, that seemingly precluded the possibility of procreation. She was adult and a consenting partner who might even be described as enthusiastic. When accused he lied which I presume is par for the course for married men similarly accused. He is said to have perjured himself by lying about a non-criminal event. But why did he have to testify, under oath, about a non-criminal event?

This week Clinton was in the Middle East trying to put the peace process back on the rails. His speech to the Palestinians was one of the best made by an American President in recent times. He spoke the truth in the circumstances, which took some courage to do. Meanwhile, back at the homestead, he was being assailed by this nonsense. I am no great fan of Clinton's. He can be an unscrupulous opportunist, like his pal Blair, in politics as in everything else, as Monica found out. That he philandered in the Oval Office is terribly heinous, his critics say. Come off it! The Oval office has been the scene of plots to overthrow governments, in Chile and elsewhere in Latin America. Around that famed desk was no doubt discussed the defoliation of Vietnam, the bombing that drove Cambodia back to the middle ages, the dropping of the atom bomb, the Bay of Pigs, the plot to murder Castro and a host of other heavy metal dastardly deeds. Yet so enfeebled is the moral fibre of Republican Congressmen that dalliance between a President and a young woman is considered more grave than all these things, and probably many other things, much worse, put together. In a sense this shows, once again, that the United States is unworthy of world leadership. She has it, but by might, not right. Think of this. The grim situation in the Middle East could set the world ablaze. America, at present, is the only power with the clout to avert that catastrophe. The American President cannot fully apply himself to this problem because of something that is basically the personal business of him, his wife Hillary, and Monica, who, poor lass, will forever be the butt of risqué jokes, not because of what she did or didn't do in that White House cupboard but by the unscrupulous antics of politicians on the make.

Morality is about a helluva lot more than sex. And politics, primarily, should be about that which constitutes the helluva lot more. I, of course, add that the sexual humbug in British politics is nearly as bad. What is it about Anglo Saxons that makes them so hung up about sex? 'Twas they that first covered the genitals of nude male statues with fig leaves while erecting statues, in all sorts of public places, of men shouldering the really destructive weapons of war and mass destruction. I still adhere to the uplifting ethos of the afore-mentioned Robert Burns.

> The deities that I adore are social peace and plenty,
> I'd rather be the cause of one than be the death of twenty.

A few other things have made me pause in my perusal of the week's news. How can public support for human and civil rights be considered a defect in the veracity and objectivity of the Law

Lord Hoffman? Failure to support these causes in such a person should cause worry, not his support. I've always felt that Pinochet would eventually be returned safely to Chile but desperately want to be proven wrong. In his book *Spanish Testament* Arthur Koestler defines his concept of war crimes. He starts from the premise that in wars, given the nature of war itself, there will be excesses, even atrocities that happen but are not planned. In Spain he showed that terror was the actual strategy of Franco and his generals. He argued that terror is the strategy of all military coups. The Military must cow and terrorise the people or fail, that's the nature of the beast. Pinochet led a military coup, not a civil war. The government he overthrew was democratically elected. Pinochet destroyed democracy with terror. The crimes against humanity that took place were not brought about by the crude over-zealousness of subordinates but were the settled strategy laid down by him and his commanders. He did the same as Hitler on a much smaller scale. For the dead and disappeared it wasn't small scale at all, but total. He should be brought to justice, and if the law doesn't affirm this, the law is an ass.

I am now convinced that the peoples and nations of these isles must be integral parts or part of the European Union. There is no other viable option though the arguments for involvement are more positive than that. We urgently do need a debate throughout the UK on all related matters. We won't get one if the Prime Minister continues to bad mouth those who disagree with him as lunatics and headbangers. That's the language of abuse, not debate.

EXPLODING THE MYTHS OF BLAIR'S SPIN DOCTORS

6 JANUARY 1999

ANOTHER resignation. Who's next to go? Will it be Alastair
Campbell? What a good idea! Prescott/Brown challenge Blair.
What about? It certainly ain't about politics. There are no dissidents in the Cabinet. They've all been on message since well
before the General Election. New Labour's message has material-
ised. New Labour is honouring its electoral pledges. That's the
problem. Its economic strategy is the most reactionary in Europe.
You cannot have a reactionary economic strategy *and* progressive
social policies. One precludes the other. That reality now confronts
us. It will get worse. Spin doctors might try to obscure this reality
but reality will out.

Spin doctors can only spin. It matters not to them if what they
spin is false. They spin deception and peddle myths. When things
go wrong they go on spinning. That is their only ploy. Spin, more
spin, more spin. Dizzy with supposed success they tend to lose
their equilibrium and then, atishoo, atishoo, they all fall down. If

we're lucky they stay down.

New Labour's spin doctors have deceived members of the Labour Party and the British people by creating a myth that flew in the face of all the known facts. The scenario was as follows: Labour was unelectable until Tony Blair became leader, and then, with the help of his two trusted courtiers, Peter Mandelson and Philip Gould, Blair remade Labour into New Labour, and then thrashed the Conservative Party at the 1997 General by becoming more Tory than the Tories. The rest as they say is history. But it's tainted history, easily exposed by facts.

After Labour's defeat in the 1992 General Election, Neil Kinnock resigned as Party leader and was replaced by John Smith. In the month following that election opinion polls showed the following support for Labour: Gallup—39.5%; ICM—34%; Mori—38.5%. As leader, John Smith got rid of Peter Mandelson and Philip Gould, who had both been involved in the defeat of 1992. I'm not sure that Smith had anyone working for him who could be called a spin doctor. Yet in June 1994 opinion polls showed support for Labour as follows: Gallup—50.5%; ICM—48%; Mori—51.5%. John Smith died in 1994 and Blair became Party leader. He reinstated Mandelson and Gould. In April 1997, just before the General Election, the opinion polls showed support for Labour as follows: Gallup—50.5%; ICM—48%; Mori—50.5%. Look at these figures, for they prove that the big breakthrough in Labour support came during John Smith's leadership. Blair added nothing, and John succeeded without the services of Mandelson and Gould.

New Labour actually polled 43.2% at the '97 election, amounting to 13.5 million votes. In 1992 the Conservative Party led by John Major polled 14 million votes, 500,000 more than Blair in '97. Yet Mandelson and his cohorts, helped by the vagaries of Britain's bizarre electoral system, spun these figures into a miraculous conception fertilised solely by the genius of Blair. There's been nothing like it since Stalin airbrushed Trotsky out of the Soviet Revolution. It's a deception, of course, not a conception. Labour Party members

in particular have been deceived. The big advance for Labour
came during the period when John Smith was leading the party
and telling Britain that with a Labour government would also
come job security for every worker from the first day of their
employment. He believed it morally essential that full employment should be the prime goal of any Labour government, and
said so. He was saying these things, now deemed taboo by the
Blairites, when Labour was forging ahead in terms of popular
support. New Labour, it goes almost without saying, has reneged
on all these principles.

Another interesting aspect of the last election was that 1.3 million fewer voted than in 1972. This too doesn't tally with the
picture painted of resurgent Britons flooding to the polls in '97 to
return a New Labour government. Tory voters stayed away, particularly in the South of England. Significantly, so did Labour
voters in traditional Northern English strongholds. A possible
portent of what is to come.

The current opinion polls have to be looked at in context. In
Scotland voters think they have a viable alternative in the SNP,
and the opinion polls reflect this. New Labour up here is in trouble
compared with New Labour down South. That is in contradistinc-
tion to what applied over the last decades when Labour was in
trouble in England and very strong up here. But today there is no
viable alternative down there. Who in their right minds would
vote for Hague's mob even though he, himself, has been surpris-
ingly effective in Parliament? It's interesting that the Scottish Tories
are trying to distance themselves from their comrades south of the
Border, and who can blame them. The Liberal Democrats are
paying the price for Ashdown's perceived obsequious involvement with New Labour. I don't think Ashdown will be able to
hold back his troops for much longer.

Some time ago I gave up all hope in Westminster. It is too far
removed from us in ways more important than geography. The
Imperial past hangs over the place like a dark malignant cloud,

fostering preposterous illusions of global grandeur. To see New Labour Ministers recently rocket-rattling in the Middle East was symptomatic of this malaise and in every sense pathetic. There is about Westminster a corruption not necessarily personal but born of outmodedness. Blair wants Westminster to lead Europe. To be at the centre of Europe. For the City of London to be the financial centre of Europe even if outside the EMU. This is empty posturing. The Europeans know the score. They identify him as Thatcher Mark 2.

Two trends face us. The EU, if it is to work effectively, will have to be ceded powers, both economic and political. This must also mean, as a counterbalance, more sovereign power exercised by the peoples in their communities and nations. To my mind this means the Scottish Parliament and its relationship with Europe. In this context Westminster would become less important for us. To make this work our Parliament must be fundamentally different, with a different ethos and political culture. To have a Scottish Parliament controlled by politicians in London through their emissaries up here would be disastrous.

I don't think New Labour can be changed. Power is now too centralised in the Party. Talk of Gordon Brown leading the fight to resurrect Labour principles is risible. He was and is a major player in turning Labour into a party of the Right. Geoffrey Robinson was/is his mate and advisor. Brown is now the darling of the City. The fire in his belly was extinguished years ago. Most of his colleagues never had any fire. What a mess. Oh what a blessing it would be to have an independent Scottish Labour Party free of Tammany Hall et al. Pity we won't have it by next May.

IF IT'S ALL THE SAME TO YOU

18 JANUARY 1999

THE PRIME MINISTER says "soon we will all be middle class".
That baffles me. The middle class is a social group with a locus
somewhere between the capitalist class and the working class. If
we are all to be middle class then it presupposes the disappear-
ance of the working class and the capitalist class. If these two
classes disappear there is no need of a middle class. The concept
becomes redundant. We would be living in a classless society.
What then would the middle class be the middle of? A classless
society is a socialist society. Is the Prime Minister promising us
that, and soon? Maybe he's conned the capitalists into believing he
is one of them only to plunge the dagger into their collective heart.
Oh Mr Murdoch your Sun is setting. Beware the Ides of March.
Does it mean that the Prime Minister has been a closet Trotskyist
all along?

On the other hand it could be that he has got so tied up in his
own verbless soundbite rhetoric that he is in danger of disappear-
ing up his own nether regions. Or, alternatively, he is trying to con

us. His strategy, and he makes no bones about this, is to have a second term as Prime Minister, through prising Middle England from the Tory camp by embracing the Thatcherite values so beloved by Middle England, as evident in General Election after General Election over the last 20 years. Middle Scotland has just as resolutely rejected these values, if you can call them that, over the same period. His problem is how to pander to the basic conservatism of Middle England without totally alienating Labour's core working-class vote throughout the UK. Thus far he is getting away with it in England where people have, as yet, no viable alternative, but not in Scotland where they do.

He then has to develop a rationale which cloaks the reality of this strategy. What better than to assert that we are all, in a sense, like Middle England. We are all middle class. The ploy is not new. The Tories peddled the same line. They claimed that we were all living in a "property owning democracy". That class was a thing of the past. John Major argued at the last election that Britain was already a classless society. Thatcher sold off Council houses in the expectation that as property owners the former tenants would automatically vote Tory. That a worker who owns a mortgage for a two-room-and-kitchen in Govan would automatically think politically like his boss always seemed far fetched to me. In the latter years of the old Gorbals the great majority owned their own slum dwellings and Gorbals remained a safe Labour seat. You know something, workers aren't daft.

I used to claim that given certain statistics about a constituency, such as the average value of housing, average income per household, the number of cars and the type of cars per household, what schools the children went to, I could then tell you whether the constituency was a Tory or Labour stronghold. No big deal, you might say, and you would be right. What it does prove is that class and politics are indivisible. This has always been the case and will remain so for as long as classes exist. This applies whether we like it or not. I don't like it. I want to end it. That's why I've been a lifelong socialist. The snag about putting an end to all this class nonsense is that those who benefit most from any status quo believe that this particular status quo is the natural order of things, the very ultimate in the evolution of human society. To tamper with it or end it would be an offence against God, nature, or both. We have to accept as a psychologically feasible proposition that those sitting at the top of any pile may well be disposed to take a favourable view of that pile. Voltaire satirically summed up this attitude in the phrase "we are living in the best of all possible worlds", proclaimed ad infinitum in spite of the fact that humanity was surrounded by manifest cruelties, injustices, plagues and natural disasters.

The slave owner no doubt believed that slavery was the best of all possible worlds. The slave no doubt begged to differ. Feudalism was slightly less stark. The serf worked for his Lord for so many days and then some days for himself, so that he might sustain his family. This ensured future generations of serfs kept their Lord and heirs in the style to which they had become accustomed. The feudal Lords claimed authority to rule in this way through divine right. To buck the system would anger God, and all hell would be let loose, as Wat Tyler found to his cost. The Industrial Revolution and the rule of capital created a society in which the economic relations between the classes became somewhat more complex. It liberated the serfs and peasants and made them free labourers. The free labourer was allowed to exercise his free will in the field of employment. He was free to sell his labour to a master who was prepared to buy it. Or he could decide not to sell. The price of exercising the latter option was starvation. He and his wife and children were thereby forced, as free labourers, into the dark satanic workplaces of the Industrial Revolution, to work, for next to nothing, long and health-destroying hours. This was the natural workings of the free and unregulated market. The slave owners had their slaves whipped to work. The masters of industry only had to blow their factory whistles and the free labourers streamed to work, of their own free will, of course.

From the pits of this despair an anger was forged. Workers banded together in societies that became trade unions. These were made illegal by a Parliament that served only the interests of capital. The struggle joined with the fight for democracy. Battles were won and votes for women were only achieved earlier this century. Wealthy capitalists, men like Robert Owen and Frederick Engels, sickened by the inhumanities of their own system, worked for a more civilised way of life through co-operatives and socialism. The best of the middle class also sided with the workers. The Webbs, William Morris, George Bernard Shaw, Sir Stafford Cripps, Clement Attlee, and countless more.

All my life every technological change moved people from the point of production to the preparatory stages of production, or out of the productive process all together. I knew that in my teens and wrote about it in my twenties. That a worker wears a dust coat or a suit and not dungarees doesn't make him any less a worker. A worker is someone who has to sell his labour to someone who is in a position to buy it. That hasn't changed. During my years in shipbuilding and engineering I never wore a bunnet. Neither did most of my mates. In Scotland the landed gentry wear cloth caps.

The disparity between the very rich and the very poor in our society is greater than it's ever been this century. That's a fact, not an opinion. The very poor, now in their millions, have been pushed down into the abyss and threaten the fabric of our society. The mega-rich want less public spending so that they may pay even less tax. The only alternative is that we pay more taxes to fund the expenditure required to make our society more civilised. It really is as simple as that. Which side are you on?

PRINCIPLE FROM A PAST TIME

25 JANUARY 1999

I'VE BEEN interested in genetics since my mid-teens. Let me tell you how this came about. The Soviet geneticist, Trofim Denisovich Lysenko, claimed that acquired characteristics could be inherited. Stalin endorsed this theory. All other genetic theories were banned in the Soviet Union. I read about Lysenko's theories in English language booklets printed by the Soviet Union. Their tone was most unscientific. They read like propaganda tracts. I sought enlightenment in the public library through books on Gregor Johann Mendel, the Austrian monk and botanist, whose long painstaking research into the hybridisation of green peas actually founded the science of genetics. Mendelian genetics stood the test of time though of course modified in the light of new, subsequent, discoveries. It tallied with the findings of Darwin. It could accommodate the discovery of DNA. Mendelianism was condemned as a bourgeois science by the Communist movement throughout the world on Stalin's say so. At the time I was a sixteen-year-old member of the Young Communist League. I remember going to a meeting organ-

ised by the Communist Party in Glasgow where a party function-
ary was going to explain to us how and why Lysenko was right.
It soon became clear that his ignorance of genetics was more or
less absolute.

When it came to questions I tried to establish what he meant by
"acquired characteristics". He didn't really know and waffled on
about growing wheat in the North Pole. I dare say if you expose
a living organism to cold it might learn to live with that cold
providing it's within the organic temperature determined by the
genes of the organism concerned. If it goes well below or above
that temperature the organism will die. The discussion went from
absurdity to absurdity. Nobody seemed to know what were the
possible acquired characteristics they were so certain could be
inherited, but that didn't stop them from being adamant. Towards
the end I said to him jocularly, "If I acquire the ability to ride a bike
does that mean my children will inherit this acquired ability and
ride a bike without having to learn to do so?" "That's daft," he
said. "I know," said young Reid, "but you started it."

Stalin condemned cybernetics as a "bourgeois science". It was a
branch of science in which the Russians excelled. They were banned
from doing further work in this field. Cybernetics was the fore-
runner of computer science. When computers burst on to the
world's stage the Soviet Union was years behind the West. This
cost the Soviets dearly. The dead hand of Soviet dogma, the heavy
hand of Stalinist power, virtually killed off, for this century at
least, whatever creative dynamic there was in Marxism, which
was conceived by its founders as a social science. Science and
dogma are utterly incompatible. This contradiction destroyed
Soviet Communism. Man lives and works. He observes and is
capable of abstract thought. He thinks of new ways of doing
things that might work better. He tries out his theory. If it works
then that is another piece of knowledge to be used as and when he
pleases. If it doesn't quite work he will think of how it might be
modified so that it may work better. If it doesn't work at all, he

367

scraps the idea and starts anew. That is the origin of scientific methodology. It's human thought structured into a scientific discipline. We are all capable of thinking scientifically. It's natural for us to do so. Some will do it better than others, but that's true of everything. Yet today science is shrouded in a mystique that excludes and alienates the non-scientist. It's all part of a process that files us all away in various catchment areas. The homogeneity of past years has largely disappeared except, ironically, among the poorest in society. Over them a homogenous poverty prevails. A kind of social solidarity born of want.

I want the social solidarity of abundance which modern science can provide. There is no need for anyone to starve on this planet. The factor that bedevils everything in our world is that our sociology lags about a hundred years behind our technology. Political science still further back.

This affects us in many ways. The impreciseness of political thought is a case in point. How, for example, can you think the unthinkable? If something is unthinkable then it can't be thought. I know what the Prime Minister means. He wants us to think of scrapping State pensions and a lot of other things. He can't say this and instead talks a meaningless gibberish that might sound good. Make a good soundbite. You couldn't get away with that in science where preciseness is at a premium.

We are supposed to be having a debate in this country about constitutional change. The Government wants to abolish hereditary peers because they are overwhelmingly Conservative, which is true. But, presumably we would want to abolish hereditary peers even if they were all Labour. Such peers should be abolished because the whole concept is irrational.

Any system of government that retains the heredity principle, in any shape or form, cannot be fully democratic. Any assumption that royals and aristocrats have some innate capacity to rule is well outwith the bounds of reason. Blue blood was the term invoked to justify their claim to govern. Blood doesn't carry inherited characteristics; the genes do. Breeding within a confined group is genetically damaging. It maximises the recurrence of recessive genes. This is why most European sovereigns in the last 250 years were mad. At the start of this century our noble families were losing their chins, had wet mouths, looked and probably were quasi-imbecilic. In fact a strong case could be argued that they were genetically unfit to hold public office. I am bitterly opposed to peers appointed by the political establishments. All we will get from such a process will be the usual panhandlers that couldn't run a menodge. Why don't we think the thinkable and get rid of the House of Lords altogether, and turn the place into a shelter for London's homeless. If hereditary peers enshrined in an institution are untenable why is a hereditary monarch/head of state any less an affront to reason?